JOURNAL FOR THE STUDY OF THE OLD TESTAMENT SUPPLEMENT SERIES

44

Editors
David J A Clines
Philip R Davies

JSOT Press
Sheffield

THE IDENTITY
OF THE INDIVIDUAL
IN THE PSALMS

Steven J.L. Croft

Journal for the Study of the Old Testament
Supplement Series 44

Copyright © 1987 Sheffield Academic Press

Published by JSOT Press
JSOT Press is an imprint of
Sheffield Academic Press Ltd
The University of Sheffield
343 Fulwood Road
Sheffield S10 3BP
England

Typeset by Sheffield Academic Press
and
printed in Great Britain
by Billing & Sons Ltd
Worcester

British Library Cataloguing in Publication Data

Croft, Steven J.L.
    The identity of the individual in the Psalms.
    — (Journal for the study of the Old
    Testament supplement series, ISSN 0309-
    0787, 44).
    1. Bible. O.T. Psalms—Criticism,
    interpretation, etc.
    I. Title   II. Series
    223'.206   BS1430.2

    ISBN 1-85075-021-1
    ISBN 1-85075-020-3 Pbk

CONTENTS

Diagrams

PREFACE

This book represents a revised and reduced form of my doctoral thesis on the Psalms submitted to the University of Durham in 1984. I should like to record here my thanks to the many people who have contributed in some way to this work over the past six years. In particular I would like to thank Professor Douglas Jones for his careful and stimulating guidance and supervision of the work; the staff and my fellow students of St John's College, Durham (1980-1983), especially the Principal, Miss Ruth Etchells and Dr Willie Morrice; my colleagues in ministry at St Andrew's, Enfield, especially my vicar, Prebendary Peter Morgan, for their encouragement and support; Mrs Ann Clark, for hours of careful typing; the editors of JSOT Press, for giving the work a place in their Supplement series; my parents, family and friends and, finally, my wife, Ann, who has shown a longsuffering and very patient interest in the problems of the Psalms for most of our married life, for all her love and support in these and in so many other ways.

Quotations are from the Revised Standard Version of the Bible unless otherwise indicated. I would like to apologize in advance to the non-Hebraist for the fact that I have felt it necessary to retain a fair amount of Hebrew, particularly in the first two chapters of the book, where the discussion is mainly about the meaning and use of certain Hebrew words. I can only hope that the presence of the Hebrew will not be too off-putting and that you will persevere. The debt which my own work owes to that of others who have studied the Psalms will be very obvious to everyone who reads these pages. My own interest in the problems of the Psalter was begun by reading the work of Aubrey Johnson and John Eaton and, although at some points I disagree with their conclusions, their work has been a constant help and point of reference. My hope is that my own contribution will in some ways further the debate and increase our understanding of one of the central books of the Old Testament.

Steven Croft,
Enfield,
January, 1986

ABBREVIATIONS

ANET   *Ancient Near Eastern Texts relating to the Old Testament* (ed. J.B. Pritchard)

BDB   Brown, Driver and Briggs, *Hebrew Lexicon*

BJRL   *Bulletin of the John Rylands Library*

BH   *Biblia Hebraica Stuttgartensia* (ed. Elliger and Rudolph)

CBQ   *Catholic Biblical Quarterly*

CPAI   *The Cultic Prophet in Ancient Israel* (A.R. Johnson)

CPIP   *The Cultic Prophet in Israel's Psalmody* (A.R. Johnson)

CQR   *Church Quarterly Review*

HTR   *Harvard Theological Review*

HUCA   *Hebrew Union College Annual*

IDB   *The Interpreter's Dictionary of the Bible*, ed. G. Butterick et al., New York: Abingdon Press, 1962.

JAOS   *Journal of the American Oriental Society*

JBL   *Journal of Biblical Literature*

JNES   *Journal of Near Eastern Studies*

JQR   *Jewish Quarterly Review*

JSOT   *Journal for the Study of the Old Testament*

JSS   *Journal of Semitic Studies*

JTS   *Journal of Theological Studies*

KP   *Kingship and the Psalms* (J.H. Eaton)

OTMS   *The Old Testament and Modern Study*, ed. H.H. Rowley; Oxford: Oxford University Press, 1951.

PIW   *The Psalms in Israel's Worship* (S. Mowinckel)

SKAI   *Sacral Kingship in Ancient Israel* (A.R. Johnson)

TBC   *Psalms* (Torch Bible Commentary) (J.H. Eaton)

TDOT   *Theological Dictionary of the Old Testament*, ed. G. Botterweck and H. Ringgren; Grand Rapids, Michigan: W. Eerdmans, 1978 onwards.

VT   *Vetus Testamentum*

ZAW   *Zeitschrift für die alttestamentliche Wissenschaft*

INTRODUCTION

In over 90 of the 150 psalms contained in the English psalter the voice of an individual suppliant, an 'I' is heard. The person who reads or sings or prays through the Psalms today wants and needs an answer to a very natural question: 'Who is the "I" who speaks in this or that psalm?' He or she may have been told the modern view that the Psalms are no longer seen as having been written by David; nor are they, for the most part, simple expressions of individual faith and experience but that they were composed for use in public worship. But these insights have served only to raise the question of the identity of the individual in a much sharper form, both for the ordinary reader of the Psalms and for the Old Testament scholar. In several recent summaries of psalm studies this area is named as one of the two key controversial issues in the study of the psalter today.[1] Several different solutions have been proposed in the last hundred years: the individual who speaks, it is claimed, is predominantly one who is unjustly accused, or a sick man, or the king.[2] However, none of these theories can be made to fit all, or even most, of the evidence available, nor has any one theory come to command widespread acceptance. The identity of the individual in the Psalms remains an enigma.

The aim of this book is to investigate the problem of the identity of the individual in the psalms in as full a way as possible. The problem is a complex one and demands, not surprisingly, an equally complex solution. In particular, the following subsidiary questions have been raised in the study of the individual in the psalms and must be answered in the following enquiry.

(1) What is the relationship between the person or group who composed a given psalm and the person or persons by whom

the psalm was delivered in the cult? My own understanding of this relationship follows that put forward by Mowinckel, and broadly accepted by most scholars in the field: the Psalms should not be seen as autobiographical accounts of personal experience but liturgies composed for the use of certain categories of person in certain types of situation in the temple cult. Although this position is not defended in a separate chapter of the book the whole work, in so far as it gives a satisfactory account of the individual psalms, must be seen as confirming Mowinckel's view.

(2) Who are the antagonists who beset the individual suppliant in so many of the Psalms? In several studies, notably in the work of Harris Birkeland,[3] the problem of the identity of the individual is approached exclusively through the problem of the antagonists. Hence my own enquiry will begin, in Chapter 1, with a full examination of this question.

(3) What is the meaning of the different terms for 'poor' in the Psalms, especially as applied to the individual suppliant? Are they to be interpreted literally or metaphorically, as referring to the individual or to the nation? The work of several scholars including again Birkeland and Schultz[4] has focused on this issue and this second preliminary question is examined in Chapter 2.

(4) What was the cultic context in which these psalms were delivered? There is comparatively little debate about the cultic setting of the psalms of the private person and those assigned to ministers of the cult. However, no examination of the royal psalms would be complete without engaging with the theories which have been put forward in recent years, particularly by the British scholars Johnson and Eaton, on the ritual setting of certain of these psalms.[5] A new reconstruction of the royal ritual is put forward in the context of the discussion of royal psalms in Chapter 3.

Complex problems, such as those involved in the study of the Psalms, often demand complex solutions. One main weakness found in many of the studies of the question of the individual in the Psalms is that only one possible solution has been examined at a time. A given writer has argued that the 'I' is always (or mainly) a persecuted individual[6] or the nation personified[7] or the king.[8] The assumption underlying this approach, although this is not overtly stated, would seem to be that psalms which share the same basic form of individual lament must also share the same setting in the life of the cult. This is, of course, not the case and content can be taken as a reliable guide to cultic context, taking us further than the foundation given by form criticism. The human, rather than logical, consequence of this methodology has been that the hypothesis in question, because it is the only one under discussion, attracts to itself as many psalms as possible and consequently the whole case put forward by a given author is weakened.

Accordingly, my own methodology has been first to set out the available options as to a solution of a given problem; next to examine all the psalms related to that problem and, finally, to assign each psalm to the likeliest of these options allowing, where necessary, for exceptions and indicating any areas of uncertainty. The picture which emerges on the identity of the individual is less uniform than that proposed by many scholars but seems to account better for the total sum of evidence in the Psalms.

The enquiry begins then with an examination of the problem of the antagonists and of the words for 'poor'. In Chapters 3, 4 and 5 and three available options for a solution to the question 'Who is the "I" in the Psalms?' are set out and each psalm in which an 'I' occurs is assigned to one of these categories: either the individual suppliant is the king; or he is a private individual; or he is a minister of the cult, a cultic prophet, wisdom teacher or psalm singer. Within these broad categories a further division of these psalms is attempted on the basis of the situation for which the lament or thanksgiving was composed.[9]

As was mentioned above, the whole enquiry is based upon, and further substantiates, Mowinckel's arguments that almost all the Psalms were composed for use in the cult, a position which has come to command widespread acceptance in studies of the Psalms. Careful attention has been paid to content as well as to form in establishing the situation and the type of person for whom a given psalm was composed. Moreover, every attempt has been made, where possible, to link the individual psalms discussed with their wider literary and cultural context in the Old Testament and the ancient Near East.

The enquiry begins, then, with an examination of the question of the identity of the antagonists in the Psalms.

Chapter 1

THE ANTAGONISTS IN THE PSALMS

I. THE HISTORY OF THE PROBLEM

The individual in the Psalms appears beset by antagonists in the majority of hymns and prayers in which his voice is heard. On every page of the psalter there is some reference either to the wicked or to the enemies of the suppliant or the nation. Clearly the opinion we form as to the identity (or several identities) of these antagonists will affect our view of the individual in a given psalm.

The question has received a good deal of discussion in recent years and several good and detailed accounts of the problem are available.[1] Hence the general history of the subject will not be discussed in great depth here. As long as the question of the date and authorship of the Psalms could be answered by the theory of Davidic authorship then the question of the antagonists itself could also be answered in these terms. The enemies were identified with the many enemies we know from accounts of David's life in the biblical narratives. The question was raised in a more acute form however with the rise of the more critical scholarship of the nineteenth century and was linked with the question of the date and origin of the Psalms. Broadly speaking, the two groups of wicked or enemies on the one hand and righteous or faithful on the other were initially seen as two groups within Israel, rival sects of Judaism. Partly for this reason, the Psalms themselves were assigned to the post-exilic period when such groups are known to have existed during the fragmentation of Judaism under Hellenistic influence. This view in turn was challenged by the work of the early form critics, and Mowinckel in particular, who encouraged an earlier dating of many of the Psalms to the pre-exilic period; hence the problem of the antagonists as it is known in its modern form arose. Mowinckel's view, at the time of his publication of the *Psalmenstudien* was that the individual laments were mainly psalms of individuals in sickness or other adversity. However he was subsequently to renounce this theory, at least in part, convinced by the arguments of his own pupil Birkeland.

The arguments of Birkeland

Gunkel and Mowinckel both began their investigations from psalms which they held to be psalms of sickness and proceeded to eliminate those which might otherwise be held to have a national or collective reference. Birkeland however began from the other end, from what he regarded as national features and proceeded to eliminate suggested references to sickness and private enemies.[2] He discovered in the national psalms of lament and in certain individual lament psalms (9-10; 42-43; 54; 56; 59) that the enemies are explicitly identified as the foreign nations with whom Israel was continually at war. This interpretation can be supported with certainty by a further 18 psalms in the three categories of National, Royal and Individual Psalms and is supported in *Die Feinde des Individuums* (1933) with much exegesis. The overall pattern of his argument is, however, quite simple:

(1)   the antagonists[3] can clearly be identified as gentiles in more than 20 psalms

(2)   the antagonists in the other psalms are described in exactly the same way

(3)   therefore, unless some substantial evidence can be brought to the contrary the antagonists in these psalms must be gentiles also.

In reviewing the opposition to *Die Feinde* in his later book *The Evildoers in the Book of Psalms* Birkeland finds that no adequate evidence has been brought forward to contest his views. He goes on to give a succinct statement of his arguments without the detailed exegesis of the earlier work and, in fact, hardens his line. Whereas in *Die Feinde* he had been prepared to admit that certain psalms were genuinely individual as opposed to Royal or, as Mowinckel calls them, national psalms of lament in the 'I' form, in *Evildoers* he retracts that concession and argues that all the antagonists are gentiles either outside Israel and in a state of war or within Israel and representatives of the occupying power. He concludes his later book with dogmatic statement:

The evildoers in the book of Psalms are gentiles in all cases where a
definite collective body or its representatives are meant.

Response to Birkeland

Birkeland's contribution to the debate on the identity of the
antagonists in the Psalms is powerfully argued and has had a large
measure of influence even among those who would not accept this
position in its more extreme form. In particular, his study paved the
way towards regarding many more of the Psalms as royal, or as
national psalms in the 'I' form, a conclusion which was taken up and
undergirded by the arguments of Mowinckel and Eaton[4] and which
is generally supported in this study. Mowinckel's own response to
Birkeland's work in *Die Feinde* was perhaps the most dramatic and
entailed an almost complete reversal of his previous position. He is
willing to concede in his later work that the antagonists are foreign
nations in many psalms and, therefore, that these psalms should be
seen as national psalms of lament in the 'I' form. Mowinckel also
finds himself able to accept Birkeland's thesis on a common pattern
describing the wicked and the enemies when he writes:

> in Ancient Israel, as in Akkadian literature, there existed a
> traditional pattern according to which the evildoers, רשעים—the
> enemies are always רשעים—are described[5]

Mowinckel would, however, dispute Birkeland's extension of his
argument to cover all the individual psalms and his consequent
denial that there are no psalms of sickness in the psalter.[6] The
British scholar John Eaton takes a similar position in that he also
thinks that many of the Psalms are royal and so welcomes
Birkeland's main conclusion. However he regards Birkeland's
argument that the king's enemies must always be outside the nation
as rather shaky. Birkeland has not perceived that the king can be as
equally opposed to forces within the nation as to forces outside it.
With Mowinckel, Eaton sees no distinction between the different
words describing the antagonists in the Psalms. Other scholars
working in the field have generally maintained that the antagonists
are described according to a standard pattern and each term can
describe enemies either inside or outside Israel. Whilst most scholars
have therefore accepted the force of Birkeland's arguments in certain
respects all have been hesitant to accept his full conclusions for three
main reasons. In the first place, there clearly are some psalms which
do not fit into his somewhat rigid theories. In the second, Birkeland

is led by his exegesis to see in the Psalms a theology of strident nationalism. Yahweh is always on the side of a righteous Israel in her battle with the evil gentiles. This theology conflicts with that found in most, if not all, of the remainder of the Old Testament. In the third place Birkeland is working with a very inflexible view of language. His arguments, and those of Rosenbaum discussed below, depend on a term having one dominant meaning throughout the book of Psalms, irrespective of its immediate context. No variation is permitted. It seems to me that, whilst stock metaphors and standard 'pattern' descriptions do have an important role to play in the Psalms, the tradition in which the psalmists worked was a very flexible one. A standard image or word could easily be used in a new way to give a different meaning and our interpretation should not be blind to this possibility.

A challenge to Birkeland's theory: the work of Rosenbaum
It is clear then that Birkeland's primary contention that the antagonists can clearly be identified as gentiles in twenty or more psalms is well supported by the evidence. What can be questioned however is his argument that the antagonists in the other psalms are described in exactly the same way. It is this unquestioned assumption which Rosenbaum sets out to test, against the background of previous semantic field studies carried out in Old Testament Hebrew.[7] He begins by criticizing the undue influence of the *parallelismus membrorum* feature of Hebrew poetry when used in defining the meaning of Hebrew words. With Sawyer he argues that 'poetic parallels are secondary importance for semantic description, as confirmation, not independent description'. Birkeland's assumption that the two predominant terms for wicked and enemies (רשעים and איבים) rests very much on the four verses where the two terms are used in parallel (3.7; 17.9; 37.20; 55.3). Rosenbaum then goes on to demonstrate, in my view convincingly, that the two terms wicked and enemies are not synonymous in the Psalms but refer to two different groups of antagonists, Israelites who have gone astray and foreign enemies respectively. The term 'wicked' (רשע) is used 88 times in the psalter and 'enemy' (איב) 74 times—one or both terms is used in nearly half of the Psalms. Both words are used outside the psalter and it seems reasonable to infer that the meaning in the Psalms is in some degree consonant with the meaning outside. The following arguments can be adduced for separating the meaning of the two terms:

(1)   איב is used alone in 35 psalms, רשע in 28. The terms occur together in 13 psalms only.

(2)   Allegations of synonymity would depend on parallel occurrences, yet the terms are only parallel four times in the psalter. However, איב is found often in parallel with other words (27x in parallel, 49x not). At the very least רשע does not seem the most ready choice for such a parallel.

(3)   Elsewhere in the Old Testament the word איבים is found mainly in the historical books dealing with non-Israelite enemies. The word רשעים predominates in Proverbs, Job and Ezekiel where the wicked in Israel are described.

(4)   Outside the psalter the words are only found once in parallel or adjacent verses, in Job 27.7: 'Let my enemies be as the wicked, and let him that rises against me be as the unrighteous'. This particular verse supports a different meaning for the two terms: if the two were synonyms there would be no point at all in Job's curse.

(5)   There is no link outside the psalter between רשע and גוים (nations) but plenty of evidence to support a link between איב and גוים. Hence the acceptance of Birkeland's thesis involves positing a separation between language meaning in the psalms and in the rest of the Old Testament.

(6)   A comparison of opposites used with the two words again supports Rosenbaum's theory. The words צדיק (righteous) and ישבילב (upright in heart) are frequently used opposite רשעים (wicked) but hardly ever opposite איבים (enemies). The converse is true of the words גוים (gentile nations) and עמים (peoples).[8]

It seems to me, therefore, that Rosenbaum's study has produced enough evidence to support the hypothesis that the root meaning of איבים (enemies) and רשעים (wicked) can be separated and the two words are not used interchangeably within the psalter. It remains to be seen whether Rosenbaum's own definition of the terms can be substantiated. This result will now be tested out in the exegesis of the psalms in question, in the first instance the 28 psalms in which the wicked occur with no mention of the enemies.

II. THE WICKED IN THE PSALMS

The main point of the enquiry here will be to try to arrive at a satisfactory definition for רשעים which will be appropriate for most of its occurrences. The search will be both for a basic meaning for the term and for ways in which this meaning is developed or extended in particular psalms. Two important points emerge from this study of the רשעים psalms. First, in many, but not all, of the psalms discussed the wicked present no threat to the 'I' in the psalm (where one occurs), unlike the enemies who always present such a threat. Second, the wicked are more often than not associated with the theme of judgment. The typical cry of the psalmist could be said to be for salvation from his enemies but demanding judgment for the wicked. These two considerations lead me to the view that the wicked should be defined not in relation to the subject of the psalm but in relationship to Yahweh and his judgment: the רשעים are those who have turned away from the law of God.

For ease of understanding the psalms in which the רשע occurs have been divided into six groups according to the theme of the psalm and the role played by the רשעים as follows.

Didactic poems (Pss. 1; 32; 34; 39; 73; 112 and 11)

Psalm 1 is generally regarded as a post-exilic composition by virtue of its wisdom themes[9] and the high profile given to the study of Torah. It is no accident that the psalm stands at the head of the psalter: the sage presents to his hearers both a description and, implied in this description, a choice between the way of the righteous and that of the wicked. Wherever this choice is presented the רשעים cannot be taken to be foreign enemies since the possibility of choice and the presentation of a warning implies that it would be possible for God-fearing Israelites to become רשעים. We are given no indication here of the latter's crimes—only that the righteous ought to separate himself from those who do not walk in Yahweh's way. At the outset of the investigation however there is a clear association between the wicked and judgment (v. 5).

Psalm 32 consists of an introductory beatitude, an individual lament or testimony with instruction drawn from this (v. 6), what appears at first sight to be an oracle of Yahweh and a conclusion summing up the lesson of the psalm. Weiser, Jacquet and others see the piece as a psalm of testimony to Yahweh's dealings with the author.[10] However it seems better to understand the piece, with A.A. Anderson, Eaton and Johnson[11] as an example of didactic psalmody. The whole goal of the psalm is to impart the teaching given in v. 6:

> Therefore let everyone who is godly offer prayer to thee in times of distress[12]

and the testimony is subservient to this end. The only question then is whether the psalm has its origins with the cultic prophets, as Johnson thinks, since it contains a supposed oracle, or with the wisdom writers. My own view is that the psalm contains so many wisdom features and elements of wisdom vocabulary that it is best seen as a wisdom psalm. These features are seen in the beatitude (vv. 1f.); and the testimony in vv. 3-5 (cf. Ecclesiastes 1 *et passim*). The supposed oracle, unusual in a wisdom psalm, is perhaps better understood not as spoken by Yahweh but as the manifesto of the wisdom teacher, with its characteristic wisdom vocabulary (אשכלך, הבון, אורך) and can be compared to the similar invitation to come and learn in Ps. 34.11-14[13] which also follows a similar testimony to Yahweh's goodness.

As in Psalm 1, the wicked present no threat to the psalmist. Rather, the wisdom teacher is presenting a choice, by inference, to his hearers urging them to follow the way of Yahweh. Again, if the possibility exists that the hearers could become רשע, then the רשעים must include Israelites. The dynamistic view of judgment is to the fore, as in several of the wisdom psalms: sin leads of itself to suffering and punishment.[14]

The acrostic *Psalm 34* has broadly the same structure as Psalm 32: a testimony to Yahweh's goodness (v. 6) is followed by an invitation to learn, followed by instruction on the blessings enjoyed by the righteous and the unpleasant fate of the wicked. There is no hint that the wicked are anything other than miscreant Israelites. Once again mention of the רשע is accompanied by legal language: it seems they can hardly be mentioned in the Psalms without attention being drawn to their fate:

> Evil shall slay the wicked;
> and those who hate the righteous shall be condemned (v. 21).

Here for the first time also we receive the impression that the רשע may be involved in the persecution of the righteous although not necessarily of the subject of the psalm himself.

Commentators are unanimous in regarding *Psalm 39* as unique in the psalter, a 'unique dialogue with Yahweh', in Weiser's words, in which, in the manner of the protest literature in Job and Koheleth, the psalmist cries out against his own fate. Hence the psalm only fits loosely into the category currently under discussion. The רשעים occur only as those before whom the psalmist would not voice his doubts—presumably Israelites who have turned from Yahweh. The sufferings of the righteous man, the devotee of Yahweh, would, no doubt, be a source of mockery to the deistic unbeliever: what does it profit a man to believe in Yahweh if suffering results? Little else is learnt of the wicked from this psalm.

The genre of *Psalm 73* is essentially identical to that of Psalms 32 and 34 though the theology is rather more refined. The purpose of the psalm is without doubt didactic, as Anderson has described, and the form is that of the testimony beloved by the wisdom writers. What is essentially a moral or theological problem is not debated in the abstract in ancient Israel but translated into narrative, in this case a narrative which purports to describe the psalmist's own experience. Here the problem is set forth—the prosperity of the wicked and their apparent impunity—and its severity is enunciated (it calls forth doubt in the psalmist himself) and finally a theological solution is proposed: judgment of the wicked is postponed, meanwhile the psalmist finds his compensation in the praise of Yahweh.

Birkeland is right (*Evildoers*, pp. 36ff.) in so far as he sees the רשעים in the psalm as a class of 'wealthy and happy lords' (vv. 3-9). However he is wrong to declare that they must represent the ruling gentile foreign classes within Israel. He invokes v. 1 as support for this view but many scholars in fact read לְיָשָׁר אֵל for לְיִשְׂרָאֵל in v. 1 regarding the latter reading as a *later* nationalistic interpretation of the psalm.[15] לְיָשָׁר אֵל preserves the parallelism much better. Alternatively the second half of the verse may serve to qualify the first: 'to those within Israel who are upright in heart'. The verse does not justify, therefore, the reading of the wicked as gentiles. The question has to be asked in this and other רשעים psalms: if the psalmist meant the gentiles, why does he not use the word גוים, עמים or even איבים as he clearly does elsewhere? Birkeland's exegesis of the phrase מקדשי־אל is similarly weak. He thinks the psalmist is describing an excursion to the ruined sanctuaries of foreign gods which then leads him to see the eventual ruin of their devotees. Yet he rejects the much more obvious explanation that the psalmist has in some way seen the downfall and judgment over the wicked portrayed in the cult at one of the great festivals. Once again, there is a clear connection between the wicked and judgment.

Most commentators assign *Psalm 112* to the post-exilic period and draw attention to the influence of the wisdom writers on the style and theology which is that of 'good man prospers, bad man falls'. As such, like other wisdom psalms, it is didactic in purpose with the acrostic perhaps acting as a simple mnemonic if the psalm were to be learnt by heart. As in the other psalms in this group, acting rightly is a matter of choice—this is the whole point of a didactic psalm. Hence the רשע is one who has made the wrong choice and is thus an Israelite who has rejected the way of Yahweh.

Recovering the situation for which *Psalm 11* was composed is not easy. Birkeland and Eaton base their interpretation on vv. 1-2. The statement about the wicked placing the arrow on the string is to be taken literally. The psalmist is in physical danger and is most likely to be the king suffering at the hands of foreign armies. However it seems more likely to me that the psalm is a didactic piece of wisdom writing. The opening verses are best understood metaphorically, particularly as the wicked are said to shoot in the dark. Ps. 64.3 gives a clear example of arrows as a metaphor for slander. Similarly the emphasis in the psalm is not on the pseudo-testimony and deliverance, but on the teaching given in vv. 4-7: standard wisdom teaching on the fate of the righteous and the wicked. The association of the wicked with judgment can once again be noted.

Hence in the first seven of the רשעים psalms to be discussed, all examples of didactic psalmody written in the wisdom style, the wicked appear as individual Israelites who have turned from Yahweh's law and are thus subject to his judgment. They are described as scoffers (Pss. 1; 73), false and boastful (32; 34; 73), arrogant and violent (73; 11) and threatening oppression. In addition, Psalm 73 gives a picture of the רשעים as prosperous and powerful and thus able to oppress those who do follow Yahweh.

Songs of Yahweh's judgment (Pss. 50; 58; 75; 82; 97; 36; 12; 94)

Psalm 50 is a powerful psalm of Yahweh's judgment which should most probably be set, with Weiser and others, in the annual festival at which the covenant was renewed (vv. 5, 16). The psalm can be dated by the prominence of this covenant concept to the later pre-exilic period. Interpretation of the piece centres around whether the words 'But to the wicked God says' (v. 16) are original to the psalm. Birkeland, Kraus and Jacquet, supported provisionally by the BH apparatus, argue that these words are a later gloss by a redactor to make the text more meaningful to a post-exilic generation.[16] The only argument in favour of this emendation is that the offending words are an intrusion into the metre of the psalm. However it is quite common for oracles in the psalms, as in the prophetic books, to be introduced by a phrase which is outside the main structure of the poetry (cf. 81.5; 95.7; 60.6). As has already been shown, this distinction between the righteous and the wicked in Israel is quite common in the psalms and, moreover, the words do mark a complete break in sense (supported by the Selah after v. 15 in LXX). Verses 7-15 are concerned with a right understanding of the cult and of sacrifice in particular, concluding with Yahweh's invitation to the people to call upon him in the day of trouble. Is it likely that he would then turn on the same people and denounce them as unfit to recite his statutes? Verses 16-23 then turn to the moral crimes of the wicked within Israel whilst vv. 22-23 sum up the psalm offering an antithesis reflecting the balance in the piece as a whole. Psalm 50 is most appropriately seen therefore, with Johnson and Eaton[17] as an example of the work of the cultic prophets in educating the people into the right attitude to the sacrifice which is going on before them and, through the charge laid against the wicked, warning them to watch their moral conduct. The great festivals were occasions of teaching and exhortation as well as celebration.[18] The attitude towards sacrifice attacked in this and other passages in the canonical prophets is not the official line of the cult but the mistaken conceptions of the people themselves. The wicked are depicted here as those who commit primarily moral offences, associate with other sinners (cf. Pss. 1; 26) and think that Yahweh is one like themselves. The delivery of this psalm at the annual festival would be part of the continual process of keeping the congregation pure for the worship of Yahweh and warning them of the consequences of his wrath.

Two very different interpretations of *Psalm 58* are also possible depending upon how the first two lines are translated. The translation given by the RSV is preferred by most commentators. On this translation אֵלֶם, which actually means 'silence' in the introduction to Ps. 56, is regarded as being an adaptation of אֱלֹהִים or its abstracted form אֵלִים made by a later Yahwist unwilling to acknowledge the existence of other gods in his religious psalmody. The psalm can be thus understood almost as a theodicy. Evil in the world is attributed not to Yahweh but to the lower ranks of the gods who are actually responsible for judgment upon the earth. These opening lines can be regarded as spoken by Yahweh, as Weiser suggests (cf. 82.1) or by the complaining psalmist who cries out for justice. In view of the similarities with Psalm 82 this latter suggestion is to be preferred. The alternative translation followed by RSV margin and favoured by Jacquet is to translate אֵלִים as 'mighty men'. The whole psalm is then to be seen not as a theodicy but as a prophetic style tirade and sentence of judgment against the corrupt judges within Israel (cf. Amos 5.7; Isa. 1.23; 5.23 etc.). This understanding of the words seems less likely in view of the cosmic dimensions of judgment in the psalm and the parallel with Psalm 82. However, it can be said that this strong condemnation of the unjust rulers of the world would have significance for any unjust rulers within Israel. We may see here, possibly, even a veiled attack on the government and the king himself. There is once again a close connection between the wicked in the psalm and this theme of judgment. Birkeland's argument that the wicked are gentiles in Israel (*Evildoers*, p. 34) is clearly false. Nor, however, can the meaning of the term be restricted to the Israelites. They are those of any nation who turn away from Yahweh and from his justice.

Psalm 75 is to be classified with others in this group as a hymn of judgment. The oracle in vv. 2-6 is framed by a hymn in plural form at the beginning of the psalm and an individual song of praise and affirmation of judgment in vv. 9-10. The oracle itself was, in all probability, uttered by a cultic prophet[19] during the great festival in which, in all probability these great hymns of judgment should be set. As in the other psalms of judgment there is a close association between these psalms and the appearance of רשעים who are seen on a world-wide scale, not just within Israel, as those who fall foul of Yahweh's judgment. Their crimes in this case are pride and insolent speech (vv. 4-5). Birkeland's thesis that the wicked are gentiles becomes most damaging to a theology of the Psalms in the case of a psalm such as this. If Yahweh's judgment is equated merely with Israel's victory over the nations how can it be claimed to be right and just? The whole of the Psalms must be seen as a distortion of the picture of God given in the rest of the Old Testament.

Psalm 82 is another hymn of judgment in which the themes of justice and the fate of the wicked are inextricably linked. Once again the judgment is on a world-wide scale, but the cultic prophet is surely speaking through his vision of a divine assembly to the judge and nobles of Israel, setting forth Yahweh's standards for judgment. It is to be granted once again (contra Rosenbaum) that many of the wicked are to be found outside Israel, but Birkeland's view of the psalm will not bear scrutiny. The categories of those who have a right to protection in vv. 3-4 cannot be taken as metaphors for the nation but must refer to individuals within Israel and outside Yahweh's standard of justice is for all the nations, and by it those who judge are to be judged. The wicked are defined by vv. 3-4 as those who oppress the weak, the fatherless and the destitute; in other words, they include the class of wealthy nobleman portrayed in Psalm 73 and elsewhere who have all they need but pay no heed to Yahweh.

Psalm 97 is a song of Yahweh's enthronement and, with others, clearly links the judgment of Yahweh, as a festal theme, with that of his kingship. Nothing can be proved about the identity of the wicked in v. 10, who are once again associated with judgment, but there is no need at all to superimpose nationalistic categories on the psalm and make the wicked the foreign nations. It seems perfectly consistent with the psalm to see the righteous as those within Israel who are faithful to Yahweh.

Psalm 36 is grouped with these psalms of judgment as the downfall of the wicked is portrayed in the closing verse of the psalm which most commentators think refers to a symbolic act performed in the cult. The description of the רשעים accords with that found elsewhere and there is no indication that any other persons than those who turn away from Yahweh and his law are described here. As in the other psalms in this section, one of the functions of the piece is to warn those present at the festival of the fate of the wicked and thus discourage them from taking the wrong path. Conversely, the psalm acts as a comfort to those oppressed by a רשע, affirming their doom and the steadfast love of Yahweh.

Although *Psalm 12* contains an oracle of judgment this is set in the context of an appeal to Yahweh to intervene, which makes the psalm rather different from those discussed above but similar to Psalm 94 below. The picture of the רשעים as persecutors of the helpless, found in Psalm 73 and elsewhere, is more to the fore in this piece also. A picture of foreign domination underlying the psalm has been suggested by Birkeland and tentatively supported by Eaton (*TBC, ad loc.*). Further, the picture in v. 8a ('On every side the wicked prowl') may be thought to refer to Judah's being surrounded by foreign armies. Three reasons make this unlikely however. First, the psalm plainly comes from the circles of the cultic prophets, since it contains the oracle in v. 5. This being the case it seems better to see a moral degeneration depicted here along the lines of that depicted in the canonical prophets (cf. Hos. 4.1; Mic. 7.11; Jer. 5.1; Isa. 57.1ff; 59.14ff, etc.). Secondly, Anderson adduces a parallel to this type of lament from an ancient Egyptian discourse on suicide dated c. 2000 BC (*ANET*, p. 406) in which the writer laments:

> To whom can I speak today?
> Hearts are rapacious;
> No-one has a heart upon which one may rely
> To whom can I speak today?
> There are no righteous
> The land is left to those who do wrong . . .

This piece plainly refers to moral decay. Third, the content of the psalm and the description of the wicked (vv. 2 ff.) accord with those found elsewhere. The meaning of v. 8a quoted above must be seen as amplified by v. 8b which Anderson paraphrases as meaning 'when worthlessness is highly exalted among the sons of man'. In other words the verse is criticizing the moral decline in the nation in the same way as does Isaiah when he says 'Woe to you who call evil good and good evil' (Isa. 5.20).

Psalm 94 links the psalms in which Yahweh is portrayed as judge with those in which the king is central for the psalm, as Eaton and Mowinckel have argued, is a royal piece. The reference to 'wicked rulers' (literally 'thrones of destruction') is an indication of this, as is the royal style found in v. 23 and elsewhere.[20] The psalm begins with a prayer to Yahweh to intervene against the oppression by the רשעים. Birkeland's interpretation of this passage is somewhat strained since he attempts to see the terms used of the socially disadvantaged as metaphors for Israel's place in the Great Society. It suffices to say that the 'Great Society' is largely Birkeland's invention and is here imposed upon the text rather than derived from it. Neither is there a need to postulate an alien invasion as the background to this appeal, as some have done, but rather a breakdown in law and order caused by a disregarding of Yahweh's law.

The appeal for intervention in the opening verses of the psalm is followed by an oracle, presumably delivered by a cultic prophet, giving assurance that Yahweh has heard. The second half of the psalm should be seen, as will be argued at length below as the call liturgy of the king in the annual festival. Yahweh asks in v. 16 who will rise up against the רשע. The king replies that in his capacity as judge he will, with Yahweh's aid, carry forward the attack against oppression in the land.

The characteristics of the רשעים denoted by these psalms of Yahweh's judgment accord with those detected in the psalms in the group above: the wicked are deceitful, slanderers (50), forget God (36; 50; 94), keep company with sinners (50), are arrogant and boastful (75; 12; 94) and oppress the weak and helpless (94). No reference is made to their being threatening to the 'I' in the psalm specifically (except 94) and for this reason they are not described as איבים. Further evidence has been brought forward against Birkeland's view therefore that the רשעים are foreign military antagonists. Furthermore, Rosenbaum's conclusion that the רשעים are antagonists within Israel only has been challenged. Those who commit certain offences in all the nations are רשע. Psalms 94 and 82 give the impression of the רשעים found also in Psalm 73—that of oppressors of the poor, the ruling classes perverting justice in their favour. Yahweh emerges as a champion of the widow and orphan in these psalms and in 94 the king is identified as his spokesman. This idea will be followed through in the next group of psalms to be discussed.

Royal Psalms (Pss. 101; 26; 141; 91; 28)

The interpretation of *Psalm 101* and the determination of its original context has often turned around the difficult phrase 'When wilt thou come to me' which seems to imply that the psalmist, who is almost certainly the king, is involved in some sort of cultic encounter with Yahweh. However, the nature of the king's oath is often neglected, perhaps in consequence of this. In fact it can be observed that the interpretation of this psalm follows on naturally from that of Psalm 94, which bridged the gap between the two concepts of Yahweh as judge and the king as judge. Here the king can be envisaged as making a solemn confession before Yahweh of his intent to administer justice in his realm. The song opens with the words 'I will sing of thy covenant love and justice' and the king goes on to affirm his desire to uphold Yahweh's law. He declares he will know nothing of evil (v. 4) and will prosecute both the slanderer and the arrogant of heart—the two chief characteristics of the wicked in other psalms. The threefold statement in vv. 6b-7 declares that the king will choose as his ministers those who are honest and upright (the threefold style resembles that of Ps. 1.1 where the oath is a prohibition not to associate with the wicked). The final verse sums up the whole psalm: Yahweh exercises his judgment over the congregation through the king himself.

The majority of commentators regard *Psalm 26* as a prayer to be spoken by an Israelite who feels himself falsely accused (so Weiser, A.A. Anderson) in a situation such as that envisaged in 1 Kgs 8.31. However, the crimes repudiated here are not crimes against a neighbour but association with false men, dissemblers and the wicked. The psalm is a much more general protestation of innocence such as that found in Job 31 or those from the Egyptian Book of the Dead (*ANET*, pp. 134f.). It seems to me that the psalm is best suited for recitation by a public figure in the cult. Jacquet thinks of a Levite but, with Eaton, I would argue that Psalm 26 is a royal psalm. As in Psalm 101 the king is declaring his innocence before Yahweh and before the assembled congregation. As the king is judge of the people so now he invites Yahweh to judge him (vv. 1-3) and declares his innocence. As was observed in Psalm 101, association with the wicked was particularly serious for the king. The well-being of the people depended upon an uncorrupt civil service. The reference to those who resort to bribery (v. 10) would be particularly appropriate for one who judged the people. It is as a result of his innocence that the king is able to perform the rites of purification mentioned in vv. 6-7. The wicked in this psalm are once again those who have turned from Yahweh and his ways.[21]

The text of *Psalm 141*, especially vv. 5b-7, is very difficult to interpret. However, Eaton does not seem justified in seeing this psalm as full of reference to warfare or as the prayer of the king on a campaign away from Jerusalem. The psalm does have a distinct style and can therefore be grouped with other psalms in which the king declares his innocence and asks for protection from the wicked, who are once again Israelites.

Psalm 91 is best seen as an oracle delivered to the king either on the eve of battle or in the context of the annual ritual. If the former is the case then the psalm should perhaps be grouped with those few psalms in which the term רשעים describes foreign armies, as Birkeland thought. However, the blessing given is more general than a promise of victory in battle: deliverance is promised from snares, pestilence and the terror of the night as well as from the arrow that flies by day. For this reason I would argue that the psalm has a wider reference than to battle alone and should be seen in the context of the annual ritual. For the same reason therefore the phrase in v. 8, 'You will see the recompense of the wicked', is best seen as referring to the triumph of justice in the land (the root שלם seems from its limited usage to be a judicial word) whilst other verses refer to the military security which Yahweh brings through the king.

Psalm 28 is no exception to the general rule established to date that the רשע does not present a direct threat to the subject in a psalm. The piece is almost certainly a royal prayer with the king's petition reinforced by a prayer on his behalf in vv. 8f. The identificaion is strengthened by the presence of features of the royal style. The precise situation for which the psalm was written is less clear. It may well be a psalm of sickness, as Mowinckel thought. The linking of the recovery of the king from illness and the salvation of the nation is found elsewhere in the Old Testament (2 Kgs 20.6). Here the king is not threatened by the רשעים but simply prays not to share their fate, that is, death. In proclaiming the judgment of the wicked the king simultaneously implies that he is not one of their number. Hence in this sense the psalm is just as much a protestation of his innocence as those discussed above. The definition of רשע as one who has turned away from Yahweh and so deserves judgment is once again confirmed.

This group of royal psalms presents essentially the same group of offences for the רשעים as listed above: to associate with the רשע is an offence in itself (26; 101); he offers bribes (by inference) (26); he slanders and is arrogant (101); speaks dishonestly and ignores Yahweh (28).

'Incidental' appearance in hymnody (Pss. 104; 145; 146; 147)

It has been noted above that there are a number of psalms in which the רשעים appear as a category at the end of the psalm to be damned, as it were. They come in such a place in *Psalm 104*. Birkeland is forced to admit, inconsistently with his own position, that some moral tone is present in the meaning of רשעים when he writes that 'men of this (wicked) quality within Israel are certainly not excluded'. It cannot be denied that here, as elsewhere, the רשעים are envisaged among all the nations, but the רשעים cannot be all the nations *en bloc*. Otherwise, if Birkeland's hypothesis were pushed to its logical conclusions the suppliant would be wishing for the total depopulation of the world outside Israel.

In *Psalms 145-147*, the final three רשעים psalms of the psalter, the wicked make further incidental appearances as part of the universe in which the psalmist finds himself. Psalms 145 and 146 both end with this curse of the רשעים balanced, in Psalm 145, against those who love Yahweh (and so the wicked are presumably those who hate Yahweh or do not give the love which is his due) and in Psalm 146 against the righteous. Here the רשעים are clearly those who are powerful enough in the land not to need such protection and here, as elsewhere, Birkeland's position is untenable. How could the same verse be saying that Yahweh will protect the (gentile) sojourner in the land and bring ruin to the way of the nations? As in many of the other psalms also there is a fundamental concern, even when the wicked only make a brief appearance, with the theme of justice and retribution:

All the wicked he will destroy (Ps. 145.20).
The way of the wicked he will bring to ruin (Ps. 146.9).

A similar theme can be observed in *Psalm 147* where the wicked appear earlier in the psalm and are here contrasted with the down-trodden. It is here plainly apparent that this contrast, as others, is meant to be taken literally not metaphorically unless, as in Birkeland's interpretation, all language in the psalms is to be translated into metaphor.

The prayer of an accused man (Ps. 109)

There seems no reason why a situation of war should be 'discovered' as underlying *Psalm 109* (so Birkeland, Eaton), nor is there evidence that the psalmist is the king. Eaton's arguments for this interpretation rest chiefly on the appellations for Yahweh, 'my God' and 'Yahweh my God', which he regards as part of the royal style, but this is not the case.[22] Moreover the terms of the curse in the psalm apply to a civil situation: to the family of those cursed and to their land and produce. It would seem therefore that this is a psalm provided for use by one falsely accused (so Anderson, Weiser *et al.*) and so fits into the context described in 1 Kgs 8.31ff. The subject's statement of love for his accusers and prayers for them are best seen as attempts to win Yahweh's favour rather than as literal description.

The opening verse of the curse provides a clear indication of who the רשע is in this case, namely an accuser in a court of law and thus an Israelite not a gentile. The curse which follows this may be an oblique reference to the disasters which have actually befallen the speaker in the psalm, a way of saying: 'May what has happened to me happen to him also'. The situation envisaged is thus one where a poor man has got himself into debt to the extent that his creditor has seized his land, goods and family and thereafter threatens his life. The language of salvation is present in the psalm since the primary focus is on the need of the individual. However the psalm does also demand retribution against the wicked.

Three 'nationalistic' psalms (Pss. 140; 125; 129)

Finally, there are three psalms (only) in this group in which the רשעים can be identified as foreign military enemies.

Psalm 140 seems from the several references to war and to battles to be a prayer written for the king and it is hard to escape the conclusion therefore that רשעים in v. 8 refers at least in part to the foreign armies. However it is apparent from the rest of the psalm that the king is envisaged as being beset by internal opponents also, stirring up wars and laying snares. Certainly the curse formula in vv. 9ff. would seem to be directed at those in the land. Hence רשעים in Psalm 140 does not have simply nationalistic meaning only: the foreign armies are included in the designation but so also are internal opponents.

Psalms 125 and *129* are part of the collection of Psalms of Ascent and would seem, therefore, like most other psalms in the collection, to be late psalms from the post-exilic period. In both the term רשע is used of foreign enemies. The prayer in Psalm 125 is that 'the sceptre of wickedness will not rest on the land allotted to the righteous'; here we can agree with Birkeland that the fear is probably of foreign domination, but this view is tempered by the concluding verses of the psalm in which the fear is expressed that a wicked ruler will lead the people astray. Hence רשע retains its moral meaning as well as this new nationalistic content. In Psalm 129 the wicked are clearly defined as haters of Zion. In both of these psalms we can see a development in the use of the term רשעים which accords with their late date: there is good evidence to show that nationalistic or party interpretations were put onto basically moral terms in apocalyptic literature and the Dead Sea Scrolls whereas there is little evidence for this phenomenon in earlier Old Testament material.

III. THE ENEMY IN THE PSALMS

We now turn to an examination of those psalms in which the enemies occur without any mention of the wicked. Rosenbaum's contention was in agreement with Birkeland's conclusion here—namely that the term denotes foreign enemies predominantly. My own investigation supports these conclusions, at least in part, in that I can see that in 24 out of the 33 psalms in this group the background to the psalm is war and the איבים are foreign belligerents. However, in other psalms there appears to be evidence to support the view that איבים can be within the nation also, primarily as enemies of the individual. Thus more diversity can be found in the use of this term than in that of the term רשעים. The latter was found to denote those who are unfaithful to Yahweh's moral law within Israel, with an extension of meaning as Israel's concept of Yahweh developed to include such persons on a worldwide scale; only in a minority of psalms is רשעים used, by extension, in a nationalistic sense. The two different meanings of איבים, however, cannot be justified in this way, as a development, but must be two branches of the same root meaning. The word איבים in the psalms is rarely used without some qualification: it is usually 'my enemies', and occasionally 'his' or 'our' enemies etc. Hence the nature of the enemies in these psalms will depend upon who is speaking and naming these enemies as his own. The word can be said to function, therefore, as the word 'enemy' in English, as a general description of hostility without any primary assumptions as to race or status. It so happens that in the majority of the occurrences in the psalms the איבים appear to be foreign nations and these 'war psalms' will be examined first. An interesting and significant factor to note is the way in which the concept of enemies is linked strongly with that of *salvation*, whereas that of the wicked was strongly linked with the theme of judgment. Many of the psalms discussed below are not dealt with in great detail, simply because the interpretation proposed is not disputed.

War Psalms

The twenty-four psalms reflecting a background of war and foreign conflict can be divided into six groups according to the nature of the speaker, or the form of the psalm as follows:

1. *'We' psalms* (Pss. 74; 80)
A genuine historical event seems to underlie the communal lament in *Psalm 74*—most probably the destruction of the sanctuary in 587 BC (so Anderson, Johnson *et al.*). The enemy are clearly the foreign army who have carried out the sacrilege and their main crime, apart from the physical damage caused, is 'scoffing thy name'—a charge which is repeated no less than three times (vv. 8, 18, 22). There is a dominant concern with salvation in the psalm (vv. 12-17)—promises of which are based both on Yahweh's past activity in redemption and on his work as creator. As Johnson points out there is a close affinity with the prophecy of Deutero-Isaiah (*CPIP*, pp. 131-36) and a concern with prophets in general (v. 9). Hence it seems not unlikely that this particular psalm originated with the cultic prophets.

It is tempting to assign *Psalm 80* also to a specific historical occasion. Its allusion to certain tribes but not others and to 'the man of thy right hand' would seem to point to this—however nothing would prevent the psalm being used repeatedly in the cult in times of national emergency. Anderson favours the time of Josiah, Weiser the time of Hoshea, assigning the psalm to the northern kingdom and taking note of the LXX addition to the title: ὑπὲρ τοῦ Ἀσσυρίου. The איבים are national enemies, and that once again the scorn and mockery of the Israelites is a cause of great offence. Furthermore there are clear appeals for salvation from Yahweh in the refrain (vv. 2, 3, 7, 19).

2. *Mixed I/We psalms* (Pss. 44; 66)

Psalm 44 is very similar to the two psalms already discussed and probably finds its context, with Psalms 74 and 80, in national days of fasting and prayer during particular times of crisis. Once again the enemies here are clearly foreign armies but once again also the bitterness of the psalmist's fate is exacerbated by the mockery and scorn of these armies (vv. 13-14). The verses in the first person singular may be meant for the king's lips. Alternatively they may be an artistic device for variation in the communal lament. Salvation is once again prominent in the psalm.

Eaton and Mowinckel view the second half of *Psalm 66* as a royal song of thanksgiving, set within the praises of the whole nation, and this view seems well-founded, particularly in view of the size of the offering which is promised.[23] The psalm was probably composed for recital after some great national victory or deliverance: vv. 13-19 indicate that its setting is liturgical, recited before a thank offering of bulls and goats is made and that it forms the second half of a complete sequence, the first being the petition that Yahweh has answered. The situation appears once again to be one of war, though the enemies are here described as Yahweh's, not the king's or the people's. The imagery and language throughout is that of salvation, as, for example, in the reference to the Exodus.[24]

3. *Description of the king in the 2nd/3rd person* (Pss. 21; 45; 72; 110; 132)

This group consists of five of Gunkel's original royal psalms. In *Psalm 21* the איבים are plainly military enemies, though whether internal strife is excluded is not at all clear. Salvation is a clear element in the psalm and the two way, almost contractual relationship between Yahweh and the king is emphasized in v. 7.

The description of the king in the wedding song which forms *Psalm 45* falls into two sections: vv. 3-4 and 5-7, the first of which centres on the theme of the king as a *warrior* (where the איבים are clearly foreign armies) and the second section, in a text which is unclear in parts, dwells on the king in his capacity as a *just ruler*. This dual picture of the king as warrior on the one hand and just ruler (or judge) on the other recurs in the psalms and evidence will be presented in Chapter 3 for regarding these functions as the focal points of royal ideology within Israel and outside it, and both within and outside the psalms. Again there is a causative connection between the king's right conduct and attitude and his blessedness:

> You love righteousness and hate wickedness,
> Therefore God your God has anointed you with oil of gladness
>   above your fellows.

This total picture and this ideology, derived from Psalm 45, are confirmed in every respect by the most concise statement of a royal ideal in the psalms, *Psalm 72*. Once again there is a division between the king's two chief functions—as a judge (vv. 1-2) and a warrior (vv. 8-9). The איבים here are clearly the foreign nations. There is a clear causative relationship between the king's righteousness in judgment and the extension and security of his dominion (vv. 11-14). The king's activity in judgment is akin to Yahweh's in that he is portrayed as the helper of those who have no help.[25] His righteousness in judgment can be seen to secure in this psalm not only the military security of the nation but also its material prosperity (vv. 3, 15).

Psalm 110 focuses more clearly on the military function of the king either at his anointing or in the context of the festival. The enemies in v. 1 are clearly the nations of v. 6. An interesting variation in this psalm is that the king is Yahweh's instrument of judgment among the nations by military might, much as Cyrus, for example, or the Assyrians are portrayed as Yahweh's means of judgment on Israel in the prophetic literature (cf. Isa. 10.3ff.; 45.1ff. etc.).

Finally, in *Psalm 132* the enemies occur in the context of a general blessing on the Davidic house, which is also an oracle of salvation to the nation (vv. 14-18) and are most naturally taken as being foreign military enemies, though rival claimants to the throne presumably could not be excluded. It should be noted that the promise of continued favour to the Davidic dynasty is conditional:

> If your sons keep my covenant
>   and my testimonies which I shall teach them
> Their sons shall sit upon my throne for ever.

Hence it can be seen that in the psalms in this group the איבים can be identified as the foreign nations at war with Israel. Following on from the lead established in Psalm 66 a causative connection can be established between the king's righteousness, particularly in judgment, and the military security and material prosperity of the nation. Furthermore the two royal functions of judge and warrior are emerging as dominant ideas in a royal ideology, a theme which will be taken up more fully below.

4. 'I' Psalms (Pss. 18; 59; 138; 102; 27; 56; 69; 61; 89; 143)[26]

Psalm 18, as will be argued more fully below, is best seen as a song of thanksgiving after victory in battle rather than a liturgy for royal humiliation rites (as Johnson and Eaton have contended). The mythical language in the psalm is used in a secondary sense to describe Yahweh's deliverance of the psalmist, acknowledged by all as the king, as is shown by the juxtaposition of vv. 16 and 17. Further it is apparent from the military language used in the rest of the psalm that a situation of battle and war has been envisaged. Once again the language throughout is that of salvation: Yahweh is portrayed as saviour and also as warrior in the great theophany description of vv. 7-15. The reflective passage found in vv. 20-27 makes good sense in view of the connection between Yahweh's deliverance and the king's righteousness described above.

Psalm 59 takes up many of the same themes. The enemy are identified as the nations (גוים) (v. 5) and therefore the subject of the psalm must be the king. The situation envisaged is the opposite to the triumph celebrated in Psalm 18. Here the foreign armies are encamped around Jerusalem (vv. 6, 14). Note that the king's prayer is once again for deliverance or salvation from the enemies primarily—though an element of 'judgment' is present in the psalm (v. 5b). The mockery of the enemies (v. 7) is a significant factor in their behaviour for the psalmist as are the other 'sins of the mouth'—'cursing and lies which they utter' (v. 12). Once again there is a fundamental connection in the psalmist's own mind between the sin of the king and the fate of the nation—as in Psalm 66 there is a protestation of innocence before Yahweh:

> For no transgression or sin of mine O Lord,
> For no fault of mine they run and make ready.

Psalm 138 is a song of thanksgiving, a song of assurance for answered prayer—probably to be seen as a royal testimony in the cult addressed to the 'Kings of the earth' by the Davidic king of Jerusalem. There is no positive indication that the enemies are military, although this seems likely, but they may also include, as elsewhere, enemies within the nation.

Despite its unique title it is apparent that *Psalm 102* is a psalm in which the suffering of the psalmist and that of the community are intertwined. Most commentators suggest that the psalm reflects an exilic background, and this may well be correct. Given the distress of Zion it is apparent that the enemies in v. 8 are foreign belligerents whose mockery is once again a significant factor in the suppliant's distress. That distress is observed to be because of Yahweh's anger and indignation (v. 10)—there is no appeal here to innocence but an implicit confession of guilt. The appeal is directed to Yahweh's constancy manifested in the work of creation and to his grace, as in the theology of Ezekiel. Given that the psalm reflects a background of exile it is unlikely that the 'I' here is the king himself but must be some other representative person.

Psalm 27 clearly envisages a military situation (either ritual or actual) as is betrayed by v. 3. The appeal is to Yahweh's salvation from the איבים —foreign belligerents once again. The psalm is a song of thanksgiving, as is *Psalm 56*, another psalm where it can be said with reasonable certainty that the psalmist is the king and his rescue is from the peoples. This scenario is less clear for *Psalm 69*: the opening of the psalm reads like a psalm of lamentation in sickness yet the triumphant ending makes it clear that communal salvation and distress have been envisaged, and therefore the enemies must be foreign armies. Indeed this is hinted at in v. 25. The portrayal of the nation's plight in terms of the suffering of an individual, in this case and others probably the king, is clearly established as a literary genre in Israelite psalmody, as it is in the prophetic writings. In addition to this psalm, it is found in Psalms 102 and 22 and in a number of other psalms as well as passages outside the psalter. It is important to recognize however, that, although the sickness here is not real but a figure for the sickness and plight of the nation, in order for this metaphorical usage to have come about there must have been real psalms of sickness from which the metaphor could be taken.

The brief *Psalm 61* tells us little about the enemies other than that they are opposed to the king and so should probably be assumed to be national. Like Psalm 18, *Psalm 89* will be discussed at length below, but a number of features deserve note here: the enemies are foreign nations; the appeal throughout is for salvation rather than judgment. The phrase 'son of iniquity', בן עולה, in v. 22 is unusual in that it is associated generally with wickedness within the land. As occasionally with the term רשעים, the foreign enemies are branded as unjust—a ploy perhaps for winning Yahweh's assistance or justifying aggression. In vv. 29ff. the same principle of Yahweh's assistance being conditional upon the king's continued obedience to Yahweh's law is found as is revealed in other psalms.

It may well be, as Anderson has pointed out, that *Psalm 143* is a late post-exilic composition which takes into itself a number of other and motifs from earlier psalmody. However Eaton's suggestion that the psalmist is the king (and therefore that the enemies are external) is at least a possibility. The second verse of the psalm

> Enter not into judgment with thy servant
> For no man living is righteous before thee.

envisages a rather greater emphasis on the suppliant's own sin than was found in the royal psalms above.

5. *Psalms in which appeal is made Yahweh* (Pss. 78; 81; 83; 8)
Psalm 78 is an account of Yahweh's activity in salvation history leading up to the election of David and of Jerusalem. The enemies in v. 53 are obviously the Egyptians. Yahweh's activity in salvation is linked throughout with the sin of the nation and also, in the concluding verses, with the conduct of the Davidic king. In *Psalm 81* the reference to the enemies occurs in an oracle of Yahweh again in a piece with a cult prophetic background. The enemies are clearly the nations and the theology is the same as in Psalm 78:

> Oh that my people would listen to me,
> That Israel would walk in my ways.

Salvation from the enemy is related to the moral conduct of the people. *Psalm 83*, a curse type prayer to Yahweh against a foreign alliance against Judah/Israel does not reflect this or any other theology however. It merely appeals to Yahweh to destroy 'his enemies'—clearly the foreign nations. The same is apparent in the brief mention of the enemies in *Psalm 8*.

6. *Psalm 42–43*

In form this psalm is an individual lament but it is not discussed under (3) above because I do not believe that the psalmist is the king (contra Eaton). A far more plausible explanation is that the psalmist is one of the guild of temple singers whose work is reflected in Psalm 137 and elsewhere and that the song was composed in exile. The psalmist looks back on the temple workshop with longing. He looks forward to being able to praise God with the lyre (43.4). The psalm will be discussed in more detail in Chapter 5. However, for the present it is sufficient to note that, consonant with the other psalms in this group, the enemies are most probably foreigners at war with Israel and mockery forms a significant element in the suppliant's suffering.

Hence it can be shown that in twenty-four out of the thirty-three psalms in this group the איבים are foreign belligerent enemies, though in one or two cases the existence of internal enemies could not be precluded. But why should this mean that *all* the enemies in the psalms are foreign armies? Birkeland's argument was based on a false assumption of homogeneity of language and meaning in the psalms. It is hoped that the following section will substantiate the case to the contrary.

Other situations

1. *Psalm 127*

Although Psalm 127 can be discussed briefly its evidence is central to this examination since it demonstrates that the word איבים can be used, without any shadow of a doubt, for an individual's enemies within Israel—as Birkeland himself has to concede (*Evildoers*, p. 46). The important verse is verse 5:

> Happy is the man who has his quiver full of sons,
> He shall not be put to shame when he speaks with
>   his איבים in the gate.

It is widely acknowledged that the gate was the place in the town for the conducting of public business and the hearing of disputations.

Ruth 3 gives a clear example of the sort of issue which might be settled there. Here, then, the type of איבים envisaged are internal enemies. These enemies are to be found elsewhere in the איבים psalms, in the following two groups.

2. *Psalms 6; 13; 30; 54*

These psalms form a group within the איבים psalms because of their vagueness about the circumstances underlying their composition and use. The three psalms 6, 13 and 54 are all united in being laments in which the subject is suffering and in distress because of his enemies. This distress has driven him to engage in some activity in the cult, to prayer or prayers and sacrifice (Psalm 54). Each lament is followed by a short thanksgiving to Yahweh for having granted the suppliant a favourable hearing, but we receive no hint as to the identity of the suppliant. The only reasonable conjecture seems to be that these prayers were provided in the cult for the use of private persons involved in some kind of dispute such as that envisaged in Ps. 127.5. To further his chances of success the suppliant would take his plea also to Yahweh, either delivering it himself or through the medium of the cultic prophet. Psalm 30 represents a more elaborate thanksgiving after a successful outcome to the appeal.

3. *Psalms of sickness*

Two psalms of sickness in the psalter, Psalms 38 and 41, contain references to enemies. *Psalm 38* is the most likely of the two to be a royal psalm but even in this case the enemies are those who 'meditate treachery' and should be seen as enemies within the nation as well as foreign allies. *Psalm 41* bears witness, as do the four psalms in the section above, to the fact that the ordinary person in ancient Israel would undoubtedly have personal enemies, the more so if he was at all eminent. The references to desertion by friends and companions in both of these psalms are not so much autobiographical as additional features of distress incorporated into the psalm to increase the picture of the suppliant's plight and to make his case more likely to be answered by Yahweh.

4. *Psalms 25 and 35*

In *Psalm 25*, although the psalmist describes his enemies in terms which would apply well to the nation there is a positive indication in vv. 13-14, that the psalmist is not envisaged as the king but as the ordinary Israelite—the promises given there are more applicable to a number of people than to the king only. A compromise solution seems necessary therefore and the suggestion that the psalm is post-exilic liturgy is attractive. The worshipper we may envisage as a post-exilic figure whose awareness of the nation's enemies as his own impinges far more upon his consciousness than that of his pre-exilic counterpart. The psalm is shot through with the deuteronomic theology that sin will lead to disaster and eviction from the land.

The structure of the psalm can be outlined as follows:

In the opening prayer (vv. 1-7) the suppliant asks Yahweh for his continued protection, for his salvation from the enemies round about. The priest then replies, giving a promise of Yahweh's nature:

> Good and upright is the Lord,
>   therefore he instructs sinners in the way...

The suppliant then repeats the prayer for forgiveness (v. 11) and the priest replies with a word of assurance for the man who has humbled himself before God (v. 12). This oracle continues until v. 14 when the prayer resumes as the worshipper continues to 'humble himself before Yahweh'. Although the psalmist is not the king but a representative Israelite of the post-exilic age the enemies are still the foreign nations who surround the small city state of Judah.

There are two types of language present in *Psalm 35*, one of which must be understood as metaphor. If the military language in the opening verses is taken literally then the 'I' in the psalm is most probably the king. In this case all judicial language and, in particular, the reference to malicious witnesses (v. 11) must be metaphorical. However, it seems more likely that this judicial language should be given a more literal interpretation and that the suppliant is one who claims he has been unjustly accused by his enemies. It is these witnesses and accusers who are the focus of the second half of the psalm in the long curse section. There are similarities to Psalm 109 in this and other sections and the opening verses of the piece, with the cry for Yahweh's aid as counsel for the defence, takes us straight into judicial language. Hence the military language is best seen here as metaphor and the enemies are those within Israel who oppress the poor.

IV. PSALMS REFERRING TO BOTH THE WICKED AND THE ENEMIES

There are fourteen psalms only in which the two terms רשעים and איבים both occur. The chief aim of the two preceding sections has been to attempt to substantiate the theory of Rosenbaum that the meaning of these terms can be separated within the psalter. This hypothesis has been supported, it is clear, from the preceding analysis and exegesis of the terms in context in some sixty psalms. However, Rosenbaum's own conclusions, which were based more upon statistical analysis than close examination of the text, cannot be upheld in their entirety. Rosenbaum's view, it will be remembered, is that the רשעים represent individuals within Israel who have turned from Yahweh and איבים are external, belligerent armies, as Birkeland thought. In the light of the foregoing examination these definitions must be emended as follows:

a. The רשעים are defined primarily in relation to God's judgment rather than by race. They are those who offend against Yahweh's laws. As such they are mainly Israelites but the term can extend to include the wicked worldwide. A later development of the word causes it to be used in a nationalistic sense, as in Psalms 125 and 129.

b. The איבים are defined in relation to the subject to whom they are hostile. In other words the word on its own denotes no particular group of people, inside or outside Israel. In the majority of the psalms in which the word occurs, however, the איבים are foreign enemies opposed to either the king or the nation. But in other psalms internal enemies of the individual are undoubtedly meant.

There may be a number of different reasons why the two terms appear together in the one psalm. The area of overlap of meaning should be assumed to be neither simple nor straightforward, but the psalms in which the two terms occur can be divided into four groups as follows:

1. *Psalms in which the enemies are external and the wicked internal* (Ps. 106)
Psalm 106 contains a clear demonstration of how the meanings of the two terms must differ despite their being included in the same psalm. The enemies (vv. 10, 42) are clearly the foreign nations and are defined in relation to the object of their hostility. The term רשעים is

reserved for those Israelites who transgress the law of Yahweh and fall into judgment (v. 18).

2. *Psalms in which the enemies are internal*
(Pss. 37; 55; 71; 92; 119; 139)

Psalm 37 focuses, like many of the wisdom psalms, on the antithesis between the righteous and the wicked. The wicked are those who seem to prosper and who oppress the righteous, as in Psalm 73, but Yahweh's judgment will overtake them in the end. The whole point of the psalm is encouragement and moral exhortation. One of its purposes is to prevent the righteous joining the ranks of the wicked. Hence the רשעים cannot be gentiles, as Birkeland thought. The wicked man is described in v. 20 as the enemy of Yahweh by virtue of his wickedness.

Psalm 55 is an exceptional psalm, peculiar because of its extended testimony to the falsehood of a friend. A number of factors indicate that the psalmist is the king: the worshipper's sufferings merge into those of the community in vv. 9-11; in the suppliant's betrayal the community is betrayed (v. 20); and the plural forms in v. 23 indicate that the individual traitor is head of a group opposed to the Davidic king.[27] It is likely that the word עקה in v. 3 (MT v. 4) should be emended to צעקה ('cry') as a number of scholars have suggested (Weiser, BDB, *et al.*). This being the case there seems no reason to doubt that the two terms in question denote the same group of people in this psalm who are both transgressors of Yahweh's law and adversaries of the suppliant. The double description is especially applicable in view of the offences which are portrayed which are both moral (v. 11) and military. Some form of civil war is prepared. That the enemy is internal is in fact confirmed by vv. 12-15, however unusual these may be in themselves.

Psalm 71, similarly, would appear to be a royal psalm composed for the king's use when facing treachery or threats from internal enemies, and this psalm also would appear to contain specific biographical details. It is likely that here, as elsewhere, the psalmist has the king describe himself as old and frail because of the heightened picture of distress which this creates. Royal features in the psalm include instances of the royal address to Yahweh (vv. 3, 5) and the king having been a portent (מופת) to many. As Eaton aptly remarks: 'The psalm appears to be a striking example of how the king could build a powerful plea on his function as God's witness'. Eaton also refers to the instances where, as the king weakened in his old age, enemies would begin to watch for the signs that divine favour had deserted him (1 Kings 1; *ANET*, p. 149a).[28] The enemies of the king should, therefore, be seen as internal; and, in the course of his prayer to enlist Yahweh's support, the king, playing the part of the unjustly accused, seeks to brand his opponents as רשעים and thus secure their punishment at Yahweh's hand.

Psalm 92 has a cosmic dimension. The reference to the wicked must be taken on a worldwide scale. There seems no reason to exclude evildoers either inside or outside Israel. In v. 9 such men are branded as enemies of Yahweh: Yahweh is opposed to all such evil conduct. The suppliant's own enemies are described later in the psalm as שורר, a term which, as Rosenbaum has shown,[29] is the approximate semantic equivalent of איב but which is presumably used here for variety and clarity. It seems that in this particular verse the foreign armies are meant, but this does not mean that the wicked earlier in the psalm are to be identified with this group only. The movement of thought is better seen as the move from a general statement or promise to a particular demonstration in an individual circumstance, that of victory over a military opponent. It should be noted, therefore, that Psalm 92 only loosely belongs in this group. The reference is primarily to all evildoers everywhere.

The six references to the wicked and one to enemies in *Psalm 119* confirm what has already been said about the meaning of the two terms. The wicked are initially described as those who 'forsake thy law'—i.e. Israelites who have strayed from Yahweh (vv. 53, 155). However, such men are found not only in Israel but all over the earth (v. 119). They present some threat to the psalmist (vv. 61, 95, 110). The designation 'my enemies' (v. 98) probably does not refer to the same group of people but a smaller unit of men actively hostile to the subject of the psalm.

Finally, *Psalm 139* also supports a differentiation in meaning between the two terms, for the psalmist says of the wicked (v. 22) 'I shall count them my enemies'. Much as in Psalm 119 this reveals that the wicked are not automatically personal enemies of the psalmist. The רשע is defined by his conduct towards God and his law. The איב is defined by his conduct towards the object of his hostility. The most natural identity for the wicked in this psalm is as evildoers within Israel especially if, as seems to be the case, the psalmist is the king. He would then be seen as crying out against violence in the land, much as in Psalm 101.

3. *Psalms in which the wicked are external* (Pss. 68; 3; 31)
In the festal *Psalm 68* the designation רשעים is parallel to איבי יהוה and it appears similarly to refer to foreign armies (v. 21). Yet there seems no reason to suppose that the individual Israelite is excluded and the opening verses particularly do count as an effective warning to the oppressor in Israel:

> A father of the fatherless and a judge of the widows
> Is God in his holy habitation.

In *Psalm 3* the enemies mentioned (v. 7) are clearly military antagonists and the subject of the psalm is the king. There is no escaping the fact that the term רשעים is here used of this group therefore. As in some of the psalms discussed above, the king can be seen as an instrument of Yahweh's judgment against the nations, who can, therefore, be described as רשעים. Conversely, the king would describe his enemies as such in the hope of invoking Yahweh's wrath against them.

Psalm 31 is one of the most difficult prayers in the psalter to interpret and a full discussion is given below. It seems for various reasons that the psalm is best seen as a royal prayer to be delivered in a time of siege: continual reference to Yahweh as 'rock' and 'fortress' would support this view as, of course, does the reference to being besieged found in v. 21. The RSV understands this verse metaphorically, translating בעיר מצור as '*as* in a besieged city', although there is no hint of this in in the Hebrew text. The psalm also is similar in a number of ways to other psalms of siege. It follows that the antagonists in the psalm are foreign armies. As in Psalm 3, by reason of their opposition to Yahweh's anointed and his chosen nation they are described as רשעים, as those under judgment, in v. 17 of the psalm.

4. *Psalms in which the king opposes internal* רשעים *and external* איבים
(Pss. 7; 17; 9–10)
The opposition to both the military enemies of the nation and the
wicked within the nation was focused in ancient Israel in the person
of the king in his twofold function as warrior and judge respectively.
It should not be surprising, therefore, that in certain psalms such as
Psalm 3 there is an identification made between the two groups and
that in other psalms, particularly *Psalms 7, 17* and *9–10* there is an
interplay of meaning between references to the wicked and to the
enemies. It seems to me that all three of these psalms are royal and
should be given a setting within the royal ritual of Judah. In Psalms 7
and 17 the king gives account to Yahweh of his stewardship for the
previous year and seeks vindication against his accusers within the
nation. In Psalms 9–10[30] the king gives thanks for victory over his
enemies in the dramatic battle but seeks Yahweh's continued help in
the fight against the wicked and against injustice in the land.
However, since it seems these psalms can only be understood against
the background of the royal ritual (and an understanding of Pss. 9–10
requires an investigation of the terms עני and ענו) full exegesis must
wait until a later chapter. It is sufficient to point out here that it
seems more sensible to use the sixty psalms already discussed as a
guide to understanding these three pieces than to follow Birkeland
and utilize the evidence from these three difficult psalms as a
foundation for understanding the remainder.

V. CONCLUSION

On the antagonists in the Psalms
On the main point at issue in this chapter the enquiry has, I believe,
been conclusive. Birkeland's theory, shared by almost all commentators
on the Psalms, that the antagonists are described according to a
stereotyped pattern has been refuted. Rosenbaum's hypothesis that
the meanings of רשעים and איבים can be distinguished in the Psalms
has been confirmed and his own definition of the two terms has been
emended. The רשעים, as was said above, must now be seen to be those
who stand under Yahweh's judgment and are often linked with a
vocabulary of judgment in the Psalms. The רשע is rarely a threat to
the psalmist himself, although the powerful and wealthy in the land
who oppress the poor can be described as רשעים.

He is characterized by arrogance, slander, lying, boastfulness and godlessness and, if circumstances permit, oppression. The רשעים occur in many Psalms as examples to the congregation of Israel of what not to become; in others as those who are condemned or judged by either Yahweh or the king.

By contrast, the איב is defined in relation to the object of his hostilities. The איב always presents a threat to the 'I' in the psalm. In about two thirds of the איבים psalms the enemies can be seen to be foreign armies, as Birkeland thought, but in others the term does refer to hostile parties or individuals within Israel. Apart from the threat to the 'I' in the psalm, the enemy is characterized by his mockery of the suppliant's condition.

There is a certain amount of overlap between the two terms and an interplay between them. Foreign enemies and armies can be described as רשעים by reason of their opposition to Yahweh or his anointed. The king in his role as warrior and judge faces both national enemies and the wicked at home, and several psalms, some of which have yet to be fully explored and which seem to have their context in the royal ritual, refer to the king's opposition to both of these groups.

On the study of the Psalms

It is hoped that the above discussion has also validated several of the principles of enquiry laid down in the introduction to the thesis, that content must be examined as well as form and that complex solutions to the problems associated with the identity of the individual are both necessary and attainable. Primarily, however, the chapter has demonstrated that the meaning of a given term cannot be satisfactorily derived from its parallels in Hebrew poetry and that if a word means one thing in one psalm it does not necessarily have exactly the same meaning in all the others. Comparison of the meanings of the words discussed above in different psalms has been helpful in the analysis, but the immediate context in which the word stands must also play a major role in the discovery of its meaning. Allowance must be made both for the tradition and for individual usage within that tradition.

Although this chapter necessarily anticipates some of the conclusions drawn later in the thesis, it is hoped that a satisfactory solution to the problem of the identity of the antagonists has been put forward. We now move on to examine the second major problem associated with the individual in the Psalms, that of the meaning of the different terms for the poor.

Chapter 2

THE POOR IN THE PSALMS

I. THREE GENERAL QUESTIONS

The individual who speaks in many of the Psalms frequently describes himself as 'poor' and 'needy',[1] particularly in the Psalms of Lament. In seeking to understand the Psalms we must ask 'What do these words mean?' It is not enough simply to see a literal description of economic poverty implied in these words. In some psalms the whole nation can be described as poor and needy. In others, as will be shown below, the words denote more than simply poverty and are used almost as a profession of piety (cf. the poor in spirit of Matthew 5). The purpose of this chapter is to investigate the meaning of the different terms for poor as they are used in the Psalms. The following questions must be addressed before the detailed examination of psalms can be presented.

1. *Who are the* ענוים *(ᵃnāwîm)?*

As in the question of the antagonists in the Psalms, the question of the meaning of the terms for poor has generated considerable debate.[2] Much of the discussion has centred around the relationship between the two terms עני ('ānî) and ענו ('ānāw). Some have argued that the two terms are variants of one root, arising from a textual confusion, others that they are different words entirely. Rahlfs argued at the end of the nineteenth century that the two words were different and that the ענוים were a party within Israel.[3] Birkeland, in his later work, argued that, as the Book of Psalms is essentially a book describing the struggles of Israel as a nation and a religious community, the two terms are variants of the same form and denote, in the Psalms, the nation of Israel. In the great commonwealth of nations, Israel is the poor and needy one and thus the one to claim Yahweh's attention and help.[4]

The most recent comprehensive examination of the problem is that by Carl Schultz who concludes, against Birkeland, that the two words are different in origin and meaning. עניים does not describe a party, however, but is a group term for the faithful in Israel. Schultz draws attention to the long-standing distinction between the two words in the Kethib/Q'ere variants, the versions and the Dead Sea Scrolls before summarizing the arguments from the psalms as follows:

1. The psalmist never groups himself with the עניים unless he has first identified himself as an עני

2. In his affliction and suffering, the psalmist refers to himself as an עני. It is only after his deliverance from trouble that he groups himself with the עניים.

3. The עני is presented as a victim while the עניים are seen as victors.

4. The עני is in bitterness, heaping imprecations upon his tormentors, and even occasionally doubting YHWH while the עניים are seen constantly expressing praise and thanksgiving to YHWH

5. The עניים are associated with the fulfilment of vows and participation in the sacrificial meal.

6. The עניים—never the עני—are connected with the congregation in its cultic acts of worship. They are pictured as rejoicing and worshipping with the great congregation. By contrast the עני is painfully aware of being alone and desolate.

7. עני bespeaks a forced situation, one that would not have been chosen. עניים reflects a volitional posture which has resulted from that forced situation. There is only one instance (Ps. 88) where עני concludes his cry on a note of complaint and does not move on to join the עניים in praise.[5]

עניים thus emerges as a group term for the faithful in Israel, parallel to צדיק (righteous) and חסד (faithful) denoting in particular the attitude of humility before God which is also one of the senses of עני. This meaning is substantiated by most of the other uses of the term outside the psalms, including the only occurrence of its singular in Num. 12.3:

> Now the man Moses was very ענו, more that all the men that were on the face of the earth.

Schultz argues correctly that, given the context, it is Moses' humility which is here being contrasted with the self-aggrandizement of Miriam and Aaron[6] and not, as some have thought, his 'affliction'. Hence the term can be no mere variant of עני.

There is, however, strong evidence in the Kethib/Q'ere variants that the similarities between the plural forms of the two words gave rise to some confusion and that one term was substituted for the other during the different stages of the transmission of the text. The Q'ere editors plainly believed that the distinction between the two terms should be preserved and will not allow עניים to parallel אביון ('eb[e]yôn) in the four instances where the Kethib has this.[7] It may be that in these passages and in four others from the prophets which Schultz acknowledges as difficult on his interpretation (namely Isa. 11.4; 29.9; 61.1; and Amos 2.7, where the עניים are linked with other words from the field poor) that in the post-exilic transmission of the text, the terms for poor were beginning to be used increasingly as terms for the nation itself (as the following arguments demonstrate). Therefore several passages were given a more overtly nationalistic and therefore eschatological explanation by changing עניים to ענוים (eg. Amos 2.7). In other later pieces the term has been used deliberately to give this impression of the nation represented by a humble and suffering individual (so in Isa. 61.1; 29.19). The ambiguity and common meaning between the two terms עני and ענו can be understood therefore to have increased rather than diminished in time. Schultz has succeeded in maintaining however, as the above arguments show, that the meaning of the two terms should be separated within the psalter.

2. *The meaning of* עני

The meaning of עני, by contrast with that of ענוים, is somewhat more complex. Schultz argues here, in my view wrongly, that the word should not be translated 'poor' but 'afflicted'. By itself, he argues, עני never means economically poor, but the term אביון (needy) must be appended to it to give this meaning.[8] Therefore עני does not denote an economic class or group but merely describes a person in any kind of affliction. However, in three passages from the Pentateuch the עני is mentioned in the laws of Israel apart from the so called qualifier אביון (Exod. 22.24; Lev. 19.10; 23.22). These laws depend for their operation on the use of fairly precise terms: the Israelites would need to know when an עני was an עני in the sense described by these laws.

Hence the term cannot have been a general term for affliction exclusively but could clearly be used to denote the poorest of the poor classes. Whilst it is apparent, as Schultz has shown, that עני can be used as a general term for affliction—a meaning derived directly from its root verb ענה meaning (according to BDB and Schultz) 'to be bowed down, afflicted'—the use of the term for a particular class or type of affliction, that of poverty, should be regarded as an extension from this root. That a Hebrew word can cover a diversity of related meanings should occasion no surprise. Words such as נפש and רוח denote one of several different objects depending on the context in which they are used, as indeed does the term 'poor' in English. The commentator's task must be, given the possibility of several different meanings, to clarify what would otherwise be a very confusing picture.

3. *Does* עני *always refer to an individual in the Psalms?*
Schultz's answer to this third general question is an emphatic 'yes'. However his argument contains at this point a fundamental weakness. In his examination of the different occurrences of עני in the Psalms he pays a great deal of attention to the word's immediate context but often neglects the whole psalm in which it stands. All too often he passes over the question of whether a psalm is individual, royal or national in character. His work is thus an example of the type of study mentioned above in which only one facet of the many-sided problem of the individual in the Psalms is examined and answers to other facets of the problem are simply taken as unquestioned assumptions. This methodology leads him to advance the following arguments:

> The fact that the heaviest concentration of appearances is in the lament psalms should occasion no surprise since the very condition of the עני lends itself to complaint. What is significant here is the heavy concentration in *individual* laments. This, along with the above facts and those which are to follow, indicate that the term is never used to designate the entire nation of Israel.[9]

If some of these 'individual laments' are 'national songs of lamentation in the I-form' or royal in character, as many scholars have suggested and as this thesis contends, the Schultz's argument falls. Passages in the Psalms which would seem to indicate that עני can be used of the whole nation (for example in Ps. 74) are skated round with dubious exegesis which will be mentioned in the discussion of the relevant psalms below. Although Schultz notes the use of עני with עם ('*ām,* people) in Isaiah[10] he avoids confessing that in certain cases here עני denotes the nation by appealing to the cumulative evidence of the rest of the Old Testament.

It is apparent that Schultz is working, as are most writers in this field, with what has been designated above as a code concept of language: either the עני is an individual or he is the nation throughout the Psalms and indeed throughout the Old Testament. The starting point for the present thesis is that this assumption is in the first place unjustifiable as an unquestioned assumption and in the second place fails to do justice itself to the Old Testament's rich use of imagery, let alone the flexibilities of its language. My own view is that עני should in most of its occurrences be taken literally but that this meaning should be determined as much by the context in which a word stands as by its use elsewhere in the Old Testament. This opens the way, as it were, to seeing that עני is in fact used of the king and of the nation several times in the Psalms, as will be explained below. It also seems false, in the examination of עני to separate the term from others in the semantic field poor, particularly אביון, דל and ריש. Psalms which contain these words, as well as psalms which refer to עני are also discussed, therefore, in the following section.

II. THE POOR IN THE PSALMS

As has been suggested above, to attempt to catalogue and describe the uses of the terms for 'poor' in the Psalms is to attempt, in effect, to chart the different facets of one metaphor or, rather, of one concept used in a number of different metaphors, as well as in its literal sense, within the book of Psalms. This being the case, it would be good at this point to dwell further on the nature and importance of metaphor in the Old Testament and particularly in the Psalms before going on to discuss individual psalms in which the terms for poor occur.

Few commentators or readers of the Psalms can doubt the importance of metaphor either in the psalter itself or in religious language generally, but very few, so it seems, actually write on the subject. The exception here is Othmar Keele[11] whose work illustrates many of the metaphors in the psalms from the iconographic remains of the ancient Near East. His work is illuminating, but is only a partial attempt to resolve what must be seen eventually as a literary problem. Keele's method is adequate and helpful in so far as the images used by the psalmist can be portrayed visually. But the heat of the sun or the barking of dogs cannot be portrayed in this way; neither can an illness, or the taste of ashes in the mouth. Furthermore Keele has not sought to investigate the complex nature of metaphor in the psalms, both the different uses to which one image can be put and the way the varied comparisons become intertwined, making it difficult for the modern reader to perceive what is meant to be image and what literal description. The Psalms would seem to have been composed within a fairly close knit tradition over a period of several hundred years. They contain a limited vocabulary, a fair degree of what Birkeland called pattern and continually use and re-use the same series of images coming back again and again, as Caird has observed of the Bible generally, to the two metaphors of the law court and the battlefield.[12] The nature of the language is such that Culley and others have been able to detect what they see as repeated formulae which has given rise to speculation concerning a stage of oral composition in the handing down of the Psalms.[13] Within this tradition, as stock images are used and re-used, a certain amount of movement and development can be observed which should lead the commentator away from the simplistic solution and towards the more complex. By way of a preliminary, it seems to me that the following points need to be born in mind when dealing with metaphor in the Psalms:

(a)   Metaphor is not code.[14] In a code a given symbol has only one meaning. With metaphor this is not the case. To quote the examples given by Caird:

> Leaven may be a symbol for good influence or bad (Luke 13.20f.; I Cor. 5.6f.). . . . The wilderness may be a symbol of desolation, demonic power, everything that has escaped or is resistant to the sovereignty of God (Isa. 13.20-22, 34.13-15, Luke 11.24, Mark 1.13, Lev. 16.7ff, Deut. 32.10) but, because of its association with the Exodus, it may also be a symbol of innocence, sincerity, liberation and security under the providential care of God (Exod. 5.1, Jer. 2.1-2, 31.2, Rev. 12.6).[15]

(b)   Caird catalogues a number of instances where metaphors and images are piled up on top of one another for cumulative effect.[16] He does not mention the possibility of the different meanings of one metaphor being combined to give a richer content of meaning within that given tradition, as can happen in the Psalms.[17]

(c) Caird also records the different stages in the life of a metaphor.[18] When first coined it is alive and sets forth a new way of seing to those who hear it. After continued use it becomes what Caird calls a 'stock metaphor' and then eventually a dead metaphor, a new literalism. Something of this development can be seen in the odyssey of the terms for poor. From having a literal meaning the words come to denote anyone in need, and thence the nation or the king in their need. From here they come to denote merely the nation and become empty code words or symbols for the elect in the intertestamental literature.

(d) The existence of a given metaphor in a tradition does not include the possibility that the vehicle cannot be found elsewhere in that tradition in a literal sense.[19] Indeed, the fact that a scenario is used in a metaphorical way actually implies that scenario was familiar to the original audience.

Two observations must be made on the use of the words for poor in the Psalms before the exegesis is undertaken.

1. The first concerns its different range of meanings: it is confusing to speak simply of literal or metaphorical usage since, as Caird has shown, a metaphor can be many things. Similarly to speak merely of an individual or collective use of a term can also lead to inaccuracies, particularly if the role of the king in a psalm is to be considered. Hence the meaning of the terms for poor in any psalm will be plotted diagrammatically, along two different axes. The horizontal axis will indicate which meaning of the terms is thought to be demanded by the context along the following range:

AFFLICTED	DESTITUTE	IN NEED	= RIGHTEOUS	EMPTY METAPHOR

The translations given for the first three categories are those suited for עני. A psalm will be placed under 'AFFLICTED' if it is thought the root meaning of the term is implied; under 'DESTITUTE' if the term is used in the sense of economically poor; under 'IN NEED' if the term is taken to refer to a more general affliction. If the psalm is placed under '= RIGHTEOUS' then this is because in the text the עני or אביון is thought to be equated with the righteous. If, in my opinion, any of the terms is used of an individual or group whose need is not genuine the psalm will be placed under the category of 'EMPTY METAPHOR'.

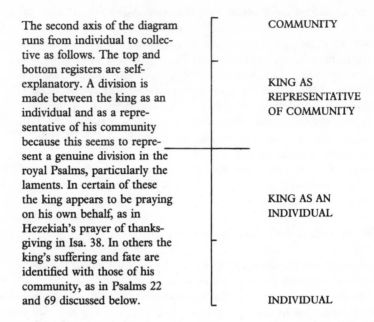

The second axis of the diagram runs from individual to collective as follows. The top and bottom registers are self-explanatory. A division is made between the king as an individual and as a representative of his community because this seems to represent a genuine division in the royal Psalms, particularly the laments. In certain of these the king appears to be praying on his own behalf, as in Hezekiah's prayer of thanksgiving in Isa. 38. In others the king's suffering and fate are identified with those of his community, as in Psalms 22 and 69 discussed below.

COMMUNITY

KING AS REPRESENTATIVE OF COMMUNITY

KING AS AN INDIVIDUAL

INDIVIDUAL

The reader may be helped in reading the exegesis of the psalms which follows by referring to the diagram on p. 70. The horizontal line used with many psalms indicates a broad base of meaning. Brackets indicate alternative positions for one or two psalms.

In one sense this diagram may seem over-complex as a way of discussing the use of the group of words for 'poor' in the Psalms. It is my view that the complexity reflected in the chart is actually represented in the Psalms, however, and such a diagrammatic representation at least gives some idea of the spread of the different uses of the term. In another sense, in attempting to give expression to the nuances of a once-living language and a text which is ever being interpreted afresh, the diagram oversimplifies and is not complex enough. It represents an attempt at compromise between the demands of the text on the one hand and the requirements of the reader of the Psalms on the other.

2. The second general point deals with what I would call 'scenario'. The complex of ideas surrounding the notion of the poor man must be remembered when dealing with any use of the term and the scenario most aptly pictured in this discussion of the terms for poor is that of the law court or legal hearing, plainly a very familiar scene

to the ancient Israelites. Within the law court the poor man is more often than not the defendant and the oppressed party. Often, therefore, he is called the righteous or the innocent at law. According to the common pattern of belief found throughout the ancient Near East, the god, in this case Yahweh, himself watches out for the cause of the widow, orphan and poor man.[20] The self-designation of the psalmist as עני and אביון may therefore be literal and descriptive, but it may also be his way of placing himself under the protection of Yahweh in the 'law-suit'—so many of the laments are in any case couched in terms of a plea for the defence. Closely connected and bound up with these ideas of Yahweh as a helper and protector of the poor is the prominent strand in Israelite theology of the necessity to humble oneself before God and to acknowledge one's dependence on him: God helps those who have no helper. The phrase אני עני ואביון ('I am poor and needy') not only acknowledges this and places the suppliant under the protection of Yahweh but also acts as a term of self-denigration parallel to others in the lament psalms (cf. 51.5).

The different psalms will now be discussed in the categories dictated by the vertical axis, beginning with psalms of the individual and ending with those in which the community is envisaged as 'poor'.

Psalms of the individual

1. *Psalms betraying a wisdom influence: the poor as objects of charity or oppression* (Pss. 41; 112; 37; 49)
It has been argued by Jacquet, Weiser and others that the opening beatitude in *Psalm 41*—'Blessed is he who considers the poor'—does not make sense in the context of the remainder of the psalm. Jacquet accordingly amends the text, without, in my view, sufficient justification, so as to read: אשרי האביון משכיל אלהים, which he translates: 'Bienheureux le pauvre qui compte avec Dieu'. Weiser, who, with Jacquet is unhappy about the use of the word משכיל in the usual translation translates: 'Blessed is he who attends to the poor' and sees דל as referring not to the impoverished but to the psalmist himself. As Kraus points out, the construction מַשְׂכִיל אֶל is in fact attested in Neh. 8.13. Whilst it must be granted that the most common meaning for the term is 'to pay attention to' the verb root can bear a number of different meanings from 'look at' to 'cause to prosper' (BDB, p. 398) and so it is not unlikely that the meaning

normally given here, to consider in a charitable sense, is actually possible but is simply unattested elsewhere. Although it seems unlikely to me that this is a royal psalm, as Eaton suggests,[21] since there are few positive indications to this effect, it remains possible that Psalm 41 was meant to be delivered by a man who would hear lawsuits and hence שכל could here retain its usual meaning. The opening beatitude does make sense if it is read with the rest of the opening section (vv. 1-3). The psalmist is quoting a wisdom saying which he then uses as the basis of his plea from misfortune. The word דל (poor man) therefore must be understood in a literal sense in this psalm.

The view of the poor found in Psalm 41, as being neither righteous nor wicked but a neutral group, treatment of whom is a measure of a man's righteousness before God, is found again in *Psalm 112*, again a psalm from the circles of the wisdom writers. The psalm portrays the blessedness of the man who fears the Lord. Like the good wife in the acrostic poem at the end of the book of Proverbs, one of the signs and causes of his blessing is that 'He has distributed freely, he has given to the poor'. It is significant that the psalm is generally regarded as a post-exilic piece since this would exclude any idea that the development of the use of the concept 'poor' was chronological along the axes suggested.

Psalm 37 also preserves this attitude to the poor as recipients of the charity of the righteous and the oppression of the wicked, though at first sight it may seem as though something more is meant by 'poor' in this case. The psalm is best seen, as was argued above, as a collection of Yahwistic wisdom sayings arranged in an acrostic form on the general theme of reward for the righteous and retribution for the wicked. Weiser puts the tenor of the psalm thus:

> The aim the psalmist pursues is to exhort the godly to cling to their trust in God and to their obedience to God in the face of the manifold temptations in which they get involved through the existence and behaviour of the wicked, be it anger or envy, poverty or affliction, fear of men, doubt about God's actions and his righteousness or getting weary of obeying moral laws.

Throughout the psalm, particularly the latter half, much the same picture can be observed concerning the righteous and the wicked as that discussed above. The righteous does not seem to be particularly poor. All the v. 16 says is that even if he is poor, he is still better off than the wicked. In v. 21 the righteous is generous and gives, in v. 25 he is 'ever giving liberally and lending'—statements which imply material prosperity. On these grounds, therefore, and on the grounds of internal consistency, it is unlikely that the righteous and the poor are to be identified on the basis of v. 14:

> The wicked draw the sword and bend the bow
> To bring down עני and אביון (the poor and needy)
> To slay ישרי דרך (those who walk uprightly).

Even though the expression ישרי דרך is often used in parallel to צדיק (righteous) the psalmist is in fact saying that the wicked man strikes at the poor who is innocent and does not deserve this harsh treatment. Hence the psalmist can assert that the conduct of the wicked man will recoil back on his own head. Therefore the poor are not *identified* with those who walk uprightly but are only *described* as such.

Finally *Psalm 49*, a late wisdom composition, begins with an invitation to listen to the teacher in the psalm, comparable to invitations embedded in Psalms 32 and 34 and found elsewhere in the wisdom writings. The invitation is to 'rich and poor together' to listen to the psalmist's wisdom. Here clearly אביון refers to an economically poor group. Although the poor here are not said to be oppressed directly, the whole does deal with the undeserved prosperity of the rich man and so this could fairly be said to be implied.

2. *Psalms of judgment: the salvation of the poor* (Pss. 82; 12; 72)

In the following three psalms to be discussed the poor appear, as it were, in a different scene of the drama. The court has been summoned and judgment is given either by Yahweh (Pss. 82; 12) or by the king (Ps. 72). In each case the judge is portrayed as a protector of the rights of the poor, although the meaning of the latter term can be seen to be taking on new content in at least two of these psalms.

In *Psalm 82* the scene depicted is Yahweh's judgment of the whole earth. It has been argued above that the oppressed classes listed are not representative of the Israel within the great society of nations. This argument can now be further substantiated by the observation that the categories of fatherless (יתום) and רש (translated by the RSV as 'destitute') are never used figuratively for the nation in the Old Testament and דל is not used figuratively in the Psalms. In accordance with the interpretation given in the previous chapter, the oppressed classes are those within all nations, not Israel herself as a nation.

Also, according to the interpretation established above for *Psalm 12*, the poor and needy here represent the disadvantaged groups within the nation rather than the nation herself. The psalm is a statement of judgment from the circles of the cultic prophets following their ethical norms. Yahweh is at one and the same time both judge and redeemer.

Complications arise, however, with the other two psalms depicting this scenario. *Psalm 72* (discussed above, p. 36) in particular seems to contain two different but not irreconcilable uses of the term עני. In v. 4 and vv. 12-14 the poor are clearly the disadvantaged groups within the nation whom the king is obliged to protect by virtue of his office:

> May he defend the cause of the עניי־עם
> Give deliverance to the אביון
> And crush the oppressor (v.4)

The phrase עניי־עם clearly indicates that the עני is only a part of the whole people here. However, earlier in the psalm the following verse appears:

ידין עמך בצדק ועניך במשפט:

The question arises, since these two terms are used in parallel, as to just what the psalmist means. Is he saying, 'May he judge thy people (the nation) with righteousness and thy poor (within the nation) with justice'—i.e. is he referring to two different groups, as A.A. Anderson thinks?[22] Or is he saying, 'May he judge thy people (the nation) with righteousness and the poor (the nation) with justice', as Weiser and Birkeland would suggest? Or, as a third possibility, does the verse mean 'May he judge thy people (the poor in the nation) with righteousness and the poor (in the nation) with justice', as Schultz would have it? The verse would then be similar in its use of עם to Isa.

3.14. On balance the last-mentioned suggestion seems the least likely: the parallel from Isaiah is a verse coined for effect and cannot be regarded as typical in its use of עם. The first suggestion has the merit of preserving consistency in the text and should perhaps be preferred on these grounds. However, the nation is identified with the poor in other texts which appear to date from the period of the monarchy and it seems that the same ambiguity of meaning which strikes us today would have occurred to the original audience of the psalm. If so, vv. 12-14 could also be taken in an ambiguous or quasi-metaphorical sense, falling as they do after the king's function as both judge and warrior has been described.

3. *Psalms of lament: the poor man's plea for the defence* (Pss. 102; 109; 70; 88; 35; 86)

Six laments are concerned with the poor man as an individual and can best be seen as cries for help from within an imagined law-court situation where God is at one and the same time both judge and counsellor for the defence. In the case of *Psalm 102* the main body of the psalm reflects the suffering and affliction of the nation rather than the individual. The later editor who inserted the heading, which is unique in the psalter, was plainly convinced by the first eleven verses of the piece that this was in fact the prayer of an individual. The picture of affliction is one of fasting, fever and physical pain: hence עני is here given its meaning of affliction rather than poverty.

Psalm 109 is rich in references to the poor and in fact all three scenarios described above are pictured at different stages in the psalm, if the lament is indeed taken as the prayer of an innocent man accused of crimes by a רשע. In v. 16 one of the crimes of the wicked, one of the reasons why he is cursed, is because 'he did not remember to show kindness but pursued עני and אביון'. In this case the psalmist identifies himself with the poor and needy in appealing to Yahweh as judge (v. 21):

> But thou O God my Lord deal on my behalf for thy name's
> sake,
> Because thy steadfast love is good deliver me,
> For I am עני and אביון
> And my heart is stricken within me.

If the curse directed at the accusers actually reflects the fate of the psalmist, as suggested above, then there is no reason why the terms עני ad אביון should not be taken literally here to denote material poverty and general wretchedness. Finally, towards the end of the psalm, the psalmist restates the basic theology on which he makes his appeal to Yahweh, counsel for the defence:

> For he stands at the right hand of the עני
> To save him from those who condemn him to death

—a statement very much in line with the theodicy sayings of Proverbs and the wisdom tradition.

Psalm 70 is a doublet of Ps. 40.13-17 although many commentators view the piece as earlier and as an independent lament in its own right.[23] Psalm 40 is probably best taken as a royal lament (see below) and Eaton wishes to place this piece also in the mouth of the king on the grounds that it is written in the royal style. In fact this is not the case. There are no indications of a royal style in the psalm. Instead, the psalm would seem to be best assigned to the small group of short general laments identified above for general use in the temple services. The suggestion made by Mowinckel and followed by Eaton that the heading למנצח (also found over Psalm 38) indicates that the psalms was intended to accompany the cereal offering is attractive. The cereal offering itself appears to have been made for atonement and in penitence and also in times of sickness (Lev. 2.2; 5.12; Num. 5.18; Sir. 38.11; 45.16).[24] The situation envisaged by the psalm may be one of illness but is more likely to have been that of legal persecution with the offering being made to secure Yahweh's favour. The terms עני and אביון may well have a quite literal reference but are suited, in this general type of psalm, to take on a wide range of meanings depending on the nature and trouble of a particular suppliant. By naming himself עני and אביון the Israelite both humbles himself before God and claims Yahweh's protection.

Psalm 88, one of the most moving prayers of the psalter, consists of one long lamentation with no glimmer of light or assurance. The psalm is normally felt to reflect some long held sickness or disease and, if this is the case, the translation of עני must be in the sense of afflicted rather than destitute.

It has been argued above that *Psalm 35*, like Psalm 109, represents the prayer of one who has been unjustly accused and that, of the two types of language in the psalm, the military language with which the piece opens can most easily be seen to be metaphorical. If so, the psalm is to be seen, like others in this group, as a plea for the defence, and as part of his plea the psalmist takes a vow of praise to the God who

> Delivers the עני from him who is too strong for him,
> The עני and אביון from him who despoils him

claiming, under the traditional theology, the poor man's right of protection from his God. The precise nature of the affliction is not made clear, however, and so, like others in this group, the psalm will be represented on the diagram with a line rather than a point.

The view is put forward in Chapter 4 below (p. 145) that *Psalm 86* is not a royal psalm (as Eaton thinks), since there are no positive indications of this. The psalm contains several late ideas and appears to be made up, to an unusual degree, of quotations from other psalms. For these reasons it seems best to conclude that the psalm is a late prayer written for the use of private persons within Israel, perhaps as a general formula for asking for a sign of Yahweh's favour. The need of the suppliant is portrayed by the psalm in the most general terms and so the terms עני and אביון must be taken as having a general reference.

4. *Other psalms* (Pss. 113; 34)

There are two psalms remaining in which the poor are to be seen as individual Israelites but which contain rather different nuances of meaning. In *Psalm 113* the language used elsewhere to describe Yahweh's care for the poor is, as it were, turned around and used as a reason and ground for praise. Yahweh is he who raises the עני from the dust and the אביון from the ash heap. He is the God who performs the impossible, the unexpected: that this is the primary focus of the verse is shown by the parallel with the situation of the barren woman giving birth (a vivid picture of the reverse of the situation given in vv. 7-8 is depicted in Job 29). Although the reference here is to the individual עני or barren woman, primarily, the two act here as symbols of Yahweh's power to bring into being that which is not. The two symbols are also found together in Hannah's song of praise, suggesting that this may have been a fairly common form of expression.

Psalm 34 is, as has been shown above (p. 21), a didactic wisdom poem. The psalmist gives no indication that he is in any real distress and lacks conviction when he declares himself an עני (v. 6). The psalm therefore appears to identify the cause of the עני with that of the righteous: the latter term is used here to denote a group (though not a party) rather than as a description for a man's innocence in court. 'Righteous' and עני are here both being used as stock metaphors:

> Many are the afflictions of the righteous,
> But the Lord delivers him out of them all (v. 19; cf. also vv. 15, 17).

The psalm is therefore placed on the chart under the heading of '= RIGHTEOUS', the only psalm so placed in this discussion.

Royal Psalms

1. *Psalms in which the king prays as an individual* (Pss. 40; 140; 116)
This group consists of three psalms which are very probably royal pieces. All of the psalms in this group and under section 2 below are laments and the scenario is in most cases similar to that described in section 3 above.

Psalm 40 provides an excellent illustration of the way in which the terms עני and אביון, initially indicative of the distress of the poor man, came to be used for any man in distress who needed Yahweh's help, including the most powerful and wealthy man in the land, the king. The lament in vv. 13-17 has been preserved elsewhere as Psalm 70, where it forms a general lament to be used by any commoner in distress. Here, however, it is part of what is clearly a royal psalm. The piece has a pronounced royal style; the 'I' is a public figure and the curious call narrative in vv. 7-8 can hardly refer to anyone but the king. In this context what is, for the oppressed suppliant in Psalm 70, a statement of fact and need becomes for the king a token of his humility and his awareness of his need of help before Yahweh. There is no indication that the king is in genuine economic or physical need, and therefore I conclude that in this psalm, with Psalm 140 in the psalter, עני is used as an empty metaphor.

It has been argued above that the most likely background for *Psalm 140* is that of a king whose allies or advisers are proposing war. The speaker not only indentifies himself with the עני and אביון (by implication) in v. 12, where there is little evidence that he is suffering other than from slander and possibly false accusation, but he is also, by implication, identifying the righteous and the upright in heart with this group also:

> I know the Lord maintains the cause of the עני
> And executes justice for the אביון.
> Surely the righteous shall give thanks to thy name;
> The upright shall dwell in thy presence (vv. 12ff.).

As in Psalm 40, therefore, עני is here being used as something of an empty metaphor. It should be pointed out that, if these psalms are royal (and hence pre-exilic) their evidence again precludes any suggestion that the development in the use of the terms for poor was unilinear and chronological from the more literary meaning to the empty metaphors contained here. Evidently a number of different meanings for the same term could exist side by side.

Psalm 116 contains one of several occurrences of עני in its verbal form and also as a noun where the term seems to have nothing to do with poverty but is wholly concerned with physical affliction (rather as דל can sometimes mean physical weakness rather than poverty). A similar meaning for the term is found at 69.29 (discussed below). As will be argued below, the psalm is best understood as a royal song of thanksgiving after illness, comparable to the song of thanksgiving used by Hezekiah according to Isaiah 38.

2. *Psalms in which the king represents the community* (Pss. 22; 69; 31)
A detailed exposition of *Psalm 22* is also given below in the context of a discussion of royal psalmody, in which it is argued that the psalm was written for a situation of starvation and siege. The speaker throughout is the king who identifies his own fate with that of the nation. His affliction therefore is not unreal but very real indeed. The meaning borne by עני must once again be 'afflicted'. As in a number of other lament psalms, once the suppliant's prayer has been answered he is able to identify with the ענוים (v. 26).

Psalm 69, like Pss. 22 and 102, portrays the plight of the nation in a skilful and moving way, employing thhe metaphor of the sick individual. The concluding verses of the psalm make it clear that it is the nation that is being described and hence that the speaker, whose plight is closely associated with that of the community, is clearly the king. The prayer towards the end of the psalm:

> For God will save Zion,
> He will rebuild the cities of Judah

would indicate that the psalm was composed for a situation in which Judah had been invaded but Jerusalem, although besieged, was not actually destroyed. Not only does the psalmist describe himself as עני and in pain (cf. 22.24) but in vv. 32f. the אביונים are identified, seemingly, with the entire congregation:

> Let the עניים see it and be glad.
> You who seek God, let your hearts revive,
> For the Lord hears the אביון
> And does not despise his own that are in bonds.

Hence for the first time in the psalms so far discussed, the theology of Yahweh's aiding the poor is invoked on behalf of the whole community. However, it should be noted that in this case, as in Psalm 22, the community really does appear to be suffering; the word is not used as an empty cipher for the nation, That עני is used in parallel with כואב here (v. 29) indicates that it again denotes physical distress, here used as a metaphor for the suffering of the land.

Finally, *Psalm 31* is the third of the psalms written for situations of siege preserved in the psalter. As is argued elsewhere in this study, this seems the only satisfactory setting for the piece. As in Psalms 22 and 69 the metaphor of the persecuted or sick individual is used as a way of describing the city's distress and of appealing to Yahweh for aid. The term עני (v. 7) is used of this suffering and can be seen here, once again, in its root meaning of 'affliction'.

Psalms of the community (Pss. 68; 74; 25; 9–10; 14; 107)

In the six psalms discussed in this group the terms for poor are used in reference to the community of Israel, rather than to the individual within the nation or the king. The three most straightforward examples of such usage appear in Psalms 68, 74 and 103. The theology underlying the use of the terms for poor for the nation is identical with that in the previous two sections. God is the helper and protector of the poor; therefore if anyone in need humbles himself and designates himself as poor he places himself under

Yahweh's protection. In *Psalm 68* Yahweh's nature as defender of the poor is affirmed in the opening hymn:

> Father of the fatherless, protector of widows,
> Is God in his holy habitation.
> God gives the desolate a home to dwell in,
> He leads out the prisoners to prosperity,
> But the rebellious dwell in a parched land.

However, in this verse, as in v. 10, the psalmist clearly sees this theology worked out in the exodus and conquest in respect of the nation:

> Thy flock found a dwelling in it,
> In thy goodness O Lord thou didst provide for the עני.

Schultz comments on the psalm[25] and acknowledges the difficulty of interpretation both in the psalm itself, adopting Albright's theory that the piece is a series of incipits, and the words used in this verse, particularly חיתך, translated by most versions, ancient and modern, as 'flock'. However he leaves one uncertain whether or not he thinks עני is used of the nation here, as it surely must be.

Psalm 74 the same theology is invoked in the context of a national psalm of lament. The psalmist prays:

> Do not deliver the soul of thy dove to the wild beasts,
> Do not forget the life of thy עני (v. 19).

and again:

> Let not the דך be put to shame
> Let עני and אביון praise thy name (v. 21).

In a situation of national emergency the whole nation is regarded as עני and אביון and needing God's help. As has been noted above, the psalm provides one of the more obvious objections to Schultz's theory that עני never designates the entire nation. He proposes that vv. 18-21 actually turn from the situation of invasion to the plight of those remaining in the land, which is plainly the case. What is not obvious, however, is that the term עני and אביון are here to be taken to refer only to the underprivileged groups within the nation. Surely they must be taken here, if nowhere else, as terms for the whole remnant left after the invasion, all of whom are now destitute and needy and crying out to Yahweh for his aid? In neither of these cases is the metaphor empty: real distress is envisaged.

As the text stands, as has been argued above, *Psalm 25* is a post-exilic liturgy for a fast day in which some representative person, in this case not the king, prays on his own behalf and on behalf of the nation. The term עני therefore (vv. 16, 18) must denote a broad range of afflictions, as with the other psalms in this group.

In *Psalms 9-10* there is an unusually rich interplay between individual and collective and between internal military enemies and the wicked in the land. The military enemies are described as רשעים (9.17) whilst opposition to both groups is focused in the person of the king. This rich use of imagery is also found in the use of ther terms for poor where the duality of reference in Psalm 72 (to both the nation and the individual poor) is heightened and amplified. In the first half of the psalm (Psalm 9) the nation is described in the image of the poor man (9.12, 18) oppressed by the nations, described therefore as רשעים. עני thus has a collective reference in this part of the psalm. In the first half of Psalm 10 however, the focus turns to the wicked in the land oppressing the *actual poor* (vv. 2, 8ff., 12). (The reason for the juxtaposition of image and actuality is given in the discussion of the festal context of this psalm below.) There is a parallel drawn in the psalm between Yahweh's power over the wicked outside Israel destroying the oppressors of the עני in the international context, with the prayer for him to intervene and save the actual עני in the nation from his oppressors. The final verses of the psalm sum up its twofold prayer: that Yahweh would continue to give Israel victory over the nations (v. 16) and that justice may be seen to be done within the land (vv. 14ff., 17).[26]

A similar situation to that found in the first half of Pss. 9-10 appears to be envisaged in *Psalm 14*. The final verse of the psalm shows clearly that a situation of military oppression is envisaged and that the evildoers are once again the nations. Hence the עני in v. 6 is once again the nation appealing, as such, for help and salvation from God. Schultz argues that this concluding verse is in fact a typical example of the convention of adding a verse lamenting the fate of the nation to an individual's lament and identifying the fate of the community with that of its member. He cites as other examples of this phenomenon Pss. 3.9; 25.22; 29.11; 51.20; 69.36, 37; 102.14; 147.2. A more satisfactory explanation for most, if not all, of these verses would seem to be that the psalms in question are not true psalms of the individual but are either national or royal in character, as is indicated by other phenomena, and this would seem to be true of Psalm 14 as well. If the psalmist is identifying his plight with that of the nation, then the nation itself must be suffering some kind of distress. The lament then cannot be seen as the prayer of an individual to be used at any time in the nation's history, but only in times of national distress. This being the case it seems more straightforward to regard the whole psalm as setting forth the plight of the nation through the metaphor of the oppression of the poor. At the same time it would, no doubt, serve as a warning to oppressors in the land. As in the other psalms in this group, there is every indication that the distress suffered by the nation as עני is real.

Finally, in *Psalm 107* it is not easy to tell whether the terms for poor refer to the nation or to the individual. The psalm is most probably to be seen against the background of the deliverance from exile and is resonant with the language of Deutero-Isaiah. As in Psalm 113, Yahweh's attitude to the poor is seen as a reason for praise in a hymn which concludes the psalm, and his treatment of the poor is, as it were, symbolic, a demonstration of the nature of a God who brings into being that which is not, who acts so as to intervene in the creation causing the unexpected to come about: rivers turn into dry ground, springs of water into thirsty land. Similarly in human life Yahweh brings down the princes and exalts the poor. If the content of the symbol is not to be lost the terms must have, primarily, a literal meaning. However, in the context of the psalm and against the background of the exile, the original audience would no doubt be able to apply the image to the fate of the nation in exile and restoration. The affliction envisaged is, of course, genuine.

III. CONCLUSION

The main thrust of this chapter has been to establish and to clarify the usage and meaning of the various terms for poor in the Psalms in the light of the conflicting theories concerning the meaning of these terms produced by Old Testament scholars in the last ninety years.

The results of the foregoing discussion can now be summarized in the following diagram:

Figure 1. The Meaning of the Terms for Poor

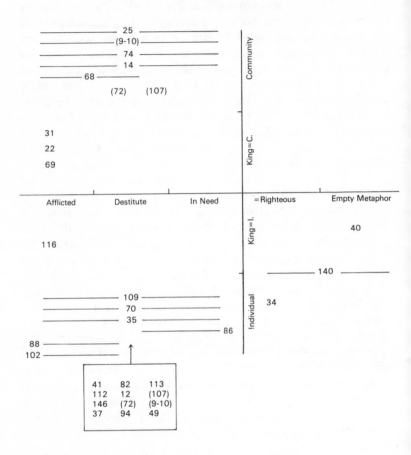

Our conclusions may be summarized as follows:

(1) Seven of the psalms in which the poor occur are not cast as
     laments of the poor man. In four of these, from the wisdom
     tradition, the poor occur as objects of either the charity or
     the persecution of their neighbours (Pss. 41; 112; 137; 49). In
     the other three pieces they stand as subjects of the judgment
     of either Yahweh or the king (Pss. 82; 12; 72).

(2) In all except three of the remaining psalms the distress
     envisaged in the psalm is real. Most of these are genuine

psalms of the individual (Pss. 102; 109; 70; 35; 88; 86). One, a thanksgiving, is royal (116). There is a spectrum of meaning in the term עני particularly. It can mean physical affliction, poverty, or any general need.

(3)   In three psalms only (Pss. 34; 40; 140) is עני used not of real distress but as a stock or empty metaphor, used casually of the suppliant.

(4)   The terms for poor are used metaphorically of the community in five (seven?) psalms. In all of these cases the need is genuine, as it is in the three psalms where the terms are used to describe the community personified in the king.

(5)   The suppliant's purpose in describing himself as poor is that by so doing he places himself under the protection of God and humbles himself before Yahweh. The term embodies both need and self-abasement.

(6)   The uses of the term found in the book of Psalms would seem to reflect accurately the uses of the terms found elsewhere in the Old Testament.

(7)   The development in the use of these terms is not chronological. Post-exilic psalms describe the poor in a literal sense; pre-exilic royal psalmody contains empty metaphor.

In the course of this investigation the three principles set out in the conclusion to Chapter 1 have been further tested and verified. These can now be restated as follows:

(1)   The psalms are not written in code, they are written in the Hebrew language. The discovery of the meaning of a term in one or several psalms does not dictate the meaning of that term throughout the psalter.

(2)   An understanding of metaphor clearly plays an important part in any general understanding of the Psalms. In particular this investigation of the terms for poor has shown how the same word can be used both literally and metaphorically in different psalms and, further, that there is a frequent use of the imagery whereby the nation is portrayed as a 'poor' individual threatened by unjust persecutors in order to secure the favour of Yahweh.

(3)   This enquiry has, it is hoped, given further validity to the basic premise adopted throughout the study that complex problems demand complex solutions and that the psalms of

the individual will not conform to pre-set exclusive theories or this or any other issue.

The first part of this inquiry has thus attempted to prepare for an examination of the question of the identity of the individual in the Psalms by providing a satisfactory solution to the related problems of the identity of the antagonists and of the poor in each of the psalms which refer to these groups. The following chapters contain an examination and classification of each of the psalms in which an 'I' occurs. As was mentioned in the Introduction, the methodology adopted here has been, first, to set out the available options for the identity of the individual in any one psalm—namely that the suppliant is envisaged as the king, or as an ordinary worshipper, or as a minister of the cult—and, second, to assign each psalm to the most likely of these three categories. The investigation begins with an examination of the royal psalms.

Chapter 3

THE INDIVIDUAL AS THE KING

It is now generally acknowledged that the king played a large part in
the cult in ancient Israel and that this royal involvement in worship
is reflected in the Psalms. My own examination of royal psalmody
falls into three sections. In the first, an attempt is made to answer the
question: 'How many psalms are royal?' The central section
addresses the problems concerning the king's involvement in the
autumn festival and in particular the question of whether he
underwent some form of ritual humiliation. A reconstruction of the
festal rites is offered which differs significantly from that put forward
by Johnson and Eaton. The final part of the chapter turns to a
classification and exegesis of those royal psalms which cannot be
assigned to the ritual but which must be seen, for the most part, as
psalms written for a particular type of crisis in the life of the king or
the nation.

I. HOW MANY PSALMS ARE ROYAL?

An outline of Eaton's position

The history of the discussion of a royal attribution for many of the
Psalms is comparatively well documented and will only be sketched
in its broadest outlines at this point.[1] Gunkel's examination of the
Psalms revealed only nine as unmistakably royal although he later
added two others;[2] of these nine only three are actually individual
psalms at all, since the other six address the king in the second or
third person. Other individual psalms in the psalter were thought by
Gunkel to be the prayerful outpourings of pious individuals within

Israel. Mowinckel's suggestion was that most of the individual laments were provided for use by ordinary Israelites seeking protection from sorcerers or other enemies but it was left to his pupil Birkeland to open the way to the interpretation of more of the psalms as royal. If the enemies of the individual are also the enemies of the nation (as they clearly are in many psalms) then the 'I' in the psalms is likely to be the king. Birkeland's arguments were subsequently taken up by Mowinckel in his new, and large, category of psalms: 'National Psalms of Lamentation in the I-Form'. Finally the British scholar John Eaton has attempted to restate the arguments in favour of a royal interpretation in the face of a general scepticism towards the theory in many more recent books. In particular Eaton has attempted to draw out a third major argument in favour of royal interpretation, that of 'royal style' in the Psalms. The first section of this chapter will attempt to assess the strengths and weaknesses of Eaton's position and restate in a clear fashion predisposing factors and arguments which indicate a royal attribution of certain psalms.

Whilst my own position is in line with that taken by Eaton, at least three general criticisms of his work may be made:

(1) As has already been mentioned, Eaton has fallen into the trap of examining the only one possible solution to the problem of the individual. The exaggerated importance which he therefore attaches to that solution diminishes the credibility of his overall position. He is also led to discuss in polemic fashion alternative explanations for the individual psalms[3] when in fact such theories remain necessary to explain the background to the twenty or so psalms which mention an individual but which Eaton does not reckon to be royal.

(2) There is a general confusion both in the opening chapter of his book and in his discussion of the psalms themselves between two different types of argument: there are on the one hand several arguments which predispose the commentator to be more open to the possibility of more royal psalms in general and there are, on the other hand, specific arguments which can be indications of whether or not a particular psalm is royal. The confusion of these two types of argument means that Eaton's case is in danger of becoming circular. The argument from the profilic use of the heading לדוד ('of David') is, for example, a 'predisposing factor' towards a more extensive royal interpretation and is rightly mentioned as such in the opening chapter, where Eaton admits that the superscription in itself cannot provide firm ground for the interpretation of any Psalms. However,

he then goes on to use the heading as an argument for royal identification in his discussion of particular psalms, which seems to me to be quite wrong. Conversely two of the strongest arguments for assigning an individual psalm to the royal group (those of 'consistent interpretation' and 'royal style') are grouped with the predisposing factors as points (ix) and (x).[4] Where so many arguments have to be used to demonstrate whether or not a psalm is royal some attempt must be made to gauge their relative strengths and the degree of interdependence involved. The justifiable fear is that fifty weak links do not make a strong chain.

(3) Finally, Eaton has not paid very much attention to the setting in life of those psalms which he does not consider to have been a part of the annual royal ritual. In effect this means he makes no attempt to group or classify over half of the royal psalms. Such an attempt is undertaken below.

Predisposing factors

The predisposing factors mentioned by Eaton may be grouped around the whole idea of the centrality of the king in the establishing of the cult in Jerusalem and in its continuing supervision and administration. The לדוד ('of David') heading over many of the psalms is evidence for this, as are the Deuteronomistic and Chronicler's accounts of the building of the temple, the provision of temple singers by the king himself and the ancient tradition that David is the founder of Israelite psalmody.[5] Comparative studies have reinforced the idea that the king's role in the religions of the ancient Near East was a prominent one and, as Eaton rightly remarks, the situation of the king in prayer is the only one of the suggested interpretations of the individual psalms which is positively attested in the Old Testament. Eaton is also correct in arguing (p. 25) that

> the narrow identification of royal psalms proposed by Gunkel and others leaves an astonishing gap. There would scarcely be any royal petitions or intercessions . . . Nor is it likely that all the king's prayers were lost while those of all and sundry were treasured in the official corpus.[6]

Arguments for a royal identification of particular psalms

Given that we are to expect that the king played a large part in

Israel's cult and should figure prominently in the psalms, how do we tell which psalms are royal and which are not? Three arguments emerge as such a means of identification:

(1) *The king is mentioned* either as such or as Yahweh's anointed in thirteen psalms. In six of these the king is referred to in the second or third person (Pss. 20; 21; 45; 72; 110; 132;) of the remaining seven the royal interpretation of three pieces (28, 61 and 63) has been disputed and is not clearly demonstrated by the mention of the king. It is possible (but in my view unlikely) that a general prayer for the king has been added to prayers actually meant for private individuals. This issue will be discussed below in the context of an exegesis of these psalms. As far as the other four psalms in this category (Pss. 2; 18; 89; 144) are concerned, there can be no reasonable doubt that the psalms are royal, as all acknowledge.

(2) *Arguments from situation.* In asking the question 'Who would have prayed this psalm in the cult?' one is clearly also asking the question 'What situation of need (or thanksgiving) is reflected in this psalm?' It seems to me that this situation of need can, in most cases, be recovered from the psalm.[7] Clearly the situations which underly some of the psalms can indicate that the psalm was probably written for the king: these include situations of war and battle, prayers to rule justly, prayers against treachery and prayers to be tested (also set against a background of national distress).

(3) *Arguments from style.* However, arguments based on the situation envisaged behind a given psalm are not, of course, always conclusive in demonstrating whether or not the psalm was intended for use by the king. Psalms in which the suppliant appears to be ill, for example may have been provided for the common people as well as for the king. Hence a third argument in favour of royal attribution for certain psalms is needed, based upon what has become known as royal style.

Gunkel, Birkeland and Eaton have all sought to show that there are general features in Hebrew poetry which appear to form such a style. Eaton's list of possible characteristics is the most complete and need not be restated here.[8] However, arguments for royal designation based upon style are not as firm as those based on situation for the following reasons.

First, in several instances the psalm in question may be a later piece in which the royal features have been democratized and applied to Israelites other than the king (as possible in Pss. 42-43, which contain a number of royal features but appear for other reasons to form a non-royal psalm).

Second, although in most cases the given term appears a number of times and these occurrences are mainly in the group of psalms which, for other reasons, would be accounted royal, there are a number of instances of this 'style' where a term does occur in pieces which would more naturally take a non-royal explanation. One such phrase is 'for thy name's sake', which occurs in Psalm 23, which is very probably royal; in Psalms 25, 31 and 143, which may be royal; and Psalm 109, which I do not think is a royal psalm. It is possible that the explanation given above is adequate here and that the royal motif has been taken up by non-royal psalmody; but it is equally possible that the term was a general one which any Israelite, king or commoner, could use in prayer. As will be suggested below, there is no need to restrict all piety, all depth of relationship with God, to the king alone. Indeed it seems very probable that the congregation themselves learned to pray in part from the prayers of their spokesman, the king, and took up his manner of addressing God in their own prayers. A similar question could be raised over the inclusion of the term 'servant' in royal style—a term which could be surely a general term of self-depreciation before God. In the remainder of the Old Testament the phrase 'thy servant' is used by, among others, the patriarchs (Gen. 18.3; 19.19), Moses (Exod. 4.10), Samuel (1 Sam. 3.10), Nehemiah (Neh. 2.5), the Preacher (Eccl. 7.12) and Daniel (Dan. 9.17).

Other elements included by Birkeland or Eaton in the royal style, but which seem more properly to be the common property of Israelite spirituality, are the ideas of the suppliant residing in God's house, the vow of praise, the suppliant speaking of 'my people', the suppliant being called by God faithful or righteous or covenant partner, God's deliverance coming to the suppliant and finally the grace of answered prayer, which is not the exclusive preserve of kings in the Old Testament.

It will be apparent also that there is a danger of circularity in this argument from style: certain features in royal psalms are designated as 'royal style' and royal psalms are those which contain features from this style. It is clear therefore that a psalm can never be assigned to the royal group on the grounds of style alone but that stylistic features can provide useful supporting arguments. In the case of most of the features in this style the number of examples is

	18	89	118	144	91	28	61	63	3	22	27	44	59	94	40	7	92	23	62	140	143	5	31	86	142	4	70	71	16	51	54	73	25	42/3	109	45	13	30	32	38	67	74	84	88	115
My God etc.*	X	X	X	X	X	X	X	X	X	X	X	X	X	X	X	XX	XX			XX	X	X	X	X	X			X		X			X	X	X	X	XX	XX		X	X		X	XX	XX
My Rock	X	X	X	X	X	X	X												X				X	X				X					X		X										
My Fortress	X		X	X	X	X							X						X				X					X					X												
The God of My Salvation	X																																X											X	
My Help			X								X				X												X			X	X				X										
My Deliverer	X			X											X					X							X	X																	
My Shield	X			X		X		X	X																																				
My King												X										X																				X	X		
My Salvation		X	X								X								X																					X	X				
My (Strong) Refuge				X	X														X						X			X				X													
My Glory							X	X											X																										
Lifter of My Head								X																																					
God of My Right																										X																			
Horn of My Salvation	X																																												
My Shepherd																		X																											
My Light											X																																		
Upholder of My Life																															X														
My Strong Tower							X																																						
My Hope																												X																	
My Trust																												X																	
My Father		X																																											
God of My Praise																																			X										
My Song	X																																												

certainly royal ·········· probably royal ·········· not royal

* includes 'Thou art my God/Lord' and 'O Lord my God', 'O Lord my Lord'

Figure 2

too small to enable any systematic analysis; but one stylistic feature, that of the numerous epithets for God to which the first-person singular suffix is attached is open to such analysis and the following investigation attempts to demonstrate that this aspect of style is certainly royal.

The reader is referred at this point to Figure 2 (opposite) which presents a breakdown of the use of these divine epithets. There are twenty-one psalms which, on the basis of the arguments from a mention of the king or from the situation given above, can certainly be described as royal.[9] Of these, fourteen psalms contain one or more of the divine epithets under discussion and these psalms are grouped to the left of the central dividing line on the chart. The other thirty-two psalms containing such an epithet are grouped to the right of the line and are ordered according to the approximate likelihood of their being royal. This group contains psalms which are very probably royal and those which are most probably non-royal. By far the most frequent epithets used are in the group which heads the left hand column: 'My God', 'O Lord my God', 'O Lord my Lord' and 'Thou art my God/Lord', which occur thirty times in the psalter—almost three times as frequently as the next most common 'My rock', which occurs only eleven times. Furthermore, occurrences of 'My God' etc. are spread evenly right across the chart and so it would seem that this group of epithets should be seen separately from the rest and not be distinctive as a mark of the royal style.

Of the other epithets, nine occur with reasonable frequency: my rock (11x), my fortress (7x), the God of my salvation (6x), my help (5x), my deliverer (5x), my shield (5x), my king (5x), my salvation (4x), my (strong) refuge (4x); whilst an additional thirteen titles for God have also survived as a part of the tradition and have only been used the once. The visual impression given by the chart, that royal psalms are more likely to contain such epithets than non-royal psalms is confirmed by a statistical analysis. The twenty-four psalms which are most certain to be royal contain thirty-two occurrences of these epithets, giving a mean of 1.33 per psalm. The other sixty-five psalms containing some reference to an individual contain only twenty-nine instances of these epithets, giving a mean of only 0.46 per psalm. Hence, even if no other psalms than the twenty-four mentioned above are royal there is still evidence of a particularly royal style present here. The demonstration of an authentic royal style in this one respect must support the wider case for a royal style although, as was mentioned above, not to the extent that royal style alone can demonstrate whether or not a psalm is itself royal. However, in a discipline in which one is constantly dealing with accumulating probabilities rather than clear proof every piece of evidence is of value.

Results of the Investigation

Eaton applies the above arguments and others to the Psalms in search of a more extensive royal interpretation. After a careful discussion of each psalm he concludes that there may be as many as sixty-four royal psalms in the psalter. Of these, eleven are Gunkel's original groups of royal psalms, thirty-one are clearly royal while a further twenty-two are less clearly royal but are probably to be seen as such.

My own research, which has been conducted with other possible interpretations of the psalms in view as well, has substantially confirmed Eaton's conclusion that there are a large number of royal psalms in the psalter, but has reduced the number of such psalms by one quarter, finding forty-eight psalms to be royal. Of these, forty-one are, properly speaking, psalms of the individual. In addition to Gunkel's eleven royal psalms I find twenty-five of Eaton's more definite group of thirty-one psalms to be royal but only eight of his less definite group of twenty-two psalms to be so. In addition, I have suggested that four psalms not discussed by Eaton may well be royal (Pss. 26; 38; 44; 60) although the last two of these only have a partial reference to an individual. The reader is referred to the detailed exegesis of the psalms in this and the following chapters for confirmation of these results. Included in the discussion in this chapter are three psalms in which the 'I' appears to be a representative of the community but, by reason of the probable dating of the psalm to the exile or later, cannot be the king.

Exegesis of the royal psalms will begin by examining those pieces which seem to have had their context in an annually repeated royal ritual.

II. THE ROYAL PSALMS AND THE RITUAL

Whilst most scholars are now prepared to admit that the king played an important role in the ritual of the major autumn festival there is still widespread disagreement on the issue of whether or not he underwent some sort of ritual humiliation or suffering in the course of this. Hence, before an exegesis of the royal psalms in the ritual is attempted, this issue must be examined in some detail in the following stages:

1. A brief summary of the scholarly consensus, so far as this has been achieved, on the outline of the main (i.e. non-royal) part of the ritual in the autumn festival will be presented. This will both demonstrate that the king did play a central role and provide the wider context into which any reconstruction of the royal ritual itself must be set.

2. The arguments of Johnson and Eaton to the effect that the king underwent a ritual of humiliation and suffering in the midst of the ritual battle will be examined and found to be inadequately supported by the evidence from the Psalms, the rest of the Old Testament and comparative evidence from Mesopotamia.

3. My own reconstruction of the festival, which associates with the ritual several psalms which have not yet been brought into the debate, will then be offered; general arguments in favour of this interpretation will be advanced and finally this reconstruction of the festival will be expanded by exegesis and discussion of the relevant royal psalms.

An Outline of the Autumn Festival

Almost all scholars are now agreed that the main festival in Israel's sacred calendar was the autumn feast, known in the later literature as the Feast of Booths. The festival had a basic agricultural theme: thanksgiving for harvest and prayers for the renewal of the earth with the autumn rains. However, there is also very strong evidence to suggest an association with the celebration of the kingship of Yahweh which would seem to have been affirmed, rather than renewed, each year by a series of ritual acts. The main structure of the feast can be broken down into the following series of six stages.

1. *Preparation*
It is entirely reasonable to suppose that the great festal epiphany of Yahweh was preceded by a period of preparation, probably accompanied

by prayer and fasting. The prophets make oblique references to serious preparation being necessary before the Day of the Lord (cf. Joel 1-2; Hos. 6.1-2; Amos 5.4-6, 18f.); particularly in the Isaianic tradition there are references to the coming of Yahweh being to a parched and thirsty land, suggesting a period of dryness before the festival (Isa. 35.1ff.; 40-55 *passim*). Public fasting was frequently proclaimed in Israel in response to a national disaster or to seek Yahweh's aid in a national emergency (e.g. Jeremiah 36; 2 Chron. 20.3ff. etc.). Hence, if Yahweh's aid was sought in this way before a real military encounter it is reasonable to suppose a parallel time of fasting before the ritual battle. Moreover, we know from comparative evidence both ancient (as in the account of the Babylonian Akitu Festival) and modern that fasting and preparation almost always precedes a great festival. In Israel's feast this would take the the form, most probably, of repentance by king and people for any sin committed and prayers for Yahweh to arise to face the enemies of the nation in the mock battle.

2. *The ark procession*

This 'arising' of Yahweh to confront his enemies was symbolized by the procession of the ark, now agreed by almost all scholars to have been the central act of the festival.[10] The procession was most probably, it seems to me, an 'out and back' event: Yahweh arises from his temple, confronts the enemies of Israel outside the city and returns in triumph to be acclaimed king. Psalm 132 is best seen as a prayer for Yahweh to arise from the temple rather than to return to his resting place.[11] There may well be allusions to the victorious return procession of the ark in 2 Samuel 6, though it seems unlikely that this represents a full 'ark liturgy'[12] and also in the account of Solomon's transfer of the ark to the temple in 1 Kgs 8.1-6. A liturgy arising from the procession is more probably to be found in Psalm 68, whilst Psalm 118 and 24 also allude to this part of the ritual.

3. *The ritual battle*

There also seems to be sufficient evidence from the Old Testament texts themselves to deduce that in the course of this procession Yahweh, whose presence is symbolized by the ark, encountered his enemies and vanquished them.[13] Psalms 46 and 48 in particular, as Johnson has pointed out[14] tend to this conclusion. Both psalms are most probably to be linked with the festivals by way of their dominant themes: the election of Zion and the kingship of Yahweh, celebrated, in this case, by his martial victory over the nations. In Psalm 48 particularly some sort of fight ritual seems to be described:

> For lo the kings assembled, they came on together,
> As soon as they saw it they were astounded,
> They were in panic, they took to flight,
> Trembling took hold of them there,
> Anguish, as of a woman in travail (Ps. 48.4-7).

This impression is confirmed by the following verses:

> As we have heard, *so we have seen*
> In the city of the Lord of Hosts,
> In the city of our God,
>   which God establishes for ever and ever.
> We have portrayed[15] your steadfast love, O God,
> In the midst of the temple (Ps. 48.8-9).

The evidence for the ritual battle is also supported by Psalm 118, a processional psalm containing many festal themes in which the king appears to have taken part in the festal ritual as the representative of Yahweh in the battle (see below). Psalm 68, the other great processional psalm, also contains several references to bloodshed and battle and Yahweh's triumph which are otherwise difficult to explain.

4. *The entry of the ark into the temple* is also acknowledged by all to have been a central event and the ritual to which Psalm 24 bears clear witness. Yahweh returns from battle and is proclaimed as king. Psalm 118.26ff. also offers testimony to this part of the ceremony and to the king's involvements in this event also.

5. *Yahweh is proclaimed as king* as the ark comes to rest once again within the Holy of Holies. The enthronement psalms identified by Mowinckel find their context in this part of the ceremony (Pss. 93; 96; 97; 98; 99). Yahweh's once-and-for-all victory over the forces of chaos is celebrated (Pss. 93; 95.4; 96.5) as is his 'vindication' of Israel by his victory over the nations (Ps. 98.1-3).

6. *Yahweh pronounces judgment*
As Whitelam and others have shown,[16] according to the royal

ideology of the ancient Near East, kingship consisted of the exercise of the two functions of the warrior and the judge and these two were interconnected: a king validated his right to judge or to govern by victory in battle over the nation's enemies. Conversely righteousness in pronouncing judgment secured victory in battle. In the ritual thus far Yahweh, the divine king, has shown his 'strong right arm' by his defeat of the nations. He now takes his throne and pronounces judgment over all the wicked. The theme of judgment is extremely prominent in the enthronement psalms themselves (96.10, 13; 97.2, 8, 10f.; 98.9; 99.4ff.). It appears from other psalms which have survived that judgment would be pronounced over the lesser gods (Psalm 82), over the nations (Psalm 58; cf. also the prophetic oracles against the nations which would also have been delivered at this point) and over Israel herself (Psalm 50). This element of the festival is made much of by Weiser who sees here the renewing of the covenant which is, for him, the central event of the festival.[17]

Reconstruction of any aspect of the ritual in ancient Israel is, of course, hampered by a lack of direct evidence from sources outside the Psalms and so no one version of the festival can ever be validated conclusively. The above structure is however derived from the Old Testament texts themselves and represents a reasonable conjecture, I would contend, as to the focal events of Israel's main annual festival.

It can thus be seen that very many of the psalms and texts which provide evidence for the ritual of the autumn festival also give us strong evidence that the king played a major role in it (e.g. Pss. 132; 1 Samuel 6; 1 Kgs 8.1-6, etc.). This observation is also supported by comparative evidence from other ancient Near Eastern cultures where it seems that, as Halpern has argued, the renewal of the earthly kingship was closely connected with the renewal or affirmation of divine kingship in the annual festival. Hence, certain of the royal psalms, usually at least Pss. 2, 110, 72 and 132, have been attached to the autumn festival as part of its liturgy by most scholars. The royal ritual has been very much extended, however, in the work of the two leading British scholars in the field, Johnson and Eaton, and their theories on the 'ritual humiliation' of the king will now be examined.

A royal humiliation ritual? The work of Johnson and Eaton

In Johnson's initial programmatic essay on the subject of royal humiliation rites[18] he attempts to link Psalms 89 and 18 to the oultic drama, as well as Psalm 118, and he sees these psalms as the prayers of the king during and after the ritual battle with the kings of the earth. His later work supports the arguments given in *The Labyrinth* with more exegesis and includes other psalms, such as Psalm 101, in the ritual drama. Eaton's work in *Kingship and the Psalms* extends the notion of royal ritual still further. He argues that all of Gunkel's original royal psalms should be assigned to the ritual (with the possible exception of Psalm 45) and he adds a further ten which he thinks were created for the festival (some of which were also used by Johnson) namely Pss. 51, 101, 91, 121, 75, 22, 23, 118, 36 and 92, and a further nine which could possibly be added to this group: Pss. 3, 52, 57, 61, 86, 116, 120 and 129, giving a total of twenty-eight psalms linked with the king's humiliation before Yahweh and his reinstatement. In his later book *Festal Drama in Deutero-Isaiah* this bold approach is modified somewhat and only Pss. 22, 23, 91, 118 and 121 are added to Gunkel's festal group; Pss. 9–10, 40 and 71 also illustrate the festival directly, whilst Psalms 51 and 102 disclose other ceremonies of atonement.[19]

Whilst the general notion of kingship renewal has been accepted as part of the autumn feast by the majority of scholars, the royal humiliation rite (so-called) has become a bone of contention and strong objections have been raised by such eminent workers in the field as Mowinckel and Mettinger.[20] My own view is that, whilst it is not intrinsically improbable that a proportion of the royal psalms should find their context in the festival, the 'humiliation' element which is thought to be present by Eaton and Johnson and which accounts for the inclusion of many of the lament psalms into the ritual rests on very slender evidence indeed. Johnson's case for the inclusion of Psalms 18 and 89 in the ritual rests on two arguments, the first being that it is inherently probable that the Israelite ritual contained some form of humiliation rite in which the king was reminded of his place before the god similar to that contained in the Babylonian akitu liturgy; the second is that Psalm 118, which clearly has its origins in the ritual, alludes to the king being 'hard pressed' in the midst of the battle. This leads him to the hypothesis that the 'suffering' of the king took place in the midst of the mock battle and that, therefore, other psalms which appear to contain laments or songs of triumph from the midst of battle also reflect the king's humiliation and reinstatement. Once this has been admitted, of course, the door is open for almost any number of royal psalms reflecting a background of war, particularly any containing references to festal themes, to be given a place in the ritual. This is the reason why Eaton is able to expand the number of psalms placed here in *Kingship and the Psalms*.

However, the two arguments which support the overall case are not strong. In particular, Johnson has drawn wrong conclusions from the account of the king's disinvestiture in the akitu liturgy. The 'humiliation' of the Babylonian king takes place before the god and consists of the king being stripped of his royal regalia by the priest, being forced to his knees in an act of obeisance, a ritual washing of the hands and a negative confession:

> I did (not) sin, lord of the countries,
> I was not neglectful of the requirements of your godship
> (I did not) destroy Babylon
> I did not command its overthrow
> (I did not ...) the temple Egasil
> I did not forget its rites
> (I did not) rain blows on the cheeks of a subordinate
> I did (not) humiliate them
> (I watched out) for Babylon
> I did not smash its walls.[21]

The significance of this prayer is clear: at the end of another year as king, the monarch gives account of his stewardship before the god. The place of this ritual in the overall context of the akitu festival should be carefully noted. This 'giving of account' by the king takes place in the preparation section of the festival (the equivalent of section (1) above) and before Marduk goes out to do battle. In return for his humble confession before the god the king receives a promise of continued support and in particular victory over his enemies (to be represented dramatically later in the festival):

> The god Bel will bless you for ever,
> He will destroy your enemy, fell your adversary

—after which the king is re-invested and there takes place the ritual of the slapping of the king's cheek, which completes this part of the ceremony.

It is very difficult to see how this account from the akitu liturgy can be made to support Johnson's case for ritual humiliation in the midst of battle. Johnson's 'humiliation rite' is set in a military context, in a different place in the festival and contains *not one* of the elements found in Babylon. Conversely, in the Babylonian account there is no hint of battle or of danger to the king's life. The focus is not upon his suffering but upon the account given of his stewardship. Although the account in the akitu liturgy does seem to have a parallel in the Israelite kingship rites, it gives no support to the Johnson–Eaton position that the king's humiliation took place in the ritual battle.

Once this has been agreed, Johnson's other argument, based on the mention of the king's difficulties in Psalm 118, begins to look extremely shaky. The king is said here to have been in distress in battle (v. 5), to have been saved by Yahweh and to have been chastened sorely but not given over to death. This does not seem to be evidence sufficient to warrant assigning in Johnson's case three or four and in Eaton's case far more psalms to this place in the ritual in the absence of other supporting arguments. It is, of course, extremely difficult to deny absolutely that a particular psalm had a part in the ritual at this point. However, as will be argued below, all of the psalms assigned to the ritual by Johnson and Eaton and not assigned to it here can be understood perfectly well against a background of actual war or siege. In other words the proposed ritual humiliation of the king is not the only possible interpretation of these psalms. The most we can infer from the evidence of Psalm 118 is that the king may have uttered a prayer for Yahweh's aid from the midst of the ritual battle.

In the light of these arguments, Johnson's position now looks weak whilst Eaton's case can be seen to go way beyond the available evidence. This impression is confirmed when the ideology behind the 'humiliation rite' is examined. According to Johnson, the purpose of the rite was to 'remind the king that in the ultimate he holds office by will of the divine overlord whose responsible servant he is'. This is certainly the idea behind the Babylonian rite and my own under-standing of the festival put forward below, but it is not immediately apparent that this end would be accomplished by the ritual suffering of the king in the mock battle.

Eaton seeks, however, to deepen our understanding of the king's suffering in the festival still further both in these rites and in possibly separate rites of atonement.[22] The most extreme statement of this hypothesis comes in Eaton's description of Psalm 22 which, on the grounds of the king's suffering described in Psalms 18 and 89, is assigned to the ritual. Psalm 22 is described as:

> The ultimate in humiliation, the cry from the dust and dissolution of death followed by a great scene of restoration where the emphasis is on the enhancement of God's kingship and the access of life in the farthest regions. This text thus belongs to the very centre of the sacrament of death and life, covering the moment of transition ... Psalm 22 certainly supports our conclusion from Gunkel's royal psalms that the celebration of God's choice of his king was elaborated with a sequence of affliction and restoration, heavy with significance for all the world.[23]

Here there is clearly an extension of the ideology of the humiliation rite so as to see reflected in the *sham* suffering of the king a quasi-mystical statement about death and life and, clearly, a precursor of Christ. It seems to me that an adequate 'general historical' interpretation can be put forward for Psalm 22 (see below). Furthermore, this extended ideology goes beyond that found in the ancient Near Eastern parallel texts. Is it likely that in Israel, where the emphasis upon the king as a quasi-divine figure and upon history as a pattern of cyclic renewal were both considerably less than in the surrounding nations, these rites of the king suffering to the point of death (annually) and being raised again would have been so much more developed in form and significance than those found in these surrounding nations? Such a degree of royal suffering in the ritual would also destroy the pattern of correspondence between the celebration of Yahweh's kingship and the affirming of the Davidic ruler's reign which has been established by Halpern[24] and for this reason also must be rejected.[25]

As a final point, there is, of course, no direct or circumstantial evidence elsewhere in the Old Testament which could be brought forward to support Eaton and Johnson's arguments that the king suffered to an extensive degree in the context of the ritual battle in the festal cult.

Given that Eaton and Johnson's reconstruction of the festival can be shown to be inadequately supported by the evidence, my own reconstruction of the rites will now be put forward.

An alternative reconstruction of the royal ritual

According to the analysis of the main ritual events in the autumn festival discussed above, the festival can be seen to have fallen into three parts: a period of preparation; the procession of the ark and the ritual battle; and the enthronement of Yahweh and the pronouncing of judgment. It seems to me that the affirmation of the Davidic king's right to rule for another year should be seen as taking place alongside the affirmation of the kingship of Yahweh.[26] Accordingly, therefore, the royal ritual itself should be divided into the same three parts and the content of each can be summarized as follows:

1. *Preparation.* As will be argued below, the king is affirmed in the festival in his two functions of mighty warrior and righteous judge. These two functions are interconnected in so far as any unrighteousness in the king will affect the support Yahweh gives him in battle (either ritual or actual); conversely the king's continued victory in battle ensures and vindicates his right to continue to judge or govern Israel. In the preparation period for the festival, therefore, I would suggest that the king gives account to Yahweh for his previous year in office and answers any accusations made against him by the people or their representatives. Along with the people he appeals for Yahweh's help against the wicked within the land and for his military aid against enemies round about. His divine calling is renewed and he is designated king for another year. His prayer throughout is that Yahweh, whose presence is symbolized by the ark, will arise (קומה) and confront the enemies of Israel in the ritual battle to come.

2. *Procession and battle.* The ark arises and leads the forces of Israel, themselves led by the king, to do battle against the foe in some form of dramatic representation. With the aid of Yahweh the king is victorious and returns in triumph to the temple, leading the ark in procession.

3. *Confirmation of kingship and judgment.* The king, vindicated by his victory in battle, is now confirmed in his kingship by the pronouncement of oracles of Yahweh and begins himself to pronounce judgment over the wicked in the land. The following discussion of these elements of the royal ritual and the exegesis of the royal psalms given below will attempt to demonstrate the probability of this hypothesis.

1. *The preparation for the festival*
The preparation for the festival, so far as the king was concerned,

would be in the context of prayer, fasting and preparation undertaken by the people as a whole and was composed of two elements: his giving of account for his rule over the past year and his designation as Yahweh's representative in the coming battle.

a. *The king's confession of innocence* (Pss. 26; 17; 7; 5; 139)
As was mentioned above, the central act in the preparation of the king for the akitu festival in Babylon was not his physical suffering or protestation at this, but his confession of innocence. The significance of this prayer as the king's giving an account of his reign before the god has also been made clear above. Given the degree of correspondence established by Halpern and others between the Babylonian akitu liturgy and Israel's main festival it is not unlikely that the Israelite kingship ritual would have included some parallel confession of innocence. Moreover, the psalter contains several confessions, or negative confessions, similar in form to that given in the akitu liturgy, several of which appear to be royal psalms. It seems very possible, therefore, that some of these psalms should find their context in the royal ritual at just this point and the most likely psalms for such a context appear to be the following.

Although *Psalm 26* is regarded by the majority of scholars (including Weiser, Anderson and Kraus) as the prayer of an innocent accused finding its context in some situation such as that described in 1 Kgs 8.31f., the psalm is actually far too general in content for such a setting. The 'I' in the psalm can clearly be seen to be taking part in public worship (v. 6) and also to have a part in the giving of judgment (hence the mention of bribes in v. 10); moreover he stands in the role of witness to the wonderful deeds of Yahweh (v. 7). The most likely conclusion to be drawn from this evidence is that Psalm 26 is a royal psalm.[27]
    Once this has been agreed, the psalm must be given a context in some situation in which the king is subjecting himself to the judgment of Yahweh, as is indicated by the fourfold plea to be judged in the opening verse, yet no specific crime is envisaged or repudiated by the king. It seems very probable, therefore, that Psalm 26 should be set in some form of royal ritual in which the king, the judge of Israel, gives an account of himself before Yahweh in the manner of the Babylonian monarch:

> I do not sit with false men,
> Nor do I consort with dissemblers,
> I hate the company of evildoers
> and I will not sit with the wicked. . . (vv. 4f.).

(association with the wicked is similarly repudiated in Psalm 101) and:

> Redeem me and be gracious to me,
> My foot stands on level ground
> In the great congregation I will bless the Lord (vv. 11f.)

The opening verses of the psalm also contain a prayer for Yahweh to act—to vindicate his judge the king. This vindication, difficult on most interpretations of the psalm, can be seen to refer here to Yahweh's defeat of the nation's enemies and those of the king in the battle to come. By this means Yahweh will declare that the king has been a faithful judge of Israel.

An additional and supporting piece of evidence for this interpretation is that the psalm contains a reference to the king 'washing his hands', which is also the accompanying rite in the Babylonian akitu ritual.

Psalm 17 is also commonly regarded as the prayer of an innocent accused within Israel (so Anderson, Kraus, Jacquet).[28] However this psalm, like Psalm 26, is manifestly inappropriate for such a situation in that it contains general, rather than specific, protestations of innocence. In addition the psalm contains a notable feature of the royal style: the special relationship between God and the king demonstrated by the reference to the king as 'the apple of the eye' (v.8) and his appeal to 'hide me in the shadow of thy wings'. Psalm 17 should accordingly be seen as a royal psalm.

What then of the situation in which the king stands as he recites this piece? Eaton, with Birkeland, regards this as being a situation of military need. This view is made more likely by reading in v. 11 the plural suffixes attached to the verbs.

Even if the RSV translation is followed, however, some military confrontation is envisaged. But several considerations would seem to favour a setting in the preparation for ritual rather than actual combat. Clearest among these is, first, the connection made between victory and the vindication of the king, together with the declaration of innocence made by the monarch, comparable with that made in Psalm 26 and in the akitu liturgy:

If thou triest my heart,
If thou visitest me by night,
If thou testest me,
My mouth does not transgress.
With regard to the works of men,
by the word of thy lips,
I have avoided the ways of the violent.

Second, this interpretation of the psalm would satisfactorily explain the use of the two terms איבים and רשעים in the psalm. The foreign nations and transgressors within Israel are both opposed to Yahweh and his king and the two terms can be used of both groups almost interchangeably in this and in one or two other psalms. Third, the king's cry for Yahweh to arise (קומה יהוה) which is the technical cultic term used when addressing Yahweh's presence symbolized by the ark, would also support this interpretation. The same cry is found in Pss. 132.8; 68.1; Num. 10.35, in a similar cultic situation (but may be used in Psalm 3 for a situation of actual warfare). As a final strand of evidence for setting Psalm 17 in this ritual context, the psalm is clearly meant to accompany a rite of incubation (vv. 3, 15). We have no evidence that incubation was used as a means of obtaining divine guidance prior to setting out for war but 1 Kings 3 does record a case where incubation is associated with kingship accession. Solomon's dream at Gibeon, and particularly his prayer, appeal to the righteousness of his father as grounds for Solomon himself being granted the kingdom. As Gray remarks[29] this may be taken from, or have set the pattern for, the accession renewal rites (save only that an already reigning king may have appealed to his own right conduct in the preceding year). Solomon's prayer is followed, as in the Babylonian akitu ceremony, by a promise affirming the kingship and by celebration and sacrifice, significantly, before the ark.[30]

The fact that the king appeals here and in Psalms 26 and 7 for vindication from Yahweh and refers to the wicked in the land preparing to destroy him leads to the impression that he considers himself unjustly accused. This opens up the possibility that at the annual festival there was an opportunity in the ritual, or perhaps merely in the context of a large public gathering which the festival provided, for open criticism of the monarch. A number of factors suggest that this may have been the case. The direct testimony of Isaiah 8 asserts that in times of distress and darkness the people would not only turn to superstition but:

> They will pass through the land greatly distressed; and when they
> are hungry they will be enraged and curse their king and their God
> (Isa. 8.23).

Moreover, there was in Israel a tradition of the people turning against its leaders from the traditions of the Exodus and the murmurings in the camp to the secession of the ten tribes from David's heirs after the accession of Rehoboam on the grounds of unfair treatment. The care taken by the court chronicles to demonstrate the righteousness of David and Solomon in all matters is evidence that there was a need for such a precaution even under the united monarchy.[31] The frequency of coups or attempted coups in both the northern and southern kingdoms, in most cases organized with the aid of priests or prophets, also illustrates how careful the king had to be not to offend those zealous for the cause of Yahweh. The prophetic tradition bears witness to an eloquent series of accusers of kings and leaders from Elijah, the 'scourge of Israel' and the northern prophets, who were, in a real sense, the makers and breakers of royal houses[32] to Jeremiah himself in the southern kingdom. Jeremiah 36 records how the message of Jeremiah, a severe warning to king and people alike, was proclaimed by Baruch in the temple precincts (since Jeremiah was debarred from the temple) on a public fast day (though admittedly in the ninth month). With such a prominent and vigilant independent tradition in the land every king would need to take care to declare himself righteous before Yahweh and one way of doing this would be to give account each year at the occasion of the renewal of his kingship. A precursor of this ritual from the end of the period of the judges can be found in the traditions preserved in 1 Samuel 12 where Samuel actually invites the people to accuse him before Yahweh as a means of declaring himself innocent at a public festival:

> Here I am, testify against me before the Lord and before his
> anointed. Whose ox have I taken? Or whom have I defrauded?
> Whom have I oppressed? Or from whose hand have I taken a bribe
> to blind my eyes with it? Testify against me and I will restore it to
> you (1 Sam. 12.3).

Psalm 17 would seem, therefore, to fit this situation of the king's declaration of his innocence at the autumn festival better than either the situation of the innocent accused or of the king faced by a military crisis.

There would seem also to be a strong case for assigning *Psalm 7* to this preparatory stage in the ritual. Again the psalm is often seen as the prayer of an accused innocent but the cosmic scale of the judgment envisaged in vv. 6-8 surely precludes this. The preoccupation of the psalm with judgment and the fate of the wicked would seem to be a barrier to seeing the piece as a prayer before an historical battle. On the other hand there are several indications that the prayer was spoken by the king as part of his giving account and facing any charges of mal-administration over the previous year's reign. The opening verses of his prayer describe the situation as desperate; pursuers are on his heels and there is none to stand beside him, common feature of royal style in the ancient Near East. There then follows a negative confession couched in a formula of self-cursing which becomes particularly appropriate if set before the mock battle:

> O Lord my God, if I have done this,
> If there is wrong in my hands
> If I have requited my friend with evil
> Or plundered my enemy without cause,
> Let the enemy pursue me and overtake me,
> And let him trample my life to the ground
> And lay my soul to the dust.

There then follows, as in the other psalms in this group, the cultic cry for the ark to arise:

> Arise, O Lord (קומה יהוה) in thy anger,
> Lift thyself up against the fury of my enemies

together with a summoning of the cosmic judgment in which the king himself, the judge of Israel, gladly and freely submits himself to the judgment of Yahweh:

> The Lord judges the peoples;
> Judge me, O Lord according to my righteousness
> According to the integrity that is in me (cf. 26.1-2).

The remainder of the psalm takes up the fate of the wicked; by victory in battle both Yahweh and the king will be affirmed in their right to judge and punish the רשע. Verses 12-16 should probably be seen as a salvation oracle against those who have accused the king, with v. 17 as the king's response, addressing Yahweh by his festal name, Elyon. Once again both the enemies of the nation and the wicked within are opposed to the king and this opposition is focused in the cultic battle to come; this accounts for the use of the two terms in parallel here.

Psalm 5, it seems to me, also fits this context of the king's declaration of his own innocence extremely well. It is clear that, with Eaton, we should see this piece as a royal psalm. There is reference to public rejoicing (v. 11), to the suppliant's enemies having rebelled against Yahweh (v. 10) and to Yahweh himself as 'my king'. The opening verses of the psalm, instead of being translated as the beginning of a lament, should be seen as a general plea to Yahweh to hear the prayer which follows:

> Give ear to my words, O Lord,
> And attend to my prayers[33]
> Hearken to the sound of my cry, my king and my God.
> For to thee do I pray.
> O Lord in the morning you hear my voice,
> In the morning I present myself before you and watch.

The verb אערך has no object supplied in either the Hebrew or the Greek. Some commentators, who see the 'I' in the psalm as one falsely accused, supply the object 'my cause', drawing attention to the parallel in Job 23.24. Eaton and others, favouring a royal interpretation, supply the object 'my sacrifice' (so RSV). However, ערך is used with a wide variety of such objects and any choice seems arbitrary. A not unreasonable conjecture is to follow the Greek rendering (παραστήσομαί) and take the verb in a reflexive sense. The original reading may have been the (otherwise unattested) niphal form אֵעָרֵךְ.

According to the interpretation pursued here, vv. 4-6 are not an allusion to the king's enemies but take up the theme of his presenting himself before Yahweh in the early morning to 'watch'—part of the vigil of preparation for the feast. In listing the crimes which prevent men from standing before Yahweh and then saying he himself is fit to worship in effect once again declares the king's own innocence before God and people (vv. 4-8). Only at this point does the psalmist ask for Yahweh's aid against his enemies in the forthcoming battle and judgment. The fate of the enemies is balanced in the celebration to come by the rejoicing of the righteous. Here, as in other psalms discussed above, the two hostile groups of foreign enemies and the wicked in the nation are identified almost as one in their opposition to Yahweh and the king.

Finally, a relatively strong case can be established for seeing *Psalm 139* against this context of the king's declaration of his innocence before the ritual battle. There are several indications that the 'I' in the psalm is the king: he counts Yahweh's enemies as his own (vv. 21f.); he stands in a special relationship with God, as is revealed by vv. 14ff.; he is continually led by God's hand and is always in his presence (vv. 1-12). The focus of the psalm, as several scholars have noted, is not in fact the long meditation on the suppliant's closeness to God but his prayer to be searched and tested:

> Search me, O God, and know my heart,
> Try me and know my thoughts,
> And see if there be in any wicked way in me,
> And lead me in the way everlasting.

This plea to be searched by Yahweh is parallel to that found in Psalm 26, 17 and 7 and so it seems reasonable to assume that this piece also belongs to a similar place in the ritual. The cursing of the enemies, which precedes this passage, also points to such an interpretation: the king is beset by accusers within the land and prays that Yahweh might drive them away by vindicating his anointed one. The reference to the everlasting way (דרך עולם) in v. 24 can also be seen in this light as a reference to the sacred way followed by the ark in its procession (cf. the reference to פתחי עולם in the festal Psalm 24). On this reading the long passage of meditation with which the psalm begins is also appropriate: the passage both reminds Yahweh of his duty to protect the king and the king of his obligation to Yahweh and dependence upon him, ideas very much in keeping with this part of the festival.

b. *The renewal of the king's vocation* (Pss. 94; 101; 141; 91; 27)
Halpern has drawn attention to the fact that a pattern runs through many different manifestations of martial leadership and kingship of 'designation—victory in battle—affirmation of kingship'. This is the pattern of Marduk's accession to the kingship in the Enuma Elish, and although Israel's theology prevents it being traceable at a divine level in Israel (other than in vestigial form) it is observable in Israel's political structures. In particular, Halpern finds this pattern in the meaning of the term *nāgîd*, as one anointed to the kingship but not

yet confirmed in it;[34] in the pattern which emerges from the accounts of the rise of the judges Jephthah[35] and Gideon[36] and can also be traced in reconstructions of the coronation ritual in the period of the monarchy.[37] Given the prevalence of this pattern it seems not unlikely that the king, after his confession of innocence and prayers for vindication, underwent some form of designation ritual before the procession and mock battle.

But what form would this designation take in Israel? Again, Halpern has analysed accounts of the rise to power of various leaders and reaches the conclusion that the divine call was an important element in this. The phenomenon of a divine vocation occurs frequently in Israel's ancient traditions: Abraham, Jacob and Moses were called by Yahweh, as were many of the judges, from Jephthah to Samuel, whilst the divine call to Saul and to David was mediated through a prophet. Solomon was granted an encounter with Yahweh in his dream at Gibeon. Several of the canonical prophets (most interestingly for our purposes Isaiah) also continue in this tradition. Hence it would not be inherently surprising if Israel's kingship rites contained a call as part of the ritual. As will be argued below, Psalm 94 seems to give direct evidence of this phenomenon and, conversely, the 'call' event in the ritual gives a satisfactory setting for an otherwise difficult psalm. Other psalms which may belong in this portion of the ritual are also discussed at this point, namely two pieces which may have formed the king's vow to rule justly (Psalm 101 and 141) and two songs of celebration and assurance which follow this renewal of the king's vocation (Psalms 91 and 27). Finally, to conclude this discussion of the preparation section of the festival, Psalm 132 will be discussed as a psalm which seems to reflect the people's prayer for the king at this stage of the ritual.

The call of the king: Psalm 94

Commentators have suggested various dates and opinions to account for the different passages in *Psalm 94*, including giving the piece a late date (Kraus, for example, dates the piece to the Persian period) and dividing the psalm at v. 11. There can be no reasonable doubt, as was argued above, that the 'I' in the latter half of the psalm is the king (so Mowinckel, Eaton). There are also at least two good reasons for connecting the psalm with the Autumn Festival: first, the psalm is embedded in the psalter among other enthronement psalms and takes up several of their themes (particularly in v. 2); and second, the psalm, as Eaton mentioned, was used at the later feasts of booths according to the Talmud (*b. Sukka* 53a).[38]

It seems to me that the psalm is to be set, unlike the others in this portion of the psalter, before Yahweh's festal epiphany and before his procession to battle. The first section describes a world in need of Yahweh's kingly rule shattered in particular by social injustice. As in Psalm 17 and the others above, and also, although less directly, in Psalm 101, the appeal to Yahweh is to rise up (הנשא) as judge and king against this injustice.

> O Lord, thou God of vengeance,
>> thou God of vengeance, shine forth!
> Rise up, O judge of the earth,
>> render to the proud their deserts!
> O Lord how long shall the wicked,
>> how long shall the wicked exalt?
> They pour out their arrogant words
>> they boast, all the evildoers,
> They crush thy people O Lord,
>> they afflict thy heritage.
> They slay the widow and the sojourner
>> and murder the fatherless
> And they say, The Lord does not see,
>> The God of Jacob does not perceive.

This much we may imagine to have been sung by the 'full choir', as it were (for a true understanding of the psalm involves seeing the piece, like others from the festival, as a liturgy). At this point Yahweh speaks in the person of a cultic prophet:

> Understand, O dullest of the people!
> Fools, when will you be wise!
> He who planted the ear, does he not hear?
> He who formed the eye, does he not see?
> He who chastises the nations, does he not chastise?
> He who teaches men knowledge, the Lord,
>> knows the thoughts of men,
> That they are but a breath.

The choir respond to the oracle from Yahweh, their attention focusing now on the king, prepared by prayer and fasting and depicted, according to the ideal, as struggling to see right prevail.

> Blessed is the man whom thou dost chasten, Yahweh,
>> and whom thou dost teach out of thy law

To give him respite from the days of trouble
    until a pit is dug for the wicked
For Yahweh will not abandon his heritage;
For justice will return to the righteous
    and the upright in heart will follow it.

At this point the speaker changes again and, in my judgment, v. 16 is to be put into the mouth of the cultic prophet who spoke vv. 8-11 rather than into the mouth of the 'I' in the latter half of the psalm. Yahweh asks the congregation:

Who rises up for me (יקום לי) against the wicked?
Who stands up for me against evildoers?

This interpretation is defended on the grounds that it makes the best sense of the psalm and preserves its essential unity as a liturgy. There seems little sense in the appeal in v. 2 for Yahweh to rise up if the psalmist is to testify in v. 16 that he has already risen up on the king's behalf. The oracle has already spoken once in this piece and there seems no awkwardness in his speaking again. Furthermore, v. 16, on this understanding, would have a close counterpart in the question asked in Isaiah's vision:

Whom shall I send and who will go for us?

The latter also takes place in the context of Yahweh's (presumably festal) epiphany in the temple where we assume the call of the king to have been made. It may be that the Isaiah passage borrows this element among others from the festival celebrations. Certainly the motifs of a deaf and blind people and of the 'chastiser of nations' recur there, as well as the ritual question 'How long?' (Ps. 94.1; Isa. 6.11). The interpretation also solves the difficulty of the imperfect tenses in vv. 17-21 which otherwise have to be taken as referring to the past by reason of their context (so Dahood, *ad loc.*).

The king's reply to this question falls into the pattern in the call narratives noted by Halpern in which the intial question by the god is met with humility and self depreciation.[39] He declares both his dependence upon Yahweh and his confidence that the wicked in the land will be punished and overcome by Yahweh's might. Hence it seems reasonable to argue that in Psalm 94 there is preserved a liturgy for the renewal of the king's vocation in the annual festival.

The promise: Psalms 101; 141
Following his confession and call it is not unlikely that the king will
have made a promise to Yahweh for the coming year, renewing his
oath of allegiance. Although there is no direct evidence for this act,
Psalm 101 and 141 would fit such a context (and no other)
exactly.

Psalm 101 is the psalm which Mettinger regards as the surest
evidence for an annual festival for kingship renewal.[40] The lament
metre of the psalm and the otherwise difficult phrase אלי תבוא מתי
('When wilt thou come to me?') are both adequately explained by the
fact that the king, having made his confession, probably in the ritual
dress of sackcloth and ashes and with fasting, is now waiting for his
vindication in the festal epiphany of Yahweh. The oath or promise,
for the future in vv. 2b-8 forms the counterpart to the earlier
confession: having given account of his stewardship over the
previous year he promises to continue to show righteousness in all
his dealings in the year to come. Again the psalm demonstrates the
importance of right ruling for the ideal monarch and how this was
made one of the two key elements in the kingship ritual.

Psalm 141 is cast, similarly, in a metre and style of lament and would
seem to be a prayer for Yahweh's vindication from the accusations of
the wicked in the fight which is to come. At the centre of the psalm
lies a prayer for purity very similar to that found in Psalm 101, which
is followed by a reference to the coming fate of the wicked in the
judgment which will follow Yahweh's being proclaimed king. The
prayer in v. 5:

> Let a good man strike or rebuke me in kindness
> but let the oil of the wicked never anoint my head[41]

may well refer to two of the ritual acts in the preparation rites: the
slapping of the king's cheek, which is attested as a part of the akitu
liturgy, and the anointing with oil which would be a part of the
designation ceremony. The prayer, like Psalm 17, is to be said in the
evening, perhaps at the end of the second day of the festival.

Celebration and assurance: Pss. 91; 27
The final part of the preparation for Yahweh's arising would seem to
have taken the note of assurance for the king in answer to his prayers

and in preparation for the ritual battle to come. *Psalm 91* is a blessing pronounced over the king, presumably though a cultic prophet. The person blessed is clearly the king as one who:

> dwells in the shelter of the Most High,
> who abides in the shadow of the Almighty.

Yahweh is addressed here, as in other ritual psalms, as 'Elyon', Most High, a title which, as Johnson has pointed out, is particularly associated with the festival. The blessing pronounced over the king, as was mentioned above, is general in tone, referring to the ritual battle to come, but also to the king's security from sickness and his ability to judge the wicked. The faithfulness of the king in seeking Yahweh by prayer and fasting, by giving faithful account of his rule over the preceding year and by answering Yahweh's call is again answered itself by the promise of Yahweh:

> Because he cleaves to me in love I will deliver him,
> I will protect him because he knows my name,
> When he calls to me I will answer him,
> I will be with him in trouble,
> I will rescue him and honour him,
> With long life I will satisfy him,
> And show him my salvation.

Finally, *Psalm 27* could well be the king's response to such a prayer. Indeed, no other explanation has yet accounted for the unusual juxtaposition in the psalm of confidence and assurance followed by lamentation, to the extent that several commentators (including Weiser and Anderson) suggest that two psalms should be seen here, with the division in the text at v. 6. The psalm bears many marks of the royal style, in particular in envisaging a situation of war and in the epithets for Yahweh, and therefore should be attributed to the king and seen as a song of assurance after promises of aid, but also as a final prayer for aid before the ritual battle. The opening verses echo the note of assurance found in Psalm 91 and draw attention to the two dangers facing the king: those who accuse him of corruption within the nation and also external enemies:

> The Lord is my light and my salvation,
> > whom then shall I fear?
> The Lord is the stronghold of my life;
> > of whom shall I be afraid?
> When evildoers assail me,

uttering slanders against me[42]
my adversaries and foes,
　　they shall stumble and fall.
Though a host encamp against me,
　　my heart shall not fear;
though war arise against me,
　　yet I will be confident.

The following verses refer back to the king's prayers and the answers he has received, whilst v. 6, with its emphatic ועתה, looks to his coming triumph in battle:

And now my head shall be lifted up,
　　above my enemies round about me,
And I will offer in his tent,
　　sacrifices and shouts of joy,[43]
I will sing and make melody to Yahweh.

However, the battle has yet to be joined and so vv. 7-12 return to the note of prayer and supplication. The phrases 'Seek ye my face' in v. 8 is very probably another reference to the prayers for the ark to arise: פני is a usual synonym for the ark elsewhere.[44] Verse 11 takes up the theme of the king being taught by Yahweh found in Psalm 94 whilst v. 12, difficult on any other interpretation, refers back once again to the king's accusers in the opening rite. The psalm ends on a note of confidence and an appeal, once again (cf. Ps. 101.2a) to 'wait for the Lord', for his festal epiphany (again a reference which cannot easily be explained on any other interpretation).

c. *The prayer of the people: Psalm 132*
Psalm 32 is generally seen as a song to accompany the return of the ark to Jerusalem in triumph. On this understanding v. 8, which reads in the Hebrew קומה יהוה למנו חתר, is translated: 'rise up, Yahweh, *go to* thy resting place', presumably that return must be one of triumph, as reflected in Psalms 118 and 24. Yet this mood of triumph is not reflected in the remainder of the psalm. A better context for the psalm is provided if the piece is seen as the intercession of a cultic prophet for the king in the context of the preparation for the festival. This would best account for the lament and earnest prayer in the opening verses of the psalm:

Remember, O Lord, in David's favour,
　　all the hardships he endured,

How he swore to the Lord
> and vowed to the mighty one of Jacob,
'I will not give sleep to my eyes,
> or slumber to my eyelids,
until I find a place for the Lord,
> a dwelling place for the mighty one of Jacob.'

These verses, in this context, would also allude to the vigil of the present king as he beseeches Yahweh to come to his aid. Verses 6 and 7 are the song of the congregation as they assemble at the outset of the festival, whilst v. 8, it seems to me, should be seen as continuing the more of petition found in vv. 1ff. and v. 10 and be translated:

Rise up, O Lord, *on behalf of* your resting place,
> thou and the ark of thy might,
Let thy priests be clothed with righteousness
> and let thy servants shout for joy;
For thy servant David's sake,
> do not turn away the face of thy anointed one.

This translation has the merit of preserving consistency in the lament section of th psalm. Also, as D.R. Hillers has indicated, there is no evidence elsewhere in the Old Testament that the preposition ל can be used with קום to indicate direction.[45] Hillers himself argues that ל must be used here like the Ugaritic *l* to mean 'from'. This is a possibility but is not without its difficulties, as Johnson has pointed out.[46] A more straightforward translation would be to see ל here as meaning 'on behalf of', a meaning which is well attested in the Old Testament[47] and which is found elsewhere with קום, in Ps. 94.16 cited above. This translation would also have the merit of preserving the meaning of קומה found elsewhere in these ritual psalms, namely 'rise up' or 'rouse thyself', with reference in particular to the forthcoming battle. The meaning is clearly that Yahweh's temple, the symbol of his kingdom and authority[48] is threatened by the forces opposed to the king. This identification between the election of David, the election of Zion and the affirmation of Yahweh's kingship is found in vv. 11-17 of this psalm and elsewhere in pieces from the festival.[49]

The subsequent section of Psalm 132 answers this prayer made by the congregation with an oracle from the cultic prophet promising a continuing dynasty in return for faithfulness to Yahweh's testimonies. The reference to Yahweh teaching the king himself takes up a theme also found in Psalms 94 and 27.

The closing verses of the psalm link the continuation of the Davidic dynasty with continued blessing for Zion whilst v. 18 looks forward once again to the coming confrontation:

> His enemies I will clothe with shame,
> but upon himself his crown will shed its lustre.

Hence Psalm 132 is best seen as a festal prayer made before the ark procession in which the conditional promises to David's line are renewed on account of the previous testimonies given by the king to his faithful conduct (Pss. 7; 17; 26) and his promise for the future (Pss. 141; 101) and rites of vigil and fasting which precede the ark procession.

2. *Procession and battle: Psalm 118*[50]

Broadly speaking, the other consituent elements in the festival discussed here are commonly agreed to have been present and the interpretation of the relevant psalms is not disputed. Discussion can therefore be fairly brief. The tone of Psalm 118 is completely different from that of the laments described above. It is throughout a song of rejoicing for victory: the ritual battle has taken place; Yahweh has prevailed and has rescued his king from the onslaught of the nations. In the course of the psalm the returning procession reaches the gates of the temple and passes through into the temple courts. It can now be seen that the references to the prayers which Yahweh has answered (v. 21) need not be to prayers from the midst of battle but prayers delivered in the preparation for the battle. The self-depreciation of the king in v. 22 in the light of the foregoing discussion can also now be seen as the appropriate response by the king to his divine calling. The note of prayer continued in v. 25 refers, as do similar prayers in other psalms of triumph, to future battles to be fought in the coming year: Yahweh's victory in the ritual battle guarantees success in these actual encounters.

3. *The confirmation of kingship*

Following his triumphal return to Jerusalem and as Yahweh himself is acclaimed king in the enthronement psalms, the Davidic king, vindicated by his victory in the cultic battle, is now affirmed in his kingship in the coming year. Some eight psalms can be assigned to this portion of the festival, four of which are for the king to recite in the first person and four of which are oracles or promises or intercession delivered by a third party, presumably a cultic prophet.

a. *Psalms recited by the king* (Pss. 2; 144; 92; 40)
Psalm 2 portrays the consternation among the nations now that Yahweh has vindicated his king and come in triumph to Zion. In response to this the king recites Yahweh's promise made at his designation as king and confirmed by victory over the nations in the ritual battle (cf. Pss. 94; 132). In the present he gives a solemn warning to the nations to beware of Yahweh's judgment which is to follow.

Psalm 144, rather like Psalm 118, is a song of thanksgiving for victory in battle and is probably, in this instance, to be regarded as arising from the royal ritual. Such a setting would explain why the king gives thanks for a battle already over and won (vv. 1f.), yet also appeals for Yahweh's aid in the future from the aliens (vv. 6-8, 11). The most appropriate explanation would seem to be that victory in the sham fight, as in Psalm 110, in some way assures king and people of victory in the actual battles to be fought and other dangers to be encountered. A further indication of a festal setting for the psalm, as Eaton has remarked (*KP*, pp. 127-29) is the final prayer linking together the king's victory with the prosperity and fertility of the land. However, Eaton's own understanding of the psalm as the king's prayer from the midst of his 'humiliation' in battle does not seem to do justice to the mixture of praise and blessing on the one hand and appeal for protection on the other. Also, Eaton is inclined to see a quasi-mystical connection between the king's 'passion rites' and the fertility of the land. There is a far more natural connection between the kingship rites and the prosperity of the land, however. The safety of the land from foreign invaders has been sought from Yahweh and obtained in the royal ritual; the kingship has been renewed, and in an agricultural society only a strong king could provide the protection necessary for prosperity and well-being.

Psalm 92 appears to be another psalm in which the king, as in Psalm 144, rejoices over the victory in the ritual battle which has taken place. It stands in the collection of psalms which clearly come from the festal ritual. Again we see what, on any other interpretation, would be the paradox of thanksgiving for victory and prediction of victory in the same psalm. On the one hand the king, possibly through the medium of a cultic prophet, declares:

> For lo thy enemies O Lord,
>> for lo thy enemies shall perish,
>> all evildoers shall be scattered.

Yet on the other hand he gives thanks:

> But thou hast exalted my horn like that of a wild ox,
> I am anointed with fresh oil,
> My eyes have seen the downfall of my enemies,
> My ears have heard the doom of my evil assailants.[51]

This verse alone is sufficient to indicate that the 'I' in the psalm is the king and he looks back, as do the congregation in Psalm 48, on the ritual battle which has taken place (there is no reference here, it should be noted, to the king suffering in the battle). As was noted above, there is the same identification of the two groups, of evildoers within the land and the foreign antagonists, found elsewhere, in those festal psalms in which the king plays a central role.

Psalm 40, as Eaton has noted, again fits this context well. Because of the unusual structure of the psalm in which thanksgiving is followed by lament (cf. Psalm 27) and the fact that vv. 13-17 are found elsewhere in the psalter as a separate psalm for a private person in distress, the psalm is often seen as a late and somewhat disjointed composition. In fact, as Eaton remarks, the psalm fits the festal context extremely well. In the first half of the psalm the king proclaims his deliverance from the ritual battle and affirms his vocation in v. 7, the surest indication that the piece is a royal psalm:

> Then I said, 'Lo, I come,
>> in the roll of the book it is written of me
> I delight to do thy will O God,
> Thy law is within my heart'.

Again in vv. 9f, the king affirms that he has fulfilled his role as witness to Yahweh's saving deeds. In the second half of the psalm, employing the metaphor of a private and poor man in danger, he reminds Yahweh of the real destroyers which still face the nation and asks for his deliverance in the actual situations of need to come.

b. *Psalms recited by a third party* (Pss. 110; 72; 21; 61)
Psalm 110, like many of these psalms of victory, very much

highlights the king's role as warrior winning his victories with Yahweh's aid. The psalm opens with an oracle inviting the king designate to be enthroned at Yahweh's right hand and conferring upon him an everlasting priesthood 'after the order of Melchizedek'. As Yahweh defeated the nations in the ritual battle so he will march with the king to battle and the king himself, like Cyrus in Isaiah 45, will be an instrument of Yahweh's judgment.[52]

Psalm 72, the psalter's finest prayer of intercession for the king, takes up many of the themes discussed above and in particular the king's twofold function of warrior and judge. As Eaton aptly remarks (*KP*, p. 120), 'peace reigns also among the commentators' in that all are convinced of the psalm's origin in the annual celebration of the king's accession. The twofold function of the king is brought out in vv. 1-4, 12-14, on the one hand (the king as judge) and vv. 8-11 on the other hand (the king as warrior). The latter verses also pick up language already familiar from Psalms 2 and 110. Prayers that the king will bring peace and justice are coupled with intercessions for his long life and for the prosperity of the land which, as was remarked above, will follow only from the stable social conditions deriving from a strong leader.

Psalm 21, another of Gunkel's original royal psalms, should also be given a place at this point in the festival. The enthronement has already taken place (v. 3) and prayers have already been answered. The oracle of the worshipper, most probably a cultic prophet, is that the ritual victory will now be translated into actual victories against Israel's enemies. Again the appeal is to Yahweh Elyon (v.7) and ends with the worship of the God himself, now also enthroned in the festival. The Divine Warrior gives his strength and support to his earthly counterpart.

Finally *Psalm 61*, which contains an intercession for the king given in the third person and not dissimilar to that found in Psalm 72, is most probably to be seen as a royal psalm throughout. The first section of the psalm contains several examples of the royal style and this being the case, the psalm can most appropriately be set at this point in the ritual as the king looks back to prayers already answered (v. 5) and forward to new dangers (v. 3). As such it forms the last of the psalms attached to this portion of the festival.

4. *Psalms 9-10*

Finally, the reconstruction of the festival offered above, when coupled with what has already been said concerning the royal ideology, the identity of רשעים and איבם, עני and ענו, can be used to offer what I believe to be a satisfactory festal interpretation of Psalms 9 and 10. Debate about the unity of these psalms has plainly been longstanding: although the LXX presents the piece as one, guided by its acrostic structure and common themes, the MT in fact separated the two halves of the poem probably on the grounds of the very different situations portrayed in each:[53] the situation in Psalm 9 is basically one of national need whilst that in Psalm 10 pictures the persecution, apparently, of individuals within the nation. Modern commentators have, without exception, accepted the unity of the psalm, but do not as yet seem to have come up with a context for the piece which accounts for its diverse parts: the balance between praise and lament and the interplay between the enemies of the nation and the wicked in Israel, between the fate of Israel as a nation and of the poor within the nation.

The key to understanding the piece lies in seeing the psalm both as a royal psalm and as one set in the festival. Birkeland, Eaton and Mowinckel all see the psalm as royal—and indeed it is difficult to avoid this conclusion given the explicit references to victory over the nations —but account, in so far as they mention it, for the picture of the poor in Psalm 10 as a metaphor which continues to describe the plight of Israel as a nation. Weiser, by contrast, does set the psalm firmly in the festival but gives more prominence to the individual lament. In the psalm as a whole, he argues, a persecuted individual draws on the great festal themes and applies these to his own situation of need. Birkeland acknowledges that the psalm should have a festal setting, but his blinkered vision of the problems of the psalter prevents his exploring the richness of the piece.

The psalm is best seen, then, as a festal piece, and the suppliant throughout is the king. The psalm is set at the point in the festival where Yahweh has been enthroned as king (vv. 4, 7), having vanquished the nations in the mock battle, and the second part of the ceremony, the pronouncing of judgment, is now envisaged. The psalm in fact links the two concepts together.

The psalm opens (vv. 1-2) with a hymn of thanksgiving for the king's deliverance in battle, which has already taken place. The king in his role as witness now proclaims his salvation to the congregation bearing testimony to the God who saved him:

> I will give thanks to the Lord with my whole heart
> I will tell of all thy wonderful deeds,
> I will be glad and exult in thee,
> I will sing praise to thy name O Most High.

He goes on to describe the victory over the nations in the mock battle linking this victory, in this case, with the judgment of Yahweh which is now to be proclaimed. As in the other psalms from the festival, the king's deliverance is seen as his vindication before God and the people; conversely, therefore, the defeat of the nations must be viewed as their condemnation. They have been tried and defeated, found guilty and are now to be sentenced:

> When my enemies turned back
> They stumbled and perished before thee,
> For thou hast maintained my just cause.[54]
> Thou hast sat on the throne to give righteous judgment.[55]
> Thou hast rebuked the nations (גוים),
> Thou hast destroyed the wicked (רשע),
> Thou hast blotted out their name for ever and ever.
> The enemy has vanished in everlasting ruins;[56]
> Their cities thou hast rooted out,
> The very memory of them has perished.

The term רשע is used here as referring to one convicted under Yahweh's judgment and hence can aptly be applied to the nations. As was mentioned above, its use here does not entitle us to assume a correspondence between the two terms thoughout the Psalms. The reference to everlasting ruins and the destruction of cities takes up into the festal mock battle the past, and therefore the guaranteed future, triumphs of the Israelites over their warlike neighbours.

The focus of the psalm now turns from the victory which has been celebrated before the eyes of all present (cf. 48.9) to Yahweh who is now enthroned as judge in the second aspect of his divine kingship. In particular, the chief concern of the judge is brought to our attention: his concern for the poor and the needy (cf. Chapter 2 above):

> But the Lord sits enthroned for ever;
> He has established his throne for judgment
> And he judges the world with righteousness.
> He judges the peoples with equity.[57]

Yahweh is a stronghold for the oppressed,[58]
A stronghold in times of trouble;
And those who know thy name put their trust in thee,
For thou, O Lord, hast not forsaken those who seek thee.

A connection is begun here which is sustained throughout the psalm
between (a) Yahweh's judgment against the nations who oppress on
behalf of the afflicted Israel and (b) Yahweh's judgment within the
nation, expressed explicitly in Psalm 50, against those who oppress
the poor themselves. Verses 11-12, perhaps sung by a choir, at this
point take up more explicitly the notion of prayer and thanksgiving
for Yahweh's salvation:

Sing praise to the Lord, who dwells in Zion
Tell among the people his deeds,
For he who avenges blood is mindful of them
He does not forget the cry of the עניים.[59]

On this understanding, and indeed on any understanding of the
psalm which aims to be consistent, the textual emendation which
involves a change in the pointing only in v. 14 seems most attractive.
Several scholars, including Weiser and Kraus, emend חֲנֵנִי to חָנְנֵנִי
and רְאֵה to רָאָה, an emendation supported by Aquila and Jerome.[60]
There is also support for the reading in the triple נ of the present MT:
many MSS have, in fact, altered the imperative to the more normal
חָנֵּנִי, and this would be the only recorded instance of the deviant form
of the imperative.[61] The verse can, therefore, be translated (with
Weiser):

The Lord was gracious to me,
He saw my affliction
and lifted me up from the gates of death,
that I may recount all thy praises
and in the gates of the daughter of Zion may rejoice in thy
    deliverance.

The king refers here to Yahweh's deliverance in the mock battle
when, as is mentioned in Psalm 118, the king is portrayed as being
hard-pressed and crying out for help. It is significant for the
interpretation of the psalm that the warrior king recounts his
salvation in the *gates* of Zion, given the prominence of these gates or
doors in other festal psalms (so Pss. 118; 24). The four verses which
follow again draw the connection between the king's salvation and
victory in battle and the judgment of the nations, again described as
רשעים:

The nations have sunk in the pit which they made;
In the net which they hid has their own foot been caught.
Yahweh has made himself known, he has executed judgment;
The רשעים are snared in the work of their own hands.

After the pause indicated by 'Higgaion Selah' in the Hebrew text, the following verses sum up the conclusion to the first half of the psalm—a moral lesson drawing attention, as in so many of the psalms discussed above, to the fate of the wicked and, by contrast, the poor. The moral lesson itself is given in v. 18 and is drawn from the preceding dramatic ritual but is applied to conditions in Israel in both halves of the psalm:

The רשעים shall depart to Sheol,
All the nations that forget God.
For the needy shall not always be forgotten,
And the hope of the ענוים shall not perish for ever.

Finally, to close Psalm 9 itself the appeal is made to Yahweh in language familiar already to the festal worshippers from the calling out of the ark to the mock battle, to rise up and seal the judgment of the nations, to sentence them finally, as it were, and to confirm the judgment implied by their defeat by the king in the cult; the congregation, perhaps, joins at this point in the cry:

Arise O Lord (קומה יהוה: cf. Psalm 132 etc.),
Let not man prevail,
Let the nations be judged before thee,
Put them in fear O Lord,
Let the nations know that they are but men.

At this point the attention of the congregation is turned once again by a lament style prayer uttered, possibly, by the king or by a cultic prophet. Given that Yahweh has established justice among the nations, why is there so much confusion and injustice on the home front? This section of the psalm has often been misconceived as a personal lamentation over individual misfortune. In fact this is not the case at all and the appeal is made to Yahweh on behalf of sufferers in general: it is not the 'I' in the psalm who is suffering but the poor in the community. The continuation of thought from the first half of the psalm is that since Yahweh has prevailed gainst the nations and earned the right to sit enthroned as king and judge then he must now set matters to right in Israel itself and it is perhaps fitting, therefore, to see that the king, as in his warrior capacity he appealed to Yahweh for aid in overcoming the nations, so in his judge capacity he brings the plight of the nation before the divine throne. The prayer in the opening verses is that the wicked in the nation may share the fate of the nations. The rather lengthy description of the plight of the poor (Ps. 10.1-11) is followed by a prayer for Yahweh to arise this time in judgment over the internal רשעים, parallel to the prayer for judgment over the nations in 9.19f.:

> Arise O Lord (קומה יהוה)
> O God lift up thy hand
> Forget not the עניים
> Why does the wicked renounce God
>   and say in his heart 'Thou wilt not call to account' (vv. 12-13)

which in turn is followed by a couplet of assurance that God hears based on the confidence in God provided through the ritual drama:

> Thou dost see; yea thou dost take note of trouble and vexation.
> That thou mayest take it into thy hands
> The hapless commits himself to thee;
> Thou hast been the helper of the fatherless.

The concluding verses of the psalm contain another appeal for action from Yahweh and further link together his judgment on the nations with that in Israel herself:

> Break thou the arm of the wicked and evildoer;
> Seek out his wickedness till thou find none;
> Yahweh is king for ever and ever (a recurrence of the festal theme),
> The nations shall perish from his land

and the psalm ends on the note of assurance:

> O Lord, thou wilt hear the desire of the meek,
> Thou wilt strengthen their heart;
> Thou wilt incline thy ear
> To do justice to the fatherless and the oppressed,
> So that the man who is of the earth might strike terror no more.

Psalms 9-10 are best seen, then, as a liturgy for the festival which links together Yahweh's victory over the nations and salvation of the king in the mock battle, firstly with his judgment of the nations themselves and secondly with his setting things to rights within Israel herself.

Conclusion

This section of the chapter has attempted to define a context for some twenty-one royal psalms which seem to have been composed for recitation in the royal ritual within Israel. An alternative reconstruction of the royal rites has been put forward in which the king prepares for the ritual battle by giving an account of his stewardship before God. The following section will examine the remaining twenty-seven royal psalms not assigned to the ritual here.

III. GENERAL HISTORICAL ROYAL PSALMS[62]

The psalms discussed above are, it seems to me, the only psalms which can be assigned to the royal ritual with any degree of confidence. Most of the other royal psalms fall into the category of general historical pieces: psalms written with particular types of crises in the life of the king and of the nation in mind to be used as and when these crises occur. Of the thirty psalms discussed below by far the majority reflect, as Birkeland and Eaton have argued, a background of war. Others reflect crises which are more personal to the king: treachery within the nation, or sickness for example. On the positive side the psalter also contains several psalms which can be grouped as psalms of assurance to be pronounced, perhaps, in the cult as appropriate at the overcoming of any particular crises. Each of these categories will be examined in turn and an attempt will be made to illuminate each context from other accounts of Israel's life under the kings.

War psalms

An examination of the history of the monarchy in both Israel and Judah reveals an impression of almost continual war. The king lived under perpetual threat of three things: (1) violent revolt and overthrow from his own compatriots; (2) border wars and skirmishes with neighbouring states; (3) less often, clashes with the 'superpowers' on the Nile and in Mesopotamia.[63] It is not surprising, therefore, that the psalter should contain a great many psalms which seem to have been written for use in these situations of national crisis. The war psalms discussed here are divided into four groups: (1) prayers before battle; (2) prayers after battle; (3) prayers from a situation of siege; (4) pieces where the royal attribution is less certain.

1. *Prayers for aid in battle* (Pss. 3; 44; 56; 57; 60; 108; 69; 89; 20)
The psalter's provision of prayers for aid in battle is more plentiful
than it provision of songs of victory to be sung afterwards and varies
from vaguely expressed prayers for protection to full-blown laments
over a defeat which has already taken place. *Psalm 3*, which appears
to be a short prayer for protection in battle to be uttered by the king,
falls into the former category. The military metaphor (shield, v. 3),
the reference to foreign armies and the general martial confrontation
envisaged by the psalm are sufficient to indicate that the psalm is
royal, as most commentators have agreed.[64] Jacquet is happier to
follow Schmidt's suggestion that the psalmist is an accused individual
but evidence for this is slight. Why should an accused be so
frightened on account of the number of his enemies? Why should the
deliverance brought to the paslmist then affect the nation (v. 8)?
Why, too, should the psalmist use so many military 'metaphors' but
give no hint of a judicial situation? Similarly there seems no reason
to follow Kraus's suggestion that the psalm is by an individual who
'puts himself in the position of the king'—why not simply admit that
the psalm is royal? Weiser sees the psalm as stemming from the royal
ritual in the cult and this, as Eaton has acknowledged, cannot be
ruled out. There is what may be a reference to the cultic act of
incubation (v. 5) and the cultic cry for the ark to arise (v. 7), which
has been noted in the festal psalms. However, v. 5 may well be a
simple expression of trust and confidence in God rather than a
reference to the rite, as may be the parallel phrase in Psalm 4;[65] other
references to the ritual, such as the cry to God to arise, may well be
examples of festal motifs taken from this context and used in
situations of historical need. The description of the enemies and
particularly their mockery in v. 1, which is not recorded elsewhere in
a certainly ritual psalm, incline me more to the view that the psalm
should be treated more as a general historical piece revealing, as do
most of the psalms in this section, the king in his capacity as warrior
supported by Yahweh. The festal theology is put into practice here in
a situation of real need.

By contrast with Psalm 3, *Psalm 44* is more clearly a cry from a
situation of actual distress. Several commentators (Anderson, Weiser
et al.) draw attention to 2 Chron. 20:4ff., which describes a prayer
offered (significantly) by the king in a situation of national crisis.
Although Psalm 44 is mainly a communal piece, vv. 4-8, in the first

person singular, are probably best seen as spoken by the king rather than by any other representative individual for these reasons: when compared with Psalm 3 the piece contains the two features noted there, namely the mockery by the enemies of the nation as an important factor in the appeal (vv. 13-16); and the cry to Yahweh to 'arise' (vv. 24ff.), here clearly not in a festal setting. On the latter point Weiser sees the psalm as having a context in the cultic covenant renewal festival taking place after a recitation of the *Heilsgeschichte*, but it does seem as if a situation of real national distress is envisaged here. It may be that some such recitation would be built into the other ceremonies which would accompany this psalm.[66] It is worth noting, however, that here and in other psalms where the king appeals on behalf of the nation, appeal is made to God's activities in the past and to those actions in particular which the suppliant desires to be repeated in the present.[67] This point will be made again in the discussion of Psalm 22 below. The king appears again here in his role as warrior acknowledging his dependence upon Yahweh in each battle fought.

Psalm 56 presents an unusually difficult series of textual problems,[68] but the royal interpretation of the psalm is clearly indicated by v. 8. As Mowinckel writes[69] the psalm is an example of one of several national or royal laments written in the personal style. This interpretation is followed by Eaton—although he does place this psalm among his less clear cases[70]—Kraus, Johnson,[71] and Dahood. Anderson argues that עמים (peoples) is not necessarily an indication that the psalmist is the king, but may be part of the cult language the suppliant is using. Such an argument fails to hold water when, in every other respect, there can be no objection to the psalm being royal. The use of military language would thus be appropriate in its literal meaning here (not 'military metaphor' as in Weiser). The psalm sounds strong notes of assurance, particularly in the suspected refrain (vv. 3-4, 10-11), which are echoes of the songs of assurance also assigned to the king and explored below. The true metaphor in the psalm is that of the king as the persecuted individual standing before Yahweh to plead his case, which changes (v. 13) to that of the king as a sick man whom Yahweh has rescued from death itself. The fact that the metaphors of sickness, rescue from death and persecution can be firmly established here as metaphors which could be used for the trials and tribulations undergone by the king in war will be important for an accurate understanding of such psalms as 22, 18 and 89 (to be discussed below). Finally, it is important to note that the psalms vary in the degree to which they stress the king's special relationship to Yahweh: in some pieces (e.g. 2; 110) this is paramount; in others, such as this psalm, the suppliant appears to pray almost as an ordinary individual, making no claims upon the special promises given to the king.

The public praise given in *Psalm 57* is the most valuable piece of evidence for assuming that the psalm is royal. Who else but the king could claim to give thanks and praise among the nations? Other significant factors are God's special concern for the psalmist manifested in phrases like 'In the shadow of thy wings I will take refuge' and 'I will cry to God Most High ... who fulfils his purpose for me'. The metaphor of the wild beasts is more likely to represent foreign armies than any other kind of persecution and recurs in Psalms 59 and 22. Correspondence can be seen to be made explicit in the spears, arrows and sharp swords mentioned in v. 4. The abrupt change of mood in the psalm is best seen as the result of an oracle of salvation delivered by a cultic prophet (cf. 2 Chron. 20.14-17). Eaton's suggestion (which follows Birkeland) that the prayer is one from an incubation rite with vv. 1-4 being prayed in the evening and vv. 5-11 in the morning is a possible one in view of the cries to 'awake the dawn'. His suggestion that the psalm may well arise from the ritual seems less likely, but cannot be dismissed with any certainty: in the reconstruction of the festival offered above, the rites of incubation would take place before the danger became apparent. The frequency of war and battle in ancient society and the general background of war against which the psalms were written inclines me to the view that the piece was intended as a general historical prayer and thanksgiving.

Psalm 60 also clearly pictures a situation of war and great danger, although the mention of Edom (v. 9) indicates that this piece may well be a particular historical psalm. The psalm opens on a note of communal lament, prayer for God to intervene. This is followed by the oracle of a cult prophet (vv. 6-8) in which Yahweh's victory is proclaimed. The king, as spokesman for the people in v. 9, then asks for aid once more: if Yahweh will not give this aid then who will? The final verse expresses a renewed confidence that this help will be received.

Psalm 108 is a composite psalm built up from sections of Psalms 57 and 60 and there is no reason to doubt that the speaker is again the king and that a situation of war is envisaged as underlying the psalm.

Psalm 69 begins as if it were an individual lament, and is understood to be such by many commentators (so Anderson, Weiser). On this understanding the concluding verses of the psalm, which refer to the salvation of Zion and the rebuilding of the cities of Judah must be an editorial addition or a postscript which stands outside the main theme of the psalm. There seems no reason, other than a refusal to recognize metaphor as such, why the prayer should be subject to this treatment. In fact Psalm 69, understood in its entirety, is best seen as one of those pieces in the psalter in which the suffering of the community is expressed and focused in the suffering of one inidividual who is more than likely to be the king. As Eaton remarks (*KP*, p. 52) the communal aspect of the psalm emerges strongly in the thanksgiving and itself belies an individual interpretation. Birkeland draws attention to the prayers in the Amarna letters and of the prayers of the Egyptian kings[72] in which Pharaoh portrays himself as totally alone and afraid. Elsewhere in Israel this portrayal of the nation in terms of a suffering individual is found in Psalms 22 and 102 in a particularly striking way, as in this psalm, and of course the metaphor occurs frequently in the prophets. The opening imagery of the psalm where the psalmist sinks into deep mire and is overcome by many waters is not necessarily indicative of personal illness to the point of death but is frequently used in the psalter and elsewhere to denote the effect of a military invasion.[73] Other elements in the psalm have occurred in other royal prayers with this background: in particular the suppliant's concern about the number of his enemies (v. 4) is found in Psalm 3. The mockery of the foe is always of concern to the king and is nowhere more poignantly expressed than in this psalm. In particular the power of the nation and the power of God are closely bound together: 'It is for thy sake that I have borne reproach, that shame has covered my face' (v. 7);[74] 'For zeal for thy house has consumed me, and the insults of those who insult thee have fallen on me' (v. 9).

An element introduced in this psalm is the psalmist's concern about his own sin. He says in v. 5, 'O God thou knowest my folly, the wrongs I have done are not hidden from thee'. Apparently, therefore, the king feels he deserves some punishment but not to the degree with which his enemies are causing him to suffer. As a part of his defence he reasons:

> For they persecute him whom thou hast smitten,
> And him whom thou hast wounded they afflict still more.

A further supporting point for a royal interpretation is that the 'honour' of the psalmist's hearers is bound up with the fate of the psalmist. How could this be if the psalm was the prayer of an accused man? Finally, the curse of the psalmist includes the words:

> May their camp be a desolation,
> let no-one dwell in their tents

—assuming that the psalm does not date back to the nomadic period (by reason of the reference to the rebuilding of cities in vv. 35f.) then the words טירתם (camp) אהליהם (tents) would seem best to refer to the encampments of armies on the move rather than to private individuals.

Psalm 69, therefore, seems best understood as the prayer of a king made in the pronounced royal style of the ancient Near East by which the sufferings of the nation are portrayed as the sufferings of the monarch himself.[75]

Psalm 89 has been seen by several commentators, including Johnson and Eaton, as a psalm composed for the royal ritual which itself provides strong evidence for the so-called rites of royal humiliation. The connection with ritual is made because of the first half of the psalm and the many festal themes which predominate: Yahweh's victory over the nations; his choice of David; the promises to David's line and the reference (in v. 15) to the תרועה, the festal shout of victory.[76] Ps. 89.1-37 must have been written as a festal psalm.[77] However, there are several problems involved in seeing vv. 38-51 as originally a part of that festal psalm and which incline me more to the view that the lament was added later and was used on occasions of genuine military need.

The first reason for taking this view has been fully explored above: namely that there is really no evidence at all, either inside or outside the Old Testament, for seeing a royal humiliation of the type envisaged here to have been a part of Israel's liturgy. A second, and very strong argument, is provided by the theology of the psalm. In Psalms 118 and 144, which are from a ritual setting, all evil is attributed to the nations, as is appropriate in a cultic scene in which Yahweh is about to fight, or has already fought, for Israel. In Psalm 89, however, the evil and misfortune have come from Yahweh, not the nations (vv. 38-45). The doubts expressed in the psalm are real therefore, occasioned by historical circumstances and a wrestling with God. There would be no element of doubt if this were a ritual piece repeated every year. And this element of doubt and distress which dominates the second part of Psalm 89 nowhere shows through in the more triumphant and festal first part, which would again indicate that the lament has been appended to the hymn of praise. Although there are many common themes in the two parts of the psalm, which have been fully explored by Ward and Clifford,[78] they do not necessarily indicate that the psalm was originally written as a unity. They could equally well point to the theory that vv. 38-52 were composed as an answer to the triumphant song of vv. 1-37. Psalm 89 as it now stands, therefore, is best seen as a general historical song of lament.

Psalm 20 provides another example of a prayer composed for the king's use before battle. Unlike the other such intercession preserved in Psalm 21 this piece seems, on balance, to be a prayer for the king before a genuine military encounter rather than before the sham fight in the ritual, although in this particular case there is no way of being certain. Gunkel, Mowinckel, Anderson and Johnson (*CPIP*, pp. 175-85) all support a historical interpretation whilst Duhm, Schmidt, Weiser, Bentzen and Eaton side in favour of the ritual view. All we can say with certainty is that the psalm could be used on either occasion!

2. *Prayers of thanksgiving* (Pss. 18; 66)
As with Psalm 20, it is possible that *Psalm 18* may have been appropriate either in the festal setting or in the context of the celebration of an actual military victory. Although the psalm contains many allusions to the festal themes, Johnson and Eaton are surely wrong in seeing the piece as some sort of liturgy. According to Johnson's account of the piece in *The Labyrinth*, the psalm describes the deliverance of the Davidic king from death, his subsequent justification and vindication and his triumph over the nations.[79] Both scholars separate the mythical language and the victory described in the first half of the psalm from the more historical language and the

victory in the second half. It seems much better to see the whole psalm as celebrating one victory, which is expressed first in mythical and then in historical language. That the same deliverance is described in both sections of the psalm is shown by the juxtaposition of vv. 16 and 17:

> He reached from on high, he took me
> he drew me out of many waters,
> He delivered me from my strong enemy,
> and from those who hated me,
> for they were too mighty for me.

Given that the psalm celebrates the one victory it becomes much less self-evident that the piece should be assigned to the ritual. If assigned to the ritual, as a song of thanksgiving after the ritual battle, it still gives no further evidence for the theory that the king underwent a prolonged period of distress in the battle such as that supposedly witnessed to in Psalms 89 and 22. However, the psalm may have been composed as a song of victory after an actual triumph in battle. The psalm has the vigour and pace of the Song of Deborah, which also portrays Yahweh as a storm God and Divine Warrior and describes the divine and the human musters for battle separately. The best course is to remain agnostic on the issue.

Psalm 66, which is acknowledged by all to be a general historical psalm, provides a possible context for the psalm of praise and thanksgiving discussed above. As was remarked in Chapter 1 the second half of Psalm 66 is rightly regarded as the prayer of the king set in the midst of communal rejoicing over some national victory. Yahweh's victory is in this instance likened not to the creation but to the exodus (vv. 5-7) although many of the phrases describing salvation echo those in Psalm 18. The closing words of the king's speech described, in microcosm, the substance of Psalm 18 itself:

> Come and hear all you who fear God,
> And I will tell what he has done for me
> I cried aloud to him and he was extolled with my tongue.

One can perhaps imagine the psalm as opening a whole liturgy of celebration and praise for historical deliverance and victories, among which Psalm 18 would feature, and which would be accompanied by sacrifice and proclamation and other gestures of worship. As in Psalm 18, the king's victory in battle is closely linked to his own righteousness and consequently his righteousness is vindicated by his victory.

3. *Prayers for times of siege* (Pss. 22; 59; 31)

In all ancient warfare siege was as frequently used as a means of waging war as was pitched battle. The Old Testament narrative accounts contain references to several such sieges (e.g. Isaiah 36; 2 Kings 7) and we know of many more given in the accounts of Mesopotamian and Egyptian kings and exposed by archaeological excavation. It should not be surprising, therefore, that the psalter should provide prayers to be delivered in times of siege, just as it provided songs of lamentation and triumph before or after a pitched battle. The three psalms which seem to reflect this background are discussed below.

The interpretation of *Psalm 22* is by no means straightforward and no consensus has yet been reached. There is now general agreement as to the unity of the psalm. The dramatic change in the prayer at v. 22 is most sensibly attributed to the intervention of a cultic prophet who utters an oracle of salvation. There is also a general agreement that the suppliant is a representative personality of some kind and is most likely to be the king. The whole psalm is written on a public and cosmic scale (especially vv. 27-29) and there is also evidence that the suppliant stands in the king's special relationship to God (vv. 9-11). Once again several scholars, particularly Eaton, have argued that Psalm 22 should be assigned to the royal ritual on the somewhat shaky grounds of (1) comparative evidence from the Babylonian akitu festival (which does not in any case provide a suitable context for this psalm), (2) a supposed vagueness of language in the king's description of his distress (which would be different from parallel passages in other supposedly ritual psalms), and (3) the suddenness of the suppliant's deliverance after the prophetic sign (better seen as an anticipation of deliverance than as part of a ritual).

If, then, Psalm 22 is a royal psalm, and if it is not to be assigned to the royal ritual, what was its original context in the worship of Israel? The crisis envisaged in the psalm is not personal to the king but affects the whole community. The nation is in some form of great need and distress. The king appeals to Yahweh employing the metaphor of the poor man seeking the aid of his protector in time of need. The community's suffering is described as the suffering of the king. Yet the distress is described in terms different from that in other psalms already discussed. Enemies are mentioned, but there is no reference to battle. Taking all these factors into consideration it seems to me that the most likely context for Psalm 22 is in a situation of siege and near starvation in the community. The following evidence from within the psalm supports this interpretation.

a. The opening verses of the psalm indicate that the distress envisaged has been going on for some time. This counts against a ritual interpretation and in favour of a situation such as a siege.

b. There are several references to the suppliant, and therefore his community, being *surrounded* by the enemies, described throughout the psalm in the metaphor of wild beasts (vv. 12-13, 16). These verses find a parallel in the refrain in Psalm 59 (vv. 6, 14), another psalm reflecting the background of siege, where the enemies are also described as wild dogs encircling the city.

c. The suppliant's distress, and therefore the community's, is described in terms of starvation and drought—exactly the cry one would expect to hear from a besieged city. The suppliant's strength is gone; his tongue cleaves to his mouth; he can count all his bones. For the difficult line 'They have pierced my hands and my feet' it is best to follow the Hebrew (and Johnson[80]) to render 'my hands and feet are as a lion', again describing emaciation.

d. Not only is the distress in the psalm described in term of food shortage, but so is the promise of salvation, unusually so in the psalter. The promise is given in v. 26: 'the meek (i.e. those faithful to Yahweh) shall eat and be satisfied'.

This promise should be seen as being reaffirmed in the closing verses of the psalm. The text of these verses is difficult. The conventional reading for v. 31 is to read אֵיךְ לֹו for אָכְלוּ and translate: 'Yea, to him shall all the proud of the earth bow down . . .' (so RSV, Johnson). A difficulty with this rendering is in imagining how the perfectly sensible reading אֵיךְ לֹו became transliterated into the nonsense אָכְלוּ. It seems far better to emend the first two words only slightly to read אָכְלוּ וְשָׁתוּ and to translate the verse:

Eat and drink!
All the fat ones of the earth shall prostrate
themselves before him, all who go down to the dust,
and his soul shall not live.[81]

Those who are starving now are invited to eat. Those who have
plenty now will be humbled before God.

Hence for these reasons, Psalm 22 is best seen as a royal prayer
from a situation of starvation and siege.

It is difficult to see how *Psalm 59* can continue to be read as an
individual lament (so Weiser, Kraus) in the face of so much evidence
to the contrary—particularly the situation which underlies the
psalm, the special relationship between God and the supporting
evidence of royal style. As Birkeland recognized, the piece is a
national song of lament. The repeated refrain that the enemies prowl
around the city like dogs by night similarly takes one directly to the
situation of siege which is envisaged by the prayer. This interpretation
is also supported by the repeated references to mockery (cf. on Psalm
22 above) and to the repeated designation of God as 'my fortress'
(משגבי) in vv. 9, 16 and 17. Eaton (*KP*, pp. 47f) records still other
royal motifs in the psalm. An individual interpretation, by contrast,
requires a secondary interpretation of many concepts in the psalm,
particularly the references to the nations and to the nation of Israel
itself.

Psalm 31, like Psalm 22, is a difficult psalm to interpret, primarily in
this case because of the pattern of lament-thanksgiving-lament-
thanksgiving which runs through the psalm. Many have accordingly
suggested that the psalm be divided at v. 8 and treated as two, or
even three, separate compositions. A more satisfying interpretation,
however, is to see the 'I' in the psalm as the king and his prayer as
one from a besieged city (so Eaton, Birkeland, Mowinckel). That the
psalm is royal is demonstrated by the royal designations for God, the
public nature of the praise in the psalm and the nature of the
suppliant's enemies. That the situation is one of siege is shown by:
the structure of the psalm mentioned above (the king rejoices that he
has survived the invasion of his land, but prays for Yahweh's
complete deliverance); the phrase in v. 21 (MT 22) לי בעיר מצור which
should thus be taken literally ('to me in a besieged city'), not
metaphorically as in most translations; the numerous references in

the prayer to Yahweh being a rock of refuge or a fortress (vv. 2-3), which cause one to think of a siege situation; the similarities to Psalm 22, which include the description of distress and the fact that the suppliant is surrounded by enemies (vv. 9-13; cf. 22.14-18); and the message to hold strong and take courage which concludes the psalm (vv. 23f; cf. 22.26, 29f).

4. *Other psalms* (Pss. 140; 143; 102; 25; 51)
Five more psalms seem to a greater or lesser degree to reflect the nation at war or faced by foreign enemies. In the first two a royal interpretation is possible, though not certain. In the other three psalms (Pss. 102, 25 and 51), although the distress envisaged is that of the nation under the threat or at war, by their apparent date these pieces belong to the exile or later and so the suppliant in the psalm must be some representative person other than the king.

It has been argued that in *Psalm 140* the suppliant is most probably the king by virtue of the references to battle and to war which the piece contains, although several scholars would give late dates and this is not impossible. The situation of a king fits the psalm well, however, but this adversaries seem to be as much within the land as outside it, goading an unwilling ruler into a war he does not want.

A similar confusion about the date of the piece prevents a sure decision about whether or not *Psalm 143* is a royal prayer for Yahweh's aid against the foe or a late and general prayer that any man may make against his personal opponents. Eaton's arguments that the psalm is royal,[82] supported now in Johnson's work,[83] are generally more convincing than, for example, Anderson's contention that the psalm is late by reason of its allusions to other psalms and its innate concept of universal sinfulness. It has to be admitted, however, that the interpretation is less certain here than in many other cases.

Psalm 102, like Psalms 69 and 22, forms a valuable example of a psalm in which the suffering of the community is taken up and represented in the image of the physical affliction of the psalmist. As Eaton remarks, the piece draws on the festal traditions of God's kingship (v. 13), creation (v. 26) and a new era of salvation to come from Yahweh's epiphany,[84] but the psalm cannot be given a place in the regular ritual. Rather this particular piece, like Psalm 137, would seem to reflect the distress and conditions of the Babylonian exile. The evidence for this is clear: Zion is in distress (v. 13); there is reference to her stones and dust, the point being that the inhabitants bear a great love even for Zion's ruins. These features, together with v. 16, 'The Lord will build up Zion', imply a situation where Jerusalem has been destroyed. Although Eaton draws a comparison with a Babylonian festal prayer which asks god to restore the brick of the temple[85] the exilic interpretation seems more likely here. Further, in v. 24 the suppliant utters the words: 'take me not hence in the midst of my days'. This is sometimes regarded as a prayer against premature death[86] but this understanding is difficult. On the understanding of death in the Old Testament supposed by Johnson, Wolff and others [87] it would not be appropriate to see Yahweh as taking one to death. It seems more likely that, given the references to prisoners, the phrase is a prayer not to be taken into exile. The psalm can therefore be set, according to Mowinckel's suggestion, in a specially appointed day of fasting and repentance, perhaps in the years 597–587 BC.

Psalm 25 has been discussed at length above, where it was proposed the piece does reflect a background of national danger, but that the spokesman is more likely to be a post-exilic leader than the king himself.

Finally, any interpretation of *Psalm 51* is dependent upon whether verses 18 and 19 are considered to be part of the original psalm or are read as a later addition to it, adapting the piece to liturgical usage during the period of the exile. The traditional view has been to favour the latter alternative, on the grounds that the view of sacrifice contained in these verses contradicts the low estimate of sacrifice in vv. 16-17 of the psalm. However, several scholars, among them Jones[88] and Eaton[89] have pointed out that in fact there is no contradiction between the views of sacrifice expressed here. The view put forward is that sacrifice is ineffective as a plea for forgiveness, or a means of earning forgiveness in acts of atonement: here the appropriate response is a broken and contrite heart. However, sacrifice is an appropriate response to Yahweh's act of salvation in rebuilding the walls of Jerusalem. Once this has been resolved there is no other ground for the separation of vv. 18-19 from the rest of the psalm: no other psalm, so far as we can tell, has had such a liturgical addition appended to it. Moreover, as the above exegesis has demonstrated, there was a continual interplay between the sin and suffering of the individual in Israel and that of the community. If, as seems to be the case, vv. 18 and 19 are part of the original psalm, then the psalm itself would appear to have been composed in the period of the exile, after the walls of Jerusalem had been destroyed. Eaton's view that the psalm comes from a ritual in which the king suffered on behalf of the community has been examined above and rejected. This being the case, the speaker in the psalm, although a representative person, cannot have been the king (and indeed there is no evidence of the royal style). However, as there is clearly a strong association between the sin of the community, or of the individuals within the community, and the disaster which has befallen the nation, the psalm is grouped here with others which reflect a background of war. The psalm should be seen as forming part of a liturgy for a day of penitence either amongst the exiles or, more probably, in Jerusalem. As an additional confirmation of all these arguments it should be noted that the concept of repentance and of the grace of God, the creation of a new heart and the gift of a new spirit, and even the desire to teach sinners, are all concepts which became prominent in Israel's theology either before or during the exile in the work of Jeremiah, Ezekiel and Deutero-Isaiah.

Prayers from other situations of need

1. *Prayers against treachery* (Pss. 55; 62; 71)
As can been seen from a survey of the history of the two kingdoms, the threat to the king from internal dissent and treachery was considerable. Three psalms from the individual laments would seem to reflect such a situation and would seem to be prayers provided for use at such a time. It must be remembered, however, that once the discussion has moved from psalms which envisage a situation of war the royal identity of the speaker must be less sure in many cases. Situations of threat from enemies within the nation and also of sickness may be shared by king and commoner alike.

Psalm 55 is, however, acknowledged to be royal by both Eaton and Mowinckel[90] despite its unusual reference to what appears to be a particular event of betrayal by an intimate personal friend. In the

first half of the psalm the king portrays himself as beset by trouble
from inside and outside the nation following the convention of
painting the picture as darkly as possible to make his appeal more
effective. Both the enemy and the wicked create trouble in different
ways. Violence and strife are within the city itself and also round
about its walls. Against this background of danger, confusion and
oppression the psalm writer has given us the lasting image of the king
portrayed as a dove flying away from the city to be at rest in the
wilderness. From the general picture of strife and distress portrayed
in the first eleven verses the description focuses on the particular
need, which is plainly one of betrayal. One of the king's counsellors
or advisers has betrayed him, presumably either by an accusation or
a military betrayal to a foreign power. There seems no reason to
regard the piece as a particular historical psalm or to see the
description as depicting the genuine emotional turmoil of the psalm
writer (so Weiser, *ad loc.*). The friendship between king and betrayer
is drawn in as intimate terms as possible so as to make the appeal for
Yahweh's aid the more poignant and moving. The psalm need not,
therefore, refer to any particular broken relationship. That the king's
position could be so endangered by such a betrayal highlights his
precarious political position within the land which is attested in the
historical accounts. His appeal to his God is founded on his enemy's
lack of respect for Yahweh and his law contrasted, by inference, with
the king's own attitude. The images of battle and salvation are used
to describe the coming confrontation. These may be meant literally,
if a civil war is envisaged, or metaphorically to describe the political
encounter which must now take place. Verse 17 of the psalm gives a
further valuable hint about the way in which these complaints would
be made: frequently repeated prayers would be offered at set times of
day during periods of real crisis, presumably over several days:

> Evening and morning and noon
> I will utter my complaint and moan
> And he will hear my voice.

Two considerations make it more likely than not that *Psalm 62* is to
be read as a royal psalm. First, the danger is envisaged as affecting
primarily an individual in vv. 1-7, yet in v. 8 it is the people who are
instructed to trust in God at all times—the situation therefore seems
suitable for a royal psalm. Second, the psalm is rich in royal style,
particularly the royal epithets for God (vv. 2, 6).[91] Hence it again

seems wise to see the piece as a prayer designed to be used when the
king is politically weak and men plan to 'cast him down from his
eminence', a circumstance which would, of course, affect the stability
of the nation as well as the life of the king. Verses 8-10, with their
distinctive style akin to that of some of the wisdom psalms, are
probably to be seen as an oracle of salvation delivered after the
prayer (Ps. 55.2 may likewise be such an oracle). The king responds
to this in the final two verses of the psalm. As Eaton notes the psalm
is trustful in tone rather than a direct supplication.

As was argued above, the indications are clear that *Psalm 71* is a
royal psalm. The danger envisaged by the king appears to be from
internal enemies watching for signs that Yahweh has forsaken the
king and so the psalm can be grouped here along with other psalms
written for situations of treachery and internal dissent.

2. *Prayers in sickness* (Pss. 38; 116; 28)

It hardly needs to be said that in the days before modern medicine
illness of any kind was a much more serious and life-threatening
disorder than it is today and prayer was correspondingly a more
widespread response to sickness. The historical writings record the
leprosy of Uzziah (2 Kgs 15.5; cf. 2 Chron. 23.16-21) and, more
significantly, the sickness, prayer and subsequent recovery of
Hezekiah (2 Kgs 20.1-11 and parallels). Of particular interest in this
passage is the fact that the king's deliverance from illness is
associated with the political deliverance of the nation from Assyria:

> And I will add fifteen years to your life. I will deliver you and this
> city out of the hand of the king of Assyria and I will defend this city
> for my own sake and for the sake of my servant David (2 Kgs 20.6).

Again it is not unlikely, therefore, that the psalter would provide
prayers for the king's use in such situations of sickness although the
identification of the psalm as royal is more than usually difficult.

Psalm 38 is a psalm in which the vivid description of illness is not
used, as often, as a metaphor for the affliction which has befallen
Judah or Jerusalem but, so it seems, is used here literally to describe
actual sickness. The psalm is not included by Eaton among his royal
psalms but may nevertheless be royal. In particular the suppliant's
description of his enemies would seem to indicate that the psalm was
composed for use by the king:

Those who seek my life lay their snares;
Those who seek my hurt speak of ruin
and meditate treachery all the day long.

Those who are my foes without cause are mighty,
and many are those who hate me wrongfully.

There are in addition several indications of the suppliant's close relationship to God (vv. 9, 15, 22). The sickness in the psalm is clearly attributed to the suppliant's own sin in this particular piece: there is no protestation of innocence (vv. 3, 4, 18).

Psalm 116 would seem to be a fitting response to Yahweh's granting of the prayer made in Psalm 38. The latter, like Hezekiah's psalm of sickness, may well have been delivered outside of the temple, possibly in the king's own house, but Psalm 116, the prayer of thanskgiving, is uttered publicly 'in the courts of the house of the Lord'. The thanksgiving itself is accompanied by various ritual acts: the lifting of the cup of salvation (v. 13), the payment of vows (v. 14) and the offering of a sacrifice of thanksgiving (v. 17). The public nature of the thanksgiving inclines one to the view that the psalm is royal, as does the declaration in v. 16:

O Lord I am thy servant,
I am thy servant, the son of thy handmaid,
Thou hast loosed my bonds.

But this identification cannot be certain. There are no indications whatsoever that the psalm may have belonged to a festal ritual.[92] The interpretation of the piece as a psalm of recovery after sickness is supported by Job 33:26ff.:

Then a man prays to God and he accepts him,
he comes into his presence with joy,
He recounts to men his salvation,
and he sings before men and says,
'I sinned and perverted what was right
And it was not requited to me
He has redeemed my soul from going down into the pit
And my life shall see the light'.

The view has been put forward above that *Psalm 28* represents the prayer of a king from a situation of illness as he prays that he might not have to suffer the fate of the wicked, i.e. death. The concluding verses of the psalm may be an addition to adapt the piece for congregational use (so Anderson, *ad loc.*), but other individual psalms have not had this addition made. Also there are other signs of royal psalmody in the prayer, namely the suppliant's concern that the wicked receive their just reward (vv. 3-5) and the features of the royal style (vv. 7f.). The concluding lines of the psalm, presumably uttered by a cultic prophet, associate, with Isaiah in 2 Kings 20, the recovery of the king with the salvation of the nation.

Psalms of assurance: Pss. 23; 16; 138; 63

Five royal psalms remain to be discussed, four of which can be grouped together because their dominant theme could fairly be said to be the assurance of Yahweh's protection of the king through danger and difficulty rather than the difficulty itself.

Psalm 23 is, of course, the best known of these and there are several signs that the piece is a royal psalm: there is evidence of royal style ('my shepherd', v. 1); of a special relationship between Yahweh and the psalmist; of a banquet for the king in the presence of his enemies, signifying victory and, most significantly, an anointing with oil. As with the other psalms in this group it is impossible to tell whether or not Psalm 23 was intended to be used in the royal ritual; the reference to danger (v. 4) is too vague an indication. All we are able to say is that both a ritual and a general historical usage would be possible with all of these four psalms. All four pieces take up most markedly the theme of the king as a witness to Yahweh's salvation and his constant watchfulness.

Psalm 16, the second of the group, begins as more of a lament; however, the focus is upon Yahweh and his protection of the psalmist rather than upon any immediate danger. Again there is evidence of a royal style: 'my chosen portion and my cup' (v. 5) and of the special relationship between the king and Yahweh (vv. 7, 11). As in Psalm 23, the dangerous forces within and without the nation which threaten the life of the king are symbolized by the 'death motifs'—in this case Sheol and the Pit. The king's function as witness is again demonstrated, particularly in his declaration of allegiance to Yahweh alone (v. 4):

> Those who choose another god multiply their sorrows; their libations of blood I will not pour out, or take their names on my lips.

It is the reference to the kings of the earth praising Yahweh which makes it more likely than not that *Psalm 138* is also a royal psalm, together with its similarity in phraseology and thought to the two pieces discussed above. The psalm could easily have been used as a song of thanksgiving and praise after a successful outcome to any of the laments discussed above or in the festal liturgy itself.

Finally, *Psalm 63* reveals the depths of the psalmists' spirituality, again in a prayer written, most probably, for the king's lips. It seems most unlikely that the final verse is some kind of liturgical addition, but the psalm as a whole makes an interesting blend between the expression of the spirituality of the psalm composers and the thanksgiving of a king.

Psalm 45

Although Psalm 45 is unique in the psalter as a psalm written for the wedding (or a wedding) of the king (which under Solomon at least must have been a fairly frequent occurrence), in several respects it is a suitable piece with which to conclude this discussion of the royal psalms of the psalter. The poem contains one of the highest estimates of the relationship betwen the king and God found in the Old Testament, and the king is actually addressed as אלהים if the MT reading is followed. Furthermore, in the context of this high estimate of the king's divinity and the statement of the royal ideal, the ideology to emerge, as was pointed out above is that of the twofold function of the king as judge and warrior—a final confirmation, if one is needed, of the prominence of these two ideas in Israel's concept of ideal kingship.[93]

IV. CONCLUSION

This chapter has examined those psalms of the individual which seem most likely to have been recited by the king in the cult and which can therefore be assigned to the category of royal psalms. It has been shown, it is hoped, by the aid of the arguments for identifying royal psalms developed above, that some forty-one of the ninety-six psalms which mention an individual are very probably royal. In addition the psalter contains seven pieces which address or refer to the king in the second or third person. To this extent the thesis advanced by Birkeland and Eaton, that the psalter is to a considerable degree a royal book, has been confirmed.

However, in the course of the examination of the setting of some of these royal psalms in an annually repeated royal ritual the theory of Eaton and Johnson, that the king underwent 'ritual humiliation' in the midst of the mock battle, has been decisively rejected. An alternative reconstruction has been proposed whereby king and people kept a period of preparation before the central events of the festival. In the course of this preparation t'.e Israelite king, like his Babylonian counterpart, gave account to God of his year in office and received a renewal of his divine vocation before going on to take part in the ritual battle and be acclaimed king once again. Some twenty-one of the royal psalms have been assigned to this royal ritual.

The remaining twenty-seven royal psalms are most helpfully seen as having been composed, for the most part, with a general type of situation in mind such as defeat in battle, treachery within the nation, or sickness befalling the king. These psalms have been classified according to the situation envisaged by the psalm, in so far as this can be recovered, and these differing situations in the life of king and nation have been illustrated by reference to the historical narratives in the Old Testament. Three psalms which are not royal, but which reflect a background of national danger or distress have also been discussed in this section. By far the majority of the general historical royal psalms refer, as might be expected, to situations of war, battle or siege.

However, the satisfactory disposal of the royal psalms, as was mentioned above, by no means completes the discussion of the individual in the psalms, since there are a further fifty-two psalms which mention an 'I' of some kind or another and which do not appear to be royal. The final two chapters of this study will attempt to complete this picture by examining psalms composed to be delivered by the private person in Israel and, finally, psalms assigned to the ministers of the cult.

Chapter 4

THE INDIVIDUAL AS A PRIVATE PERSON

In my own estimation only eighteen of the individual psalms in the psalter were composed for use by private individuals within the temple cult. This may seem a relatively small number compared to the forty-one psalms assigned here to the king and thirty-three assigned to cultic personnel. It is very clear that all of the Old Testament psalms were composed against a background of private as well as communal and cultic prayer in the ancient Near East and in Israel.[1] However there is no simple relationship between that living tradition of prayer and the psalms which have been preserved in the psalter. The Old Testament psalter contains 148 psalms—only a selection, therefore, of the many hymns and prayers composed for temple worship. We can safely assume that the selection of material which was to survive, however it was made, was not a random process: the arrangement of individual psalms within the psalter is far too deliberate. In this respect, therefore, the collection of psalms in the Old Testament is different from all of the finds of comparative material (which do contain more ordinary prayers of the individual) which owe their preservation to chance and the discoveries of modern archaeology.

Once we admit that the hymns and prayers in our present psalter were deliberately chosen from a wider body of material it becomes possible to ask the question: What criteria were used in this selection by the post-exilic community and, in particular, by the temple groups who passed on the psalms to future generations? One of the main criteria appears to have been to include pieces used in public worship rather than in private prayer. Hence so many of the psalms which do mention an individual were delivered by public spokesmen in the cult: the king, the prophets, the teachers and the musicians.

The second criterion, evident from the high standards maintained through out the psalter, appears to have been one of excellence. Those individual prayers which have survived all demonstrate this excellence in different ways, as will be shown below. It is safe to assume that the efforts of the poets would be concentrated upon the psalms for public use at the great festivals, either said communally or by the king.

The psalms of the private person which have survived fall into four groups as follows: three short and general petitions (Pss. 6; 13; 54); three psalms relating to sickness (Pss. 41; 88; 30); six prayers of individuals undergoing persecution (Pss. 70; 142; 35; 109; 64; 86) and the individual pieces from the Psalms of Ascent (Pss. 120–123; 130; 131).

General petitions (Pss. 54; 13; 6)

It was argued above that Psalms 6, 13 and 54 form a small group within the psalter, each consisting of a short lamentation of the individual followed by a thanksgiving, presumably after an assurance of Yahweh's aid mediated through a cultic prophet. The three psalms share a vagueness on the circumstances confronting the suppliant which leads one to suppose that these pieces were reserved in the cult for any worshipper who wished to bring his need before Yahweh.

Both Eaton and Johnson argue that *Psalm 54* is in fact a royal psalm. However, the arguments of both writers, particularly Johnson's,[2] depend heavily on analogy from other psalms of this type: the enemies elsewhere are mainly foreigners, therefore the enemies in this psalm are also likely to be such. Eaton claims to trace a royal style in the opening lines of the prayer though the form of address shown to be royal above is itself lacking. Even Eaton has to admit that the psalm is 'somewhat lean in data'.[3] As Anderson points out, even if the alternative reading of זָרִים is preferred at v. 5, the word can still be used of those in Israel who stand outside the common relationship to Yahweh. As I argued in Chapter 1, the metaphors of the battlefield and the lawcourt are normally kept apart. Their juxtaposition in the opening verse of the psalm only adds to the impression that the psalm was intended for general use and may also be of a late date. In form the psalm divides into three sections.

(1) A carefully balanced prayer for aid begins the piece. The

repetition of אלהים at the beginning of vv. 3 and 4 gives emphasis and urgency to the prayer, each time the word is followed by exactly balancing prayers in exact parallelism.[4] The prayer is expanded by the insertion of a כי clause followed by a threefold description of the suppliant's opponents. The progressive lengthening of these clauses gives a cumulative effect to the description whilst the omission of a conjunction before לא lends abruptness to this final clause, giving a sense of shock and righteous indignation. The attitude of the antagonists to God contrast strongly with the psalmist's own which has been emphasized by the twofold repetition in vv. 3 and 4.

(2) The second section of the psalm takes the form of a brief song of assurance—delivered presumably after a favourable oracle has been received through a cultic prophet—again in carefully balanced clauses. As Johnson notes, the reference to the faithfulness of God implies some sort of covenant relationship with the worshipper, which may lend support to Vorländer's theory that the song was for one who had claimed Yahweh as his personal God.

(3) Finally, the psalmist offers a sacrifice to Yahweh in thanksgiving for an answered prayer, as was prescribed (cf. Ps. 116.7; Job 33.26f.). The praise of Yahweh's name links the end of the psalm with its opening line, demonstrating that although the piece is built up from independent verse units which could be fitted into or drawn from other psalms, it still has an independent unity of its own. The final line of the prayer could refer to a military victory, as Eaton thinks, but there are simply not enough positive indications in this psalm for it to be accounted royal. It seems better seen therefore as a possibly late prayer provided in the cult for use by anyone in need.

Despite its brevity, *Psalm 13* is unique in the psalter in beginning with an extremely forceful plea to Yahweh to intervene in the life of the suppliant, the phrase עד־אנה being repeated no less than four times at the beginning of the psalm. The psalmist's plea is made to rest in these lines upon Yahweh's forgetting the suppliant's pain and sorrow and upon the triumph of his enemies. Surprisingly Johnson does not discuss the psalm in any detail in *CPIP*, but he demonstrates there that the cry 'How long . . .', more usually in the form עד־מתי is one of the clearest indications that the suppliant is asking for a direct response through a prophet. This initial and vibrant appeal is followed by another two verses of direct supplication which could themselves begin a complaint psalm. Again the twofold threat seems to be of physical danger 'Lest I sleep the sleep of death. . .' and of oppression by the suppliant's enemies. As with Psalm 54, it is impossible to tell what situation underlies the psalm. Since the realms of sickness and oppression by personal enemies so clearly overlapped in ancient Israel's thought it is here impossible to argue that the psalm was primarily intended for use in sickness or in times of persecution (though in other psalms one or other of these elements does come to the fore). Hence it seems wiser to accept the piece as a general formula for requesting Yahweh's aid provided for any suppliant in any kind of need. Like the other two laments in this group, Psalm 13 concludes with a short three-line song of thanksgiving —the liturgical response provided in the cult for delivery once a favourable oracle has been received. As with the other elements in this psalm, the final verse could stand on its own and, presumably, be used in combination with other verse units to make up other prayers of lament.

Psalm 6 seems to be more directly concerned with the suppliant's illness, yet it contains sufficient references to other forms of danger, and particularly enemies, for the piece to have been used in various circumstances of need. As with the other two short laments preserved in the psalter, the quality of the piece probably ensured its preservation. Two negative prayers in exact parallelism form the first verse and two positive prayers, also in exact parallelism and each with a כי clause follow this. The first half of v. 4 echoes v. 3, giving a link backwards, whilst v. 4b sums up the fourfold petition in the liturgical cry 'And now, O Lord, how long?' The second lament section (like Psalm 13, Psalm 6 contains two sections of lament and one of praise) begins with a brief appeal made on the grounds of Yahweh's faithfulness (חסד cf. 13.6; 54.7, אמן) followed by a long description of the suppliant's distress couched in an extended כי clause designed to evoke Yahweh's mercy. Up until v. 7 physical suffering is in evidence but at v. 8 the psalmist reveals that enemies are involved also—and it is the theme of enemies which governs the victorious shout preserved in vv. 9 and 10. Yahweh has answered the prayer, as we are told three times; therefore the enemies will be put to shame.

Johnson (*CPIP*, pp. 237ff.) uses the psalm to illustrate the significance of עד־מתי in appealing for an answer to prayer but is rather literalistic in his interpretation of the piece as a royal prayer.

He argues that the king's sickness will have given his enemies time to plot and hence the connection between the two forms of danger points to Psalm 6 being a royal psalm. However, given the easy connection made in the psalter between sickness and enemies it does not seem that this is sufficient evidence for arguing that the psalm is royal. Rather, this psalm, like the two discussed above, has been composed as a general formula to be sung on behalf of suppliants in a wide variety of circumstances in need of a favourable answer from Yahweh.

One striking feature which emerges from a close examination of these three psalms is the fact that each can be broken down into three or more units of several verses each, which are complete in themselves as units of either lament or thanksgiving. The units themselves would be almost interchangeable between the three psalms and it may well be that we have here an insight into the working methods of the psalmists. Although I would not go as far as Culley and Ljung[5] in arguing that an oral tradition underlies the composition of many of the psalms, it is apparent from such simple prayers as Psalms 6, 13 and 54 that a number of different prayers may have been built up from the same literary units in the tradition. However, the skill of the psalmist is such that each time these units are used they are forged into a new whole so that, in the case of most of the psalms preserved, this debt to a tradition is not always apparent.

Psalms 6, 13 and 54 then, it is argued, form the prayers of the private person as they have survived in their most simple form. The other, more elaborate, psalms of the private person will now be explored from this basis: psalms in which the two dangers represented in the more simple psalms, from physical illness and from persecution by enemies, the two great perils facing the private person in Israel, can be more clearly distinguished.

Psalms of sickness (Pss. 41; 88; 30)

It is a measure of the complexity of the problems in the psalter that each of the psalms in this category is distinct from the others. A full discussion of the opening verse of *Psalm 41* was undertaken above, in which it was argued that the sayings about the man who is kind to the poor are best understood as a preface to the lament at the centre of the psalm; the psalmist quotes his text and then applies it, so to speak. The psalm is clearly a prayer designed to be made in time of sickness as both this introduction and the prayer itself demonstrate (vv. 4, 5, 9, 11). In form the psalm emerges as an elaboration of the simple lament structure examined above. To the basic lament and concluding song of assurance (vv. 12, 13) two elaborations in style are added, giving more reasons why Yahweh should answer this prayer. The first is the wisdom-style introduction to the psalm, unique in the psalter, which has already been explored. The second feature is the pseudo-autobiographical account of the attitude of the psalmist's companions, which is another example of persuasion by hyperbole. The discussion of the term עני ('poor') above has demonstrated that the suppliant will go to almost any lengths to win Yahweh's favour, representing himself as suffering in an utterly wretched condition. In this case, he argues, not only have his enemies forsaken him but his closest friend has turned traitor. Eaton argues that the prayer is in fact a royal psalm, but there are so few positive indications of this. The opening verses could be applied to any fairly wealthy Israelite in a position to bestow charity; other psalms of the private person indicate that the machinations of enemies during sickness were not restricted to the king, nor was the desire for vengeance. The desire to remain in Yahweh's presence for ever may be an indication of a royal ascription but need not be. Again the suppliant may be using hyperbole to make his point.

The psalm gives insight into the complex relationship between sickness and personal enemies in Israel. There are no overt indications here that the enemies and the sickness are causally related—no mention of a curse, for example. The reason for sickness is ascribed to sin (v. 5). But the sickness is described as the will of the suppliant's enemies and the latter are also depicted as taking advantage of the suppliant's misfortune to slander his good name—doubtless also attributing this sickness to some sin he has committed. In this case, therefore, the enemies need be no more than local rivals of the suppliant and his 'triumph' the satisfaction of seeing Yahweh as the champion of his own cause rather than theirs.[6]

The division between a psalm written for use by a private person in the cult and a psalm which is actually the composition of some person in distress can be seen to be a fine but necessary distinction when the two psalms of sickness, unrelieved by any testimony to Yahweh's goodness, are examined. Psalm 39 departs in several places from the accepted standard of piety in the psalms; the scale of suffering found in this lament outweighs that found elsewhere in the psalter and so does the degree of blame attached to Yahweh. For this and other reasons, in particular the shared world-view with the writers of Koheleth, this particular piece is best seen as a wisdom prayer and will be explored more fully in the following chapter. *Psalm 88*, by contrast, despite its similarly monochrome outlook, is much closer in style and content to the other prayers of sickness discussed in this section. That sickness is the background to the prayer cannot be disputed and there are no indications that the piece could be royal; therefore, it can safely be assigned to this group. As in other prayers of this type the suppliant's aim is to set his case before Yahweh, persuading God to have mercy upon him. An unusual number of arguments are marshalled including the persistent prayer of the psalmist (vv. 2, 9), the degree of his suffering and its extent in time (v. 15); the loneliness of the suppliant (vv. 9, 19) and the fact that praise will not be offered to Yahweh from the realms of the dead (vv. 11f.). All these motifs taken together add up not only to a picture of desolation but to a powerful argument to persuade God to intervene. It is a mistake to read such verses as 9, 15 and 18, references to the suppliant's youth or to his companions, as autobiographical data on the psalm writer himself. Rather they are included in this prayer, as often elsewhere, simply to emphasize the extent to which the suppliant himself throws himself on Yahweh's mercy. The overriding focus of the psalm is upon the death or the threat of death and the evil which has befallen the psalmist is here attributed not to the enemies but to Yahweh himself. These two features combine with the fact that the element of assurance at the end of the prayer has either not been preserved or never existed to make the psalm somewhat unusual among the laments in time of sickness, though it is still recognizable as such. It seems probable that the psalm was preserved partly by reason of these unusual characteristics.

Finally, *Psalm 30*, like Psalm 116, is a song of thanksgiving to be sung after deliverance from illness (v. 2 תרפאני can be interpreted in no other way). Unlike Psalm 116 however, there are no indications that the piece is royal and so the psalm is best assigned to this group. The relationship between sickness and enemies is the same as that discovered in Psalm 41, namely, the enemies rejoice at the suppliant's downfall but do not themselves cause it. A very different picture of the enemies is presented in the group of psalms discussed below. The psalm confirms that praise delivered after recovery from illness was to be public (v. 4) and, like other psalms of thanksgiving, contains a small testimony section (vv. 6-10) which also probably had a didactic function: 'the correct thing to do when ill is to pray to Yahweh'. The argument for being heard presented in Psalm 88—of Yahweh not being praised among the dead—is quoted here as an example of prayers to be said in time of sickness. Indeed the psalm presents such a picture of joy that it would form a fitting counterweight to Psalm 88 itself.

The corpus of psalms for sickness which have survived in the psalter is, therefore, not large, according to my analysis, consisting of four laments (Psalms 41, 88, 28 and 38, the last two being royal psalms) and two songs of thanksgiving (30 and 116, of which the latter is also probably royal). Each of these psalms is in some way distinctive and this would indicate that only a selection of the laments in sickness available to the Israelites have survived. The general petitions discussed above may of course have been used in this way and other prayers do reflect a background of physical illness: Psalm 39 may well be the autobiographical testimony of a wisdom poet and the great national psalms of lamentation take up the metaphor of the sick and lonely man in a moving way, also drawing, probably, upon the traditional songs of sickness for their imagery. Finally, of course, the book of Job has preserved a whole tradition of individual complaint and prayer in time of illness which the pieces preserved in the psalter both reflect and amplify.

Prayers in time of persecution (Pss. 70; 35; 109; 64; 142; 86)

There have been scholars, among them Schmidt and Delekat,[7] who have argued that a great many of the individual laments in the psalter find their setting in the judicial processes taking place within the sanctuary. Such theories have been largely discredited, however, as lacking the necessary external and internal evidence to substantiate the case.[8] Yet there remains a small group of prayers in the psalter, all individual laments, which show very little sign of being royal and which seem to reflect not so much general need or sickness but persecution by enemies. It is not entirely clear what the suppliant is being persecuted for, although some hints do emerge. The book of

Proverbs describes the correct attitude to take towards personal enemies at several points[9] revealing that these 'enemies' were a feature of life in ancient Israel. The persecution may have been legal, and certainly the legal metaphor is strongly in evidence in Psalm 35. Although, as Eaton remarks, there is little evidence for the temple and psalms actually being involved in a formal trial, prayers may have been provided for those facing trial for help in the coming ordeal. Again, according to the witness of Proverbs, false witnesses (and therefore trial situations) were a regular feature of life in ancient Israel.[10] Alternatively, and more probably, the persecution and oppression may well have been economic in nature even if carried out through the processes of law. Oppression of the poor is castigated in the prophets, particularly in Amos and Isaiah. It does not seem at all unlikely that, given Yahweh's stated love for the poor, the cult should have provided various prayers to be made should this form of economic oppression arise. The long curse formula in Psalm 109 may well be the suppliant wishing on his enemies what has actually happened to him and, if this is the case, the psalm would provide further evidence of this economic oppression.

As with the other categories of psalms of the private person the likelihood is that the psalter has preserved only a small selection of the prayers once available and has preserved these by reason of their outstanding merit rather than for reasons of cultic usage alone. Of the six texts discussed here Psalm 70 emerges as the simplest prayer from persecution preserved and forms a good background to the study of the more complex pieces, Psalms 35 and 109. Psalm 64 varies the pattern somewhat, as does Psalm 142, which seems at first reading to reflect a background of imprisonment rather than persecution. A discussion of Psalm 86 concludes the section. From a study of these seven psalms four elements emerge as marking this genre.

1. The fervent cry for help (a motif shared with the two categories outlined above).
2. The description of being persecuted or threatened by others.
3. The cursing of the enemies.
4. The praise of God before the congregation, a feature not found in the psalms of sickness explored above. It may be noted that one of the functions of these prayers was to enable the suppliant to declare publicly that he was being

unfairly persecuted—hence his promise to give public thanksgiving.

As has been argued above, although *Psalm 70* is a doublet of Ps. 40.13-17 it should be regarded as a lament in its own right and as the prayer of an individual rather than of the king. The psalm contains the fervent prayer for help (v. 1); a description of being persecuted or tortured by enemies (vv. 2b, 3b, 4b) and of general distress (v. 5a); the cursing of the psalmist's enemies is found in vv. 2-4. Although the psalm contains no response of praise or thanksgiving after the lament is delivered it is apparent from v. 4 that the prayer was to be delivered in public in the midst of the congregation. The only evidence that the psalm may be royal is contained in the epithets in the final verse which alone are not strong evidence for a royal ascription. The psalm has a definite literary unity, beginning and ending as it does with appeals to God to make haste and balancing the description of the suppliant's enemies with a description of the people of God (vv. 2-5). In this way the suppliant implies, quite subtly, that his personal enemies are also those who do not love Yahweh. The actual threat to the psalmist is couched in the most general terms in the description of his antagonists as 'those who seek my hurt' and 'those who say "Aha, Aha"'.

Psalms 35 and 109 may be regarded as more complex expressions of this same basic form. *Psalm 35* has been discussed above, where it was argued that the judicial language in the psalm must take precedence over the military language and that, once this has been agreed, there is insufficient evidence for understanding the psalm as royal: the piece stands as an unusually elaborate example of a prayer for a persecuted individual. The psalm proceeds in two movements, the first using military metaphor and the second returning to the judicial language which reflects the situation facing the suppliant. Each of the two movements contains each of the four elements outlined above. The first (vv. 1-10) begins with the urgent appeal to Yahweh the warrior to arise and fight for his dependant (vv. 1-3), addressed to God in a compelling series of imperatives. The tone of the psalm throughout is altogether more bold than, for example, the tone of the psalms of sickness. Psalms 70 and 109 share this belligerent stance in which the appeal is less to Yahweh's mercy than to his justice and sense of fair play. The curse formula which follows this appeal utilizes some of the same phrases as are used in the curse formula in Psalm 70.[11] The description of the suppliant's danger is again contained in the curse formula and in the כי clause which supports them (v. 7). Again the description of distress is couched in the vaguest of terms. This first movement of the psalm ends with a vow of praise promised to God should the deliverance come about (vv. 9-10) and as in Psalms 70 and 109, the suppliant is described as poor and needy (cf. above pp. 61f.).

The second movement of the psalm (vv. 11-28) begins not with fervent appeal but with the element which has received least attention so far, the description of the psalmist's distress. The suppliant contrasts his own righteousness with the conduct of his adversaries and the motif, now familiar from the prayers of sickness, of the treacherous friend reappears in a slightly different context. Again this is cited not as autobiographical detail but as evidence of the suppliant's need of help and additionally here of his right dealings when contrasted with his enemies' unfairness. The malicious witnesses, together with the appeals for vindication later in the psalm, suggest that some form of persecution in the courts is envisaged. The appeal is taken up again in vv. 17f., together with another promise of praise, and then the curse motif predominates until v. 25. Two sections of cursing (vv. 19-21, 35-36) surround a three-verse appeal to Yahweh's righteousness. The description of the persecutors expands that given in Psalm 70, but some of the same phraseology is again used.[12] In the psalms in this group there is clearly a causal link between the psalmist's enemies and the danger he finds himself in, which is not the case in the psalms of sickness: there the mockery of the enemies merely exacerbates the psalmist's suffering.

Finally, and again as in Psalm 70, the psalm ends not so much with praise as with a vow or a promise made to praise God should the asked-for deliverance be granted, and once again this praise involves not only the psalmist himself but the congregation, contrasted again with the antagonists of the suppliant.[13]

It remains safely established, therefore, that Psalm 35 is an elaboration of the type of psalm found in Psalm 70, namely a prayer provided by the cult for use by a private person undergoing persecution.

Psalm 109 shares the same four characteristic elements as Psalms 35 and 70. The psalm begins with an opening line of petition and continues with a statement of the suppliant's dire need. The motif of kindness returned with malice found in Psalm 35 and other pieces recurs here also. The long passage in vv. 6-19 is most usually understood as a curse formula pronounced by the suppliant against his enemies, although there has been much debate about this. The suggestion made by Creager and others[14] that the suppliant is repeating the curse made by the enemies against himself is, however, unsatisfactory. The shift made from plural to singular enemies, the main evidence for this view, is not so very hard to understand: in Ps. 41.6, to give an analogous example, the wicked behaviour of the enemies is summarized, as it were, in the reference to one friend's treachery.[15] The suppliant is best seen as praying that his enemy will suffer in the same way as he himself has suffered. The suppliant has been tried before a wicked man—let his accuser himself now so be tried on the principle of 'an eye for an eye'. The discussion of other psalms in this genre also makes it plain that a curse was a normal part of such a psalm, even if this particular curse is rather extended in form. As was mentioned above, if the curse does reflect back onto his accusers the suppliant's own plight, then this gives us several clues into the nature of distress suffered during persecution.

The remainder of the psalm is taken up with a further description of distress (vv. 22f.) and of fervent prayer (vv. 26f.), concluding with a song of praise which is, once again, to be sung in the midst of the congregation.

Psalm 64 falls into the category of the prayer of an individual in time of threat or persecution but the prayer is rather more meditative in tone and not nearly so urgent in its pleading. After the prayer for aid which begins the psalm (vv. 1-2) the psalmist gives a strong picture of his own plight by focusing on the machinations of his enemies (vv. 3-6). What has been implied in other psalms about the psalmist being righteous and his enemies wicked is here stated explicitly. In place of the curse motif found in the three psalms discussed above we find an assurance that God will strike these men down. As Weiser notes, this portion of the psalm is artfully constructed and there are a number of links forged between the activity of the enemies and God's punishment of them. The psalm concludes, like the others in this section, with a song of praise which, rather like the rest of the psalm, draws out the lesson of God's dealing with men from the experience of the suppliant as well as praising Yahweh directly.

Psalm 142, in my view, also falls into this category, but Eaton has claimed that the psalm is the prayer of a king.[16] He mentions as evidence the psalm's position among other royal psalms and the general similarities between Psalms 140–143 (which I would argue against in any case; Dahood helpfully points out that this is the only prayer in this part of the psalter to have משכיל in the heading); and the two features of enemies laying traps and the suppliant having no helpers, which are also found in royal psalms (to which one can object that these features are found also in demonstrably non-royal psalms). The 'bond with the god' which appears in v. 6 seems to be something a commoner could share. Most other commentators see the psalm as the lament of a private person, differing only in the nature of the distress envisaged. If the term 'prison' is interpreted literally, of course, it must be assumed that the suppliant has been imprisoned and prays for release. However, this seems to run counter to his prayer to Yahweh for sanctuary and safe refuge and would also be an unusually specific reference for such a psalm of lament. Therefore, it seems best to understand the prayer in v. 7 as a metaphorical plea for the suppliant to be released from his distress. The psalm contains three of the four elements used in the construction of the other psalms from persecution: urgent petition (vv. 1, 3, 5–7a), description of distress (3b–4) and a promise of public praise and thanksgiving (7b). There is, however, no curse motif in this psalm.

Finally, *Psalm 86* is attached to these songs from persecution because of the final third of the psalm (vv. 14–17) which does seem to envisage such a situation of danger. Eaton argues[17] that the psalm is probably royal, but I cannot subscribe to this view. The only evidence he can adduce is the title, the self-designation servant and a possible allusion to royal passion rites in v. 13. Alternatively, the psalm has been seen as constructed either from quotations and allusions to other psalms or originally to have been three separate prayers. There is probably some truth in both of these suggestions. The psalmist has made an unusually full use of the tradition against which he writes in both the introductory invocation and the song of praise. However, this does not mean that he himself was either lacking in artistry or short of original material since there are clear themes, of the psalmist's humility and of God's mercy, which run right through the psalm. It is also possible that the composer has used originally separate, longer units of tradition in building up this prayer.[18] As it stands, however, the psalm is best seen as a whole as a late, probably post-exilic, prayer written for individuals undergoing persecution and as such is a development of the earlier form explored above. It is not so much the psalm's indebtedness to tradition which gives this impression of lateness but the theological ideas which the psalm contains. Hazardous though it is to date any part of the Old Testament on these grounds, the strong emphasis here on the mercies of God, twice given in a Deuteronomistic type formula (vv. 5, 15) in the two halves of the psalm and in the central praise section on the nations going up to Jerusalem to worship Yahweh, seems to indicate a post-exilic date of composition. The latter idea is found elsewhere in the Old Testament only in exilic or post-exilic texts.[19] The elaboration of form in the psalm from the earlier pieces in this genre seems to be found in a lengthening of the introductory invocation, the omission of the curse formulae and the bringing of praise and thanksgiving into the body of the psalm itself. Instead of praises the psalm now concludes with the description of distress and the request for a sign of favour; as was suggested above, this latter section of the psalm may have existed independently as a general formula for requesting a sign of Yahweh's favour through the medium of a cultic prophet.

Individual psalms among the Psalms of Ascent
(Pss. 120; 121; 122; 123; 130; 131)

Six of the individual psalms in the psalter are found in the collection known as the Psalms of Ascent (Psalms 120–134) and, although none of these are prayers of the private person in distress in the sense described above, these psalms will be discussed at this point for the sake of completeness and clarity. There seems no need to discuss here the rival theories relating to the origins of the Psalms of Ascent.[20] The thesis proposed here is that these psalms are best seen, with the exception of Psalm 132, which is different in tone and style from the other pieces, as a post-exilic collection. Evidence for this view is found in the differences in style, form and subject matter which mark these prayers off from all the others in psalter; the presence of the late Hebrew particle שֶׁ,[21] and at least one concrete allusion to the exile and return (Ps. 126.1ff.). The focus upon Jerusalem and the asumption that the well-being of Jerusalem and of

Israel are parallel and closely related also provides evidence of a post-exilic origin. The psalms show evidence of a peculiar literary style whereby the last word of a line becomes the first word of the next line.[22] Other features which bind these psalms together are the common themes of concern with Zion, with peace and well-being, with unity and with contemplative trust in Yahweh. There is also, of course, a strong concern with the festival and with pilgrimage, which would account for the inclusion of Psalm 132 in the collection. There seems no reason to doubt the widely held theory that the original context of these psalms was as songs sung by pilgrims either at or on their way to the great festivals and that this is the origin of the unusual heading.

As far as the study of the individual in the psalms is concerned however, the Psalms of Ascent present pieces which are hard to fit into the recognized formal types. Although several of the prayers have been written, at least in part, in the style of the individual laments (cf. 130.1; 129.1; 127.1) they are in fact quite different. The first three of the prayers discussed below seem, in their different ways, to reflect the individual taking part in his pilgrimage to the holy city; by contrast in Psalms 123, 130 and 131 the focus is much more on the individual as a part of the community which, when assembled together, prays to Yahweh to have mercy on his people.

1. *Psalms of pilgrimage* (Pss. 120; 121; 122)
Psalm 120, though a relatively short psalm, is one of the most enigmatic in the psalter. There is debate, initially, over the translation of v. 1. The MT has the verbs in the past tense giving a song of thanksgiving, whereas most English versions emend so that the psalm reads as a lamentation throughout. The place names mentioned in v. 4 are, of course, very far apart (so Anderson, *ad loc.*); rather than emend the verse it seems wisest to assume that some metaphorical sense is implied. This being the case it seems very unlikely either that the psalm is pre-exilic or that the psalmist is the king, as Eaton suggest.[23] Why should the reigning monarch sojourn abroad among a warlike people in any case—still less have a psalm written to celebrate his homecoming couched in such general terms that it could be used on subsequent occasions! The piece seems far better suited to an era when many Jews did live far from Jerusalem and there would be travel back and forth from the diaspora to Zion itself, particularly at times of festival. The song is thus intended to

depict the miseries of the 'civilized man' living abroad amongst men who cannot be trusted, who continually seek wars or quarrels. When sung at the feast, either in performance by a temple poet or communally by the people, the song would evoke great joy at being 'home' for the festival itself.

Psalm 121 is similarly bristling with difficulties. Eaton sees the piece as the prayer of a king followed by a blessing pronounced over him as he goes out to war. In the first line the suppliant looks to the hills not as a source of danger but as the source of Yahweh's help in the festal epiphany.[24] Such an interpretation is unlikely however: there is no explicit reference in the psalm either to a festal epiphany or to a military battle. The phrase עשה שמים וארץ ('who made heaven and earth') occurs elsewhere in the Psalms of Ascent (124.8; 134.2) and in general tone and style the psalm is very similar to the other pieces in this part of the psalter. Therefore it seems best to associate the piece, with the majority of commentators, with the blessing pronounced over pilgrims at the annual festival, probably in post-exilic times. The blessing would be sought, perhaps, by one of the temple singers acting as a representative of the departing congregation. It seems most likely, as Anderson suggests, that the hills were a source of danger to the travelling pilgrims. A notable stylistic feature of the psalm is the step motif noted above together with the alliteration and assonance achieved by the repetition of שמר—which also brings out the main message of the psalm.

Psalm 122 contains a similar play on sound repeated with its frequent mention of both שלום ('peace') and ירושלם ('Jerusalem'). The psalm is evidently a pilgrim song. The individual appears here only in the first verse—a stylistic feature of other ascent psalms (cf. 121; 123)—as one of a group of pilgrims who are to go up (עלה) to Jerusalem, presumably for the festival. As Anderson remarks the mention of the thrones of the House of David does not preclude us from seeing the psalm as a post-exilic piece. The significance of the House of David did not end with the exile.

2. *Prayers on behalf of Israel* (Pss. 123; 130; 131)
The final three prayers to be discussed in this chapter all contain a movement from the individual to the corporate in one sense or another. *Psalm 123* is in fact a communal prayer for Yahweh to have

mercy upon Israel, but the prayer is couched as a request from one man in the community, lifting his eyes to God in expectant appeal. The circumlocutions for God in the opening verse together with the particle שֶׁ suggest a late date for the prayer. Its content then aptly describes the condition of the Jews living around Jerusalem after the exile as is reflected in the book of Nehemiah. *Psalm 130* comes closer than any other Psalm of Ascent to the form of an individual lament, with its fervent appeal for God to listen at the outset of the prayer. The message which comes at the end of the psalm—that God will redeem Israel from all *his* iniquities—is, however, directed at the nation, leading one to believe that the entire prayer was spoken for the nation as is the case in Psalm 129. Finally, *Psalm 131*, surely one of the most beautiful prayers in the psalter, calls up, like other Psalms of Ascent, an unusual yet domestic image to portray the suppliant's humble relationship with God.[25] The song of assurance given at the end of the psalm and that at the end of Psalm 130 call to mind the message of the prophets and much of the Old Testament: Yahweh will not turn away any individual or people who truly humble themselves before him.

CONCLUSION

This chapter has identified and examined the eighteen psalms in the psalter which, according to my analysis, fall into the category of psalms written for the use of private persons within Israel. Two things have been demonstrated. First, it has been shown that such psalms were written in Israel and did exist: not all psalmody was royal psalmody. However, as the introduction to the chapter argued, these psalms can only be understood against the general background of private prayer in the Old Testament and in the ancient Near East and the psalms which were written for private use in the temple cannot be used simplistically as a guide to the piety of ordinary individuals in ancient Israel.

Second, some division is possible between different groups within these psalms of the private person, as set out above. Even within this division, however, the picture given by the psalter is once again complex and no two psalms are alike, although different psalms in the same group can often shed light on one another. The psalms we have preserved appear to have survived more for their distinctiveness than for their conformity to a particular form or style. Hence the general argument maintained throughout this book that there are no simple solutions to the complex problems of the psalter is validated once again.

Finally there are only 12 psalms of the individual proper (discounting those in the Psalms of Ascent) in the psalter compared to some 48 royal psalms. This means that Eaton's contention is again, to a great extent, confirmed here and the psalter is substantially a royal book, as indeed are many of the other books of the Old Testament. One of the reasons for this must be that the psalms used in public, at the great festivals, would doubtless have attracted the attention of the psalm-composers more than the provision of songs for the use of ordinary worshippers, and also their preservation would have been encouraged by their repeated use in the cult.

Chapter 5

THE INDIVIDUAL AS A MINISTER OF THE CULT

Of the 93 psalms containing some reference to an individual some 41 have been shown to have been composed as prayers for the use of the king and another 18 to have been written for the use of the private person within Israel. Some 33 psalms now remain to be examined and these psalms, it seems to me, reflect the concerns of the ministers of Israel's cult: either the cult prophets or the wisdom teachers[1] or the temple musicians and psalm singers themselves. The focus therefore turns away from examining the identity of the person for whom the psalm was composed at this point. In the case of the psalms examined here, there ceases to be a distinction between the composer of the psalm and the person who delivered the piece in the cult. The aim of this chapter is to attempt to identify the psalms of the individual which are best assigned to each of these groups of cultic ministers and also to reach some tentative conclusions on the authorship of the remaining psalms in the psalter.

The investigation will begin, therefore, with an examination of the nine psalms of the individual in which the 'I' appears to be a cultic prophet and will go on to discuss the influence of the wisdom teachers upon the psalter, and in particular upon eleven psalms in which the 'I' seems to be a wisdom teacher. Finally, attention will focus upon the temple poets themselves and their testimony as revealed in three of the individual psalms.[2]

I. THE 'I' IN THE PSALMS AS A CULTIC PROPHET
(Pss. 78; 77; 81; 74; 83; 85; 52; 36; 20; 110)

A.R. Johnson's early work on the cultic prophets[3] established the existence of a group of professional prophets attached to the major shrines in pre-exilic Israel who had, it is clear, a dual function: (1) the giving of oracles of Yahweh to the nation and to individuals in occasions of national and personal crisis, and, (2) making intercession to Yahweh in times of either national or personal difficulty and danger. The evidence would seem to indicate that these cultic prophets 'died out' as a group in the generations after the return from exile. The Chronicler sees the guilds of temple singers as having filled the role occupied by these cultic prophets, and this, together with the close connection between the pre-exilic cultic prophets and music, led Johnson to formulate his theory that the cultic prophets as it were degenerated into mere musicians on a par with the other Levitical orders in the post-exilic period.

In his more recent work Johnson has attempted to trace the activity of the cultic prophets of pre-exilic Israel through the extant psalmody of the Old Testament. In *The Cultic Prophet and Israel's Psalmody* he identifies no less than forty psalms as reflecting the activities of these prophets,[4] and several features of a cult-prophetic style are delineated.[5] Once again the activity of the cult prophets is traced through oracles and through teaching and the offering of intercessory prayer on behalf of the nation, the king and the ordinary individual.

Although Johnson has succeeded, to a large extent, in demonstrating the considerable part played by cultic prophets in Israel's worship, and particularly in psalmody, I have to disagree with his conclusions on several major and subsidiary points.[6] In particular, it seems to me, his arguments that vicarious intercession was practised by the cultic prophets, whereby a prophet would actually pray in the person of a king or of a sick individual, does not seem to be particularly well supported by evidence. Such an understanding, it seems to me, leads the way to seeing almost all of the prayers in the Psalter as having been composed and delivered by the cult prophets. This view would have the effect, if accepted, of restricting our view of the piety of the ordinary person in Israel (when it has been argued above that each person could approach God in his own right) and of the role of the temple musicians and psalm writers. Johnson's arguments generally tend towards the view that the cult prophets *were* the psalm writers in pre-exilic Israel. It seems to me that sufficient evidence can be produced outside the psalter to demonstrate the existence of pre-exilic musicians who were not cultic prophets (see below, section 3) and that there is evidence for the work of this group within the psalter also. We should therefore see two groups (of cult prophets and musicians) at work on the composition of the psalter before the exile, one of which disappeared shortly after the return. There would, of course, be many areas of overlap between the two groups in style and subject matter and it is not always possible to make a rigid distinction between the work of one group and that of another.

An additional argument which adds weight to this position is actually made much of by Johnson and is supported by the exegesis of the cult-prophetic psalms in which the 'I' occurs, namely that there can be identified within certain psalms an actual cult-prophetic style. If this is the case, then it follows that the cult prophets can only have been responsible for the composition of a section, if an important section, of the psalms in pre-exilic Israel, and that the remainder were the work of the temple musicians.

Very much in line with this consideration, although this is not noted by Johnson or other more modern commentators, it does seem as if we have within the psalter itself a sub-collection of cult-prophetic works, namely the psalms headed לאסף (of Asaph), within which six of the eleven psalms discussed in this section are found. A.F. Kirkpatrick notes no fewer than six features of prophetic style which bind the Asaph psalms together (with the exception of Psalm 73):[7]

1. Many of these psalms, as was noted above,[8] represent God as judge in the manner of the canonical prophets (Pss. 50; 75; 81; 82).
2. God himself is frequently introduced as speaker (Pss. 50; 75; 81; 82).
3. There is evidence of the didactic use of history and teaching from tradition, so important in the cult. In Pss. 74.12ff.; 77.10ff.; 80.8ff.; 81.5ff., 83.9ff., the past history of the nation is appealed to for encouragement or in words of warning.
4. There is frequent use in these psalms of the image, employed by several of the canonical prophets, of God's relationship to Israel being that of a shepherd to his flock, as in Pss. 74.1; 70.20; 78.52; 79.13; 81.1.[9]
5. There is unusual use made of the combinations Jacob and Joseph (80.1) and Joseph and Israel (81.4f.), which Kirkpatrick thinks stems from a refusal to accept the division of the nation as permanent, again in agreement with the canonical

prophets. However, in several of these Asaphite psalms there is also a prominent concern with the election of Judah (cf. 76.1; 78.67-72).

6. Finally, the Asaphite psalms are almost entirely national psalms of intercession, thanksgiving, warning or teaching. Even where the 'I' occurs he is clearly speaking on behalf of the nation. One might also add to Kirkpatrick's observation that the collection is rather unusual in that it does not contain even one royal psalm which might have substantiated Johnson's case for vicarious intercession.[10]

Of the six psalms of Asaph which contain some reference to an individual three are concerned with the prophet teaching from Israel's history; two contain only incidental references to an 'I' and the remaining psalm contains the prophet's response to an oracle of Yahweh. On the theme of teaching in the cult, it is generally true that, while there has been intense study of the forms and structures of Israel's religion in recent years, very little attention has been paid to the way in which Israel's religion related to her social and political life.[11] The cult and the annual or thrice-yearly assembly of many in the nation at the national temple or, before centralization, at the major shrines, provided almost the only medium of mass communication available.[12] We have already observed how control of this medium was put to good use by the kings of Judah, following the practice of other ancient Near Eastern monarchs in that the central act of the main annual festival was a representation in music, drama and song of Yahweh's choice of the Davidic dynasty. The cult is being used here as an effective means of social and political control and to this extent has a role in educating the people. There is also evidence, however, that the cult was the place for more direct forms of teaching about Israel's faith and history and that this was just as much its function as prayer and sacrifice.[13] This is an aspect of the work of the cultic prophets which is taken up forcefully by Johnson[14] and which finds its expression, in part, in the three historical cult-prophetic psalms discussed here.

This educational role and in particular teaching from the historical tradition is especially evident in *Psalm 78*, the second longest psalm in the psalter, where the instruction is at two levels: the prophet acknowledges the claim of Jerusalem to hegemony over Israel yet maintains most strongly that the grace of God is closely connected with his judgment if the correct response to that grace is not forthcoming. As Kraus remarks, the opening invocation which prefaces the historical summary is cast in the styles of a wisdom teacher (vv. 1-2) and of hymnody (v. 4). There can be little doubt, however, given the overall tenor and concerns of the piece, that the psalmist is a cultic prophet. There is less argeement about the date of the psalm, and the view taken on this depends as much upon opinions held about the relative dating of other institutions in Israel such as the covenant and the prevalence of Deuteronomistic language in the earlier part of the monarchic period. Johnson and Weiser, who support an early date for the covenant concept and for many of the psalms, place Psalm 78 in the early years after the building of the Temple. A more probable date, however, in line with the consensus of scholarly opinion on these other issues, would seem to be the immediate pre-exilic period. As A.A. Anderson suggests, the general outlook of the psalm suggests that the northern kingdom has come to an end and the psalm reflects something of the Deuteronomic attitude to Zion and the high places. The opening invocation with its mixture of styles would also support this later date. The cultic setting in which the psalm, or sermon-prayer, was delivered would doubtless have been the autumn festival with its celebration of the election and renewal of the Davidic dynasty. The focus on the saga of the ark (v. 61) would also lend support to this view. Security and victory in battle can only be attained by faithfulness on the part of all the people to the demands of Yahweh's law.

If the didactic purpose of Psalm 78 is to give a warning to the people, together with an affirmation of God's grace through the election, then the didactic purpose of *Psalm 77* must be to sound a note of hope for Yahweh's deliverance. I find myself in disagreement with Eaton's interpretation of the psalm on two main counts. In the first place he describes the piece as a great intercession for the nation. This seems unlikely as there is no fervent appeal for God to have mercy in this psalm: the only note of petition is sounded in the context of a report of the psalmist's meditations. The first half of the psalm is much better seen as a testimony, in this case to the psalmist's 'wrestling with God' in the face of some great tragedy facing the nation. This being the case it seems much more likely that the individual in the psalm is a cultic prophet than that he is a king, as Eaton argues. In assigning this piece to his more doubtful group of

royal prayers Eaton admits both that 'there is no obvious royal
colouring' and that 'the psalmist is not far removed from the
prophet-leader of Habakkuk 3'.[15] It seems likely, therefore, that this
piece is the work of a cult prophet.[16] Even the 'faint clue' towards
royal ascription which Eaton finds in the closing verse of the psalm—
the mention of Moses and Aaron—points just as much to prophetic
authorship and use, if the psalmist is thought to have signed off with
an allusion to himself, as it does to the psalm having been used by the
king (cf. Deut. 34.10). The context of the psalm is clearly some great
national disaster, and there are two indications that this was the
exile: First, the psalm's position in the Asaphite psalter would
support the view, alongside other psalms which reflect this period.[17]
Second, in its oracle of salvation the psalm shares several affinities
with the prophecies of Second Isaiah, particularly in the linking
together of the two themes of creation and redemption (cf. Isa. 51.9-
11) and the use of the name Jacob to describe the whole nation of
Israel.

In context, therefore, the psalm is to be seen as the didactic
testimony of a cultic prophet in the period of the exile. The distress of
the prophet at the fate of the nation is described in the form of an
individual lament. The prophet has asked of the Lord 'How long?'
and has wrestled with Yahweh for an answer to his questions. Like
Second Isaiah he finds his answer in the past traditions of Israel
recording the mighty acts of Yahweh, which he then relates as a
ground for hope for the people facing exile. It is no coincidence that
the psalm ends with Yahweh leading forth his people by the hand of
Moses and Aaron, prophet and priest.

The use made of history is different again in *Psalm 81*, although the
point made in the teaching given in the oracle is similar to that made
in Psalm 78. Here also it seems that the psalm is the work of a cultic
prophet (cf. Johnson, *CPIP*, pp. 6ff). The psalm begins with a full call
to praise which strengthens the cult prophet's association both with
the music in the temple worship and with the regular ordained
festivals. It seems likely that this particular psalm would have been
used in the Autumn Festival calling the people to prayer and
worship. There seems no reason whatsoever to regard v. 5c (which
actually contains the only reference to an individual) as a gloss (so
NEB). These prophetic interlocutions before oracles are relatively
common in the psalter (cf. above p. 24). The oracle focuses, like the

historical summaries in Psalms 77 and 78, on the formative elements in Israel's history: the deliverance from Egypt and the giving of the law together with a promise of subjection if the people follow their own hearts or of rich blessing if they subject themselves to Yahweh. Johnson attempts to date this psalm, with many others, to the period of the judges. Although this dating cannot be disproved, there is no particular evidence which merits departing in this case from the general assumption that most of the Psalms in the psalter were composed and preseved for regular worship in the Jerusalem temple.

The structure of *Psalm 75* has been discussed briefly above: an oracle of judgment is sandwiched between a brief hymnic introduction and a song of individual thanksgiving or, if Johnson's reading of the text is followed, a summation by the prophet of what has gone before:

> For my part then here is my enduring message,
> The note which I must sound for Jacob's God—
> So I will cut off the horns of the wicked
> While the horns of the righteous shall be lifted up.[18]

The psalm, like others discussed in this section, is almost certainly to be set in the context of Israel's autumn festival and is to be seen as both warning and instruction to the faithful in Israel. This seems a much neater way of interpreting the psalm than is involved in seeing some verses from the oracle as spoken by the king (so Eaton, *KP*, pp. 55f.). The position of the piece within the Asaph psalms would also strengthen this attribution.

The two other Asaphite psalms which mention an individual do so in a very minor way and so only need to be noted briefly here. *Psalm 74* is a prophetic song, it would seem, which laments the destruction of Jerusalem. The prophet intercedes with Yahweh (called 'my king' in v. 12) to arise and rescue the nation from the grip of the enemy. *Psalm 83* also seems to be the intercession of a cultic prophet who addresses Yahweh as 'my God in v. 9. Like others in this group, the psalm refers to a particular event, as is indicated by the large number of proper names.

Psalms from the circle of the cultic prophets are of course found outside the circle of the Asaph psalms but only three such pieces have survived which contain reference to an individual, one of which is an intercession for the nation, whilst the other two both contain injunctions against the wicked. *Psalm 85*, which belongs to the Korah collection rather than that of Asaph, contains an intercession for the land once again, which is probably best dated to the period after the return when the nation was still beset with troubles, and an oracle of salvation preceded by an interlocution by the prophet:

> Let me hear what God, the Lord, will speak . . .

The purpose here, as in Psalm 77, is to rekindle hope in the people.

The prophetic influence in *Psalm 52* is recognized by the form of the injunction against the wicked: a direct challenge issued against the mighty man in the name of Yahweh which is also found in the prophets (cf. Isa. 22).[19] Eaton seems to give a correct interpretation of the piece in his Commentary on the Psalms when he writes that the psalm 'comes from the circle of the cult prophets and the figure addressed is of a general type'. However, he departs from this interpretation in *Kingship and the Psalms* (p. 73) and argues that the piece is royal (though in the less probable group). The evidence adduced for this is slight: the theme of witness can be shared by a prophet; the comparison to a tree can be made of an ordinary Israelite, not only the king (cf. Psalm 1; Jer. 17.7-8) and dwelling in the house of the Lord can also refer to the prophet's witness as well as to that of the king. The 'I' in the psalm is best seen as a cult prophet, therefore, and, given that the injunction is general in reference, the psalm must also be seen as didactic in character, teaching the familiar dictum to the assembled congregation that the wicked man will be cast down from his eminence and the righteous man exalted. The concluding verses have borrowed the form of an individual cultic thanksgiving from the prayers of persecution discussed above, and this may be an indication that the psalm is of a later date. Again, however, a date of just before the exile would seem to fit the piece well.

Psalm 36 contains a description of the wicked similar to that found in Psalm 52: arrogance, continual plotting and mischievous words are mentioned again and the doom of the wicked is pronounced, with some reference in Psalm 36 to a sign or act in the cult.[20] The chiastic structure of the psalm balances the description of the wicked with a hymn of praise to Yahweh thus:

Description of the wicked (1-4)
>   Description of Yahweh and those who love him (5-9)
>   Prayer for protection of those who love Yahweh (10-11)
Doom of the wicked (12).

The dramatic pronouncement of doom at the end of the psalm leads one to the conclusion that the 'I' in the psalm is a cult prophet speaking as a representative of the upright in the land. Like other prophetic psalms discussed here, this piece has a didactic purpose within the cult, teaching on the fate of the wicked, the nature of Yahweh and the joy which awaits those who love him.

Finally, to complete this review of psalms in which the individual is a cultic prophet, brief mention must be made of the royal *Psalms 20* and *110*, in which the person of the prophet emerges as he prays for the monarch. As Johnson demonstrates (*CPIP*, pp. 177ff. and 80ff.), the prophet acts here in his role as intercessor on the king's behalf.

Although the cultic prophets played a major role in the composition and delivery of many of the psalms in the Old Testament, the number of instances in which the 'I' in the psalms is to be seen as a cultic prophet is relatively small. All of the psalms in which the 'I' does appear as a prophet, with the exception of Psalms 20 and 110, can be regarded as in some way didactic: either teaching the correct response to Yahweh from historical traditions or by means of oracles of warning about his actions in the present. In this respect of concern for teaching Yahweh's way the 'I' in the psalms as a cultic prophet shares many affinities with the 'I' in the psalms as a wisdom teacher, although the form and the material used for instruction are very different.

II. THE 'I' IN THE PSALMS AS A WISDOM TEACHER

The nature and extent of the involvement of the wise in Israel with the production and transmission of the psalter has been, like the question discussed above, an area of comparatively intense research over the preceding decades.[21] Three areas of broad agreement have emerged as a result of this debate. First, the psalter does contain pieces which can fairly be described as wisdom psalms, that is as products of the scribal schools attached to the temple. Every list of such wisdom psalms varies somewhat although something of a consensus has emerged.[22] This identification of wisdom psalms has been made on the ground of forms used, vocabulary and thematic content.[23] Second, it has been generally agreed that there is a certain amount of wisdom influence outside of these wisdom psalms themselves: in other words, some of the wisdom forms, vocabulary and themes are also found in the remainder of the psalms. This should occasion no great surprise. The different groups in ancient Israel did not operate each in its own cultural vacuum. Furthermore, a similar borrowing of wisdom vocabulary and style had already been noted in the prophetic books. This general wisdom influence upon the psalter is thought to have extended in the post-exilic period to the actual arrangement of the present psalm collection. A particularly strong indication of this is the fact that the whole collection is prefaced by the wisdom psalm presenting the two ways, which we know as Psalm 1. The third and final point of consensus, which has already been touched upon, is that most, if not all, of the wisdom psalms are assumed to be post-exilic in origin. This hypothesis best accords with the general view taken of the development of psalmody in ancient Israel and the picture of the gradual pattern of Israel's assimilation of the wisdom traditions of the ancient Near East into its own religious life. In this latter development a line can be drawn from the earliest sentence literature preserved in the collection in Proverbs 10–31 to Ben Sira's wisdom in the early second century BC. In the former the material has more obviously been influenced by the wisdom traditions of nations outside Israel.[24] In the latter there is the complete assimilation of wisdom into the religion of Israel, to the extent that Wisdom herself can be identified with Torah and can be 'serving' in the temple itself.[25] The other wisdom collections in the Old Testament, Proverbs 1–9, Job and Koheleth, mark out points along the way and, it must be agreed, the wisdom psalms come from a fairly advanced stage of this development. Although there is evidence for conflict between the scribal wisdom of the courts and prophetic teaching in the pre-exilic period[26] this is not in evidence either in these post-exilic wisdom psalms. Nor is there any evidence of the struggle between Yahwistic and non-Yahwistic wisdom found in Proverbs. The assimilation of wisdom to the service of the cult is almost complete.

In view of this, it seems to me that Perdue's distinction, which builds in part upon Mowinckel's dismissal of the wisdom psalms as non-cultic,[27] between psalms written for the cult and psalms written as aids to teaching in the wisdom schools, is unnecessary.[28] It is to be remembered that the cult, particularly in the post-exilic period, was a multi-functional organism, one of whose chief functions was the education of the people in the way of Yahweh.[29] Hence there would be a continuing need for didactic psalmody and it appears that the wisdom writers in the post-exilic period were able to supplement the teaching psalms which had been handed on by the cult prophets with their own material. This argument will be taken up below in the context of the exegesis of the wisdom psalms.

However, it is the task of the chapter not to discuss in depth the contribution of the wisdom schools generally to the psalter but to discuss in detail those individual psalms in which the 'I' is best seen as a wisdom teacher. It appears that ten such psalms have survived, of which the largest group, of six, consists of psalms with a didactic purpose in mind, consisting of a mixture of instruction and testimony. Next, in three poems the individual appears in the form of hymns or prayers. Finally, the psalter contains one example of protest poetry, in Psalm 39. These psalms will now be discussed in order.

Didactic psalms containing instruction and/or testimony (Pss. 37; 49; 32; 34; 73; 11; 4)

Generally speaking in this group of psalms the individual teacher appears in testimony rather than instruction passages. Thus in *Psalm 37*, the psalm which most resembles the wisdom literature in Proverbs, two pieces of testimony are adduced to back up the general point being made throughout the instruction:

> I have been young and now I am old
> Yet I have not seen the righteous forsaken or his children begging
> bread (v. 25)

and

> I have seen a wicked man overbearing,
> and towering like a cedar of Lebanon.
> Again I passed by and lo, he was no more:
> Though I sought him he could not be found (v. 35).[30]

As Perdue remarks (p. 280), it is not difficult to show that the psalm is a wisdom composition since it betrays the features of the wisdom writings in form, style and content. What is less clear, however, is whether the piece was intended for use in the cult or in the schools. Perdue argues (p. 286) that the latter is more likely to be true: there is no cultic language in the piece and it is unlike any of the more usual genres of psalm. However, to be weighed against this is the fact that the whole tenor of the instruction given, which turns, as Perdue rightly observes, around the proverb in v. 22, is directed at the community of the faithful and at individuals within that community. Furthermore, the instruction given, without exception, is directed towards this and the related themes of righteousness and possession of the land. Had the psalm not been intended for cultic use we could have expected more diversity of theme as is found in the sentence literature and even in the longer collections in Proverbs and Koheleth.

The psalm is best seen, therefore, as a piece of instruction assembled in the early post-exilic period. As such the psalm contains a powerful restatement of Deuteronomic theology concerned to delineate to the post-exilic community, with their fragile grip on both the land and the tenets of Yahwism, that the way to maintain their foothold in Jerusalem was to trust in Yahweh and not to desert his way.

The text of *Psalm 49* is less well preserved than most of the Psalms. However, it is clear that the psalm is a wisdom piece, by reason of the introduction, the wisdom vocabulary and the emphasis on instruction throughout the composition. It would seem also, especially in view of the reference to the lyre in v. 4, that the psalm was intended to be used in the cult for the purposes of instructing the congregation. The theme of the psalm, as the emended title suggest,[31] is death and, especially, man's reaction to it.[32] The psalm seems by reason of some of the vocabulary and ideas it contains to be a late piece,[33] possibly, as Anderson suggests, one of the latest in the psalter. In particular the psalmist appears here to be reaching towards some concept of the afterlife, which is described in the terms available from the rest of the Old Testament tradition: the avoidance of Sheol and God taking a man up (the same word, לקח, is used of the translation of Enoch and of Elijah).

Several of the other wisdom psalms of testimony and instruction were discussed in some detail in Chapter 1 and so can be dealt with more briefly at this point. *Psalm 32* is declared to be a wisdom psalm by the forms used and its standard wisdom vocabulary.[34] As was argued above, vv. 8f. should not be seen as an oracle of Yahweh embedded in the psalm but as the wisdom writer's invocation to his audience to 'come and learn'. There seems no good reason to follow Perdue's interpretation of the psalm as a specimen thanksgiving written for use in the schools. Once it has been accepted that the cult was a place of teaching as well as of worship then psalms like this fit more appropriately into the festal setting.

Psalm 34 is seen to be a wisdom psalm by its acrostic structure and the instruction which is appended to the rather stylized song of thanksgiving which forms the first half of the piece. The instruction comes complete with the wisdom teacher's invocation to his audience to hear him and his promise to teach 'the fear of the Lord'. As was remarked above, the psalm is one of the few in the psalter in which the term עני (poor) is equated with צדיק ('righteous'). Again I would agree with Perdue (pp. 276f.) that the thought of the piece is structured around the proverb found in the final verse of the psalm and that the psalm was used as instruction and even in instruction in thanksgiving and the proper attitude to take towards Yahweh. However, I am unable to see why he removes these psalms from the context of the instruction of Israel and sets them in the wisdom schools for the instruction of schoolboys. The psalm form used at the beginning of the piece betrays its cultic origins. The wisdom teacher begins his instruction with a testimony to Yahweh's goodness couched in the traditional language of a thanksgiving song. He then changes (v. 8) from testimony to instruction, inviting his hearers to follow Yahweh and learn from him the psalmist himself. At the end of the piece the wisdom teacher returns to his original theme— Yahweh's protection of the righteous and rejection of the wicked.

Eaton argues (KP, pp. 77f.) that *Psalm 73* is the testimony of a king to Yahweh's faithfulness. However, for the reasons given above (p. 22) it seems better to see the piece, not as a private meditation of a wisdom poet, but, as the final verse indicates, as a piece of wisdom teaching intended to be delivered in public. The main difference from other wisdom pieces is that no formal instruction is included and the extended testimony section is left to speak for itself. The psalm is not unorthodox in its theology, but it uses the device of actually voicing doubts in the minds of the congregation in order to expose and put an end to those doubts and to reaffirm faith in Yahweh.

Psalm 11 was also discussed in some detail above, where it was argued that the instruction in the psalm (vv. 4ff.) takes precedence over the testimony and that the psalm is best seen, therefore, as a didactic wisdom piece.

Psalm 4 is the final psalm to be discussed in this group of sermon-psalms containing testimony and instruction and is the only piece included here which is not generally acknowledged as a wisdom psalm. Eaton's arguments in favour of a royal interpretation are insubstantial: he draws attention first to the parallels between Psalm 3 and Psalm 4.[35] However, there are also great differences between the two psalms—not least the clear fact that Psalm 3 is set against a background of military combat. The second piece of evidence is the alleged identification of the glory (כבוד) of Yahweh with that of the king in v. 3 (on this see below). The psalm, Eaton argues, is set against a background of famine which is causing his people both to forsake Yahweh and to criticize the king—hence this injunction. But there are serious difficulties in this interpretation: for what does the king pray exactly, since his prayer is clearly addressed to Yahweh in v. 1, and why does the psalm end on such a lame note of testimony and of personal faith if the piece is meant to be a warning to the people?

The 'private individual' interpretation also founders on this difficulty. According to the MT the psalm is in part an expression of thanksgiving and confidence and in part a lament, although no request is actually made. Therefore it seems that some emendation to the text must be made to make sense of the psalm, and it seems most sensible, in the first instance, to emend v. 2, with Weiser and Jacquet, to follow in part[36] the LXX text of the psalm. The Hebrew text would then read:

בְּקָרְאִי עֲנָנִי אֱלֹהֵי צִדְקִי
בַּצָּר הִרְחַוְבָתָּ לִּי
חַנֵּנִי וְשָׁמַע תְּפִלָּתִי

giving the English:

> When I cried the God of my salvation answered me,
> He gave me room when I was in distress
> He was gracious to me and heard my prayer.

It should be noted that this emendation involves no change in the consonantal text. However, even when the psalm is thus emended to give a psalm of thanksgiving throughout, the following verse still reads very awkwardly indeed. It seems better, therefore, to follow the LXX again, which has

υἱοὶ ἀνθρώπων ἕως πότε βαρυκάρδιοι
ἵνα τί ἀγαπᾶτε ματαιότητα καὶ ζητεῖτε ψεῦδος;

which would give the Hebrew

בְּנֵי אִישׁ עַד מָה כְבָרֵי־לֵב
לָמָה תֶּאֱהָבוּ רִיק וַתְּבַקְשׁוּ כָזָב

This emendation involves only the change of כ to ב, the dropping of ן after תאהבו and the insertion of ו before תבקשו, none of which is very difficult to imagine taking place in reverse. Both Kraus and Jacquet refer to this reading but dismiss it, rather hastily in my opinion, on the rather shaky and subjective grounds of metre. The emended reading seems to me to give better parallelism in the verse and to make sense of the whole psalm, for what we see now is a testimony to Yahweh's grace (v. 2) in answering prayer followed by an invocation to those listening to 'come and learn' uttered by a wisdom teacher (cf. 49.1f.; 34.11f.; 32.8f.) with the characteristic wisdom question and vocabulary (כזב, ריק) followed by five verses of wisdom instruction and testimony similar to that found in Psalms 32, 34 and 37. In the face of distress or of poverty the correct response is to trust Yahweh alone (v. 5). Hence the psalm is most aptly described as a wisdom sermon containing both testimony and instruction as do the other psalms in this group.

Psalms of praise (Pss. 111; 19; 119)

The preceding section has dealt, by and large, with those wisdom psalms which are addressed to man rather than to God. This section deals with the psalms which, although didactic in purpose, are expressed in the form of hymns of thanksgiving. *Psalm 111* is one such psalm. Its wisdom origin is marked by the acrostic structure of the piece taken together with the climax of the psalm, the final verse, which puts forward the motto of Yahwistic wisdom. The lack of continuity of thought, which is not necessarily the mark of an acrostic poem,[37] would seem to indicate that the psalm is of a late date (contra Weiser who, because of the abundant mention of ברית (covenant) wishes to set the piece in his pre-exilic covenant festival). The individual wisdom teacher 'surfaces' in the opening verse of the psalm in announcing his intention to sing the praises of Yahweh. The purpose of the psalm is as much didactic, however, giving teaching about the nature of Yahweh to the worshipper, as it is praise. An additional mark of the psalm's lateness is the praise of the precepts (פקד) of Yahweh, a theme which is, of course, central to Psalms 19 and 119 discussed below.

The first half of *Psalm 19*, with its mythological themes, is commonly agreed to have been originally separate from the second half of the psalm.[38] It is probably much older and may be of Canaanite origin. The second half of the poem, which consists largely of the praise of Torah, may have been written onto this hymn fragment or have been originally a separate composition. My own view is that the former option is the more likely. There is evidence for this process taking place elsewhere in the psalter[39] and the theory better explains why the two halves were joined together in the first place. Moreover, despite the difference in style, content and metre between the two sections, the themes fit together very well. The association of ideas between Wisdom/Torah and creation was a very strong one. Not only was Torah seen as something which was as permanent as creation but in some traditions the law or wisdom can be seen as the agent of that creation itself.[40] Hence the praise of the law of God can follow on naturally from the praise of Yahweh expressed by the creation.

There can be little doubt, whatever the origin of the first half of the psalm, that Ps. 19.7-14 is the composition of a wisdom writer from the post-exilic period, taking up the theme of the praise of Torah to be developed still more in Psalm 119. It is Torah now which makes wise the simple, which is more to be desired than silver and gold (cf. Prov. 8.10, 19). The essence of the psalm is as didactic as the others in this wisdom group and its spirit throughout is that of the pious wise man. The natural place for the teaching to be given would therefore be in the temple rather than in the schools. The psalm concludes with what amounts to a model prayer in the first person. Man's response to the silent witness of creation and the verbal witness of Torah is a prayer to be found worthy before the God who has ordained these things.

In the third of the wisdom psalms which are composed in the form of prayers rather than directed to an audience the identification between wisdom and Torah reaches its apotheosis.[41] In twenty-two stanzas of eight lines each the wisdom poet of *Psalm 119* declares his dedication to, dependence upon and praise of Torah. The poem is cast, basically, in the form of an individual lament, although almost every other form found in the psalms and elsewhere is employed and allusions to other parts of the Old Testament, particularly to other psalms, are both many and various. However, I would disagree with both Weiser, who sees the persecution referred to here as genuine and personal to the poet and Perdue, who, for once I think wrongly, considers this wisdom psalm to have been used in the cult. The piece is far too long for any such recitation. Moreover there are no allusions, other than the general form of the psalm, to cultic worship or to being among other worshippers. There is, however, evidence in this case to point to the fact that this psalm was composed for the use of young men being instructed in the pious wisdom and devotion to the law of the late post-exilic period. The acrostic structure and the repetition of the eight terms for law are an aid to memory in this respect. The person meant to recite the psalm is a young man (נער, v. 9; cf. v. 99); he is much concerned with the very meditation on the law which this psalm would provide (vv. 15, 23, 48, 97 *et passim*). His most frequently repeated prayer is for Yahweh to teach him, to give him understanding (vv. 29, 32, 33, 34, 102, 171 etc.). At the same time his devotion to Yahweh implies a daily discipline of worship in the temple (vv. 164, 172, 173). The obvious conclusion is that the psalm was composed for learning by heart and recitation by the devotees of Yahweh who learned Torah in the schools attached to the temple in the late post-exilic period. As such, references in the psalm to persecution and to sickness do not reflect the personal experience of the poet so much as the condition which the devotee of Yahweh was likely to experience to an increasing degree throughout this period. The 'I' in the psalm is not so much a wisdom teacher, therefore, as a wisdom pupil in the schools; and although the psalm is didactic it does not teach, as do the other psalms discussed here, by public proclamation, but by being food for individual meditation and recitation.

A protest psalm (Ps. 39)

The wisdom literature in the Old Testament falls into two catgories: orthodox wisdom and protest literature which had an accepted place amongst the canon of Israel's sacred writings.[42] The wisdom pieces in the psalter discussed above are undoubtedly examples of orthodox wisdom in its various forms, as one would expect from poetry transmitted through the official cult. However, the psalter has preserved in Psalm 39 a protest poem outside of the complaints in Job and Koheleth. The desolation depicted by the sage in the power of his language reaches across two millennia and more to make this in many ways the most moving prayer in the psalter. Of the writers quoted above only Crenshaw sees this psalm as the product of the wise.[43] Evidence for seeing the psalm as an example of this genre comes partly from the fact that it fits uneasily into any other category, both because of the forms used and particularly because of the unorthodox content of the psalmist's questions: only in protest poetry could Yahweh be linked to a consuming moth (v. 11) or could the psalmist cry:

> Look away from me that I may know gladness,
> before I depart and am no more.

Not even Koheleth is so vindictive towards God among the sages of Israel. Only the laments in Job plumb such depths, and these stand within the context of the book as a whole, which has a mitigating effect. The affinities with known examples of wisdom literature provide the further plank of evidence needed for wisdom attribution; in particular the vigorous questioning of God and the deliberation with self (vv. 1-2). The psalm also uses, with emphasis, the term הֶבֶל, in vain, beloved by Ecclesiastes, and deals with a question so familiar from the wisdom writings, the question of the righteous sufferer. The psalm could almost be taken as a reply to the, comparatively, rather bland instruction given in Psalm 37.

The introduction to the psalm (vv. 1-3) should be taken as being given instead of the normal invocation from a wisdom teacher to his hearers; it takes the form of a testimony to the sage's internal struggle. Because of this build-up the questions and complaints in vv. 4-6 have the effect of bursting upon the hearer of the psalm after the suspense of the first four lines. Emphasis is pursued throughout by the use of הִנֵּה (behold) (v. 6) and the impressive threefold אַךְ (surely) (vv. 6f.). The second half of the psalm, which is petition rather than complaint, continues the note of anger against God with a stately series of accusations and images. The form of the whole of the psalm from v. 4 is that of individual lament, but the content removes the piece from the normal cult worship of the community. We must conclude that here at least the psalter has preserved a genuine piece of private psalm poetry venting a wisdom writer's dissent and anger against God. The psalm is, therefore, most probably a late post-exilic composition, like the similar laments in Job and Ecclesiastes, and may have been informed, like these writings, by the suffering of the community as well as that of the sage himself.

In conclusion it may be said that the individual in the psalms can be identified as a wisdom teacher in some eleven psalms, all of which date almost certainly from the post-exilic period. The majority of these pieces have a didactic purpose, but nevertheless have their context in the worship of the temple, being sung or recited at the major festivals as the wise took their part in instructing the people in the way of Yahweh. In the later psalms the emphasis upon Torah in the wisdom writings culminates in Psalm 119, composed for the use of young adherents of the scribal schools. Finally among the wisdom writers of Israel are numbered the most unorthodox and the most independent of Israel's thinkers. The latter tradition has found expression in at least one piece in the psalter: the protest poem, Psalm 39.

III. THE 'I' IN THE PSALMS AS A TEMPLE SINGER

The preceding sections have discussed two of the groups responsible for the composition of many of the extant psalms: the cultic prophets, working mainly in the pre-exilic period, and the wisdom writers of Israel, working mainly, if not exclusively, after the exile. The fact that both of these groups have a distinctive style and reveal their own concerns in their desire to teach the people implies of itself that the origin of the remainder of the psalms in the psalter is not to be sought with these groups alone. For this we must look with Mowinckel[44] to the temple singers themselves.

Unlike the cultic prophets and the wise men, the temple singers of the pre-exilic period have not been the subject of any extensive study[45] partly because the data available is so scattered. The evidence does indicate, however, that, as was the case with prayer of the temple, the music of the temple must be set against a general background of music and its function in ancient Near Eastern culture.[46] Against this background, the fact that the cult supported the only professional singers and musicians in Israel outside the royal court would mean that the temple music would rise to a relatively high standard. We know, for example, that male and female singers were part of the tribute paid by Hezekiah to Sennacherib of Assyria after the siege of Jerusalem in 701 BC. In part because of the frequency and the way in which the psalms speak of the temple and its precincts it is extremely likely that most of the extant pieces, as Mowinckel suggests, were originally composed by these professional musicians and handed down from generation to generation within the different families and guilds.[47]

Some difficulty arises in trying to discover whether or not the 'I' in any given psalm is a temple singer, largely because there is no distinctive style outside the psalter as there is for cultic prophets and wisdom writers with which a given psalm can be compared. Concern for the temple alone is not enough to identify an individual as a temple singer as these poets' love for the sanctuary surfaces in many of the psalms written for king and commoner. In fact it seems that only three psalms in which the individual is 'in focus' to a large degree in the psalm reflect directly this group of psalm singers. In a further seven pieces the voice of the poet appears, as it were, incidentally, to introduce or conclude the piece. The latter group will be dealt with first.

Incidental appearances by the temple singers
(Pss. 8; 145; 146; 104; 103; 106; 135; 45)

The majority of psalms in which the 'I' occurs incidentally are songs of praise. There is no way of telling for certain whether the psalmist is a temple singer as opposed to a cultic prophet or wisdom writer but one can only say that this attribution seems more likely than the other two, largely because the emphasis here is less upon teaching and more upon declarative or descriptive praise. Even so, the seven hymns included in this section can be divided into songs which focus upon creation and so take up many of the wisdom themes, and songs focusing upon history taking up the themes of the cultic prophets.

Psalm 8 is a song of meditative praise. As in the creation song

embedded in Psalm 19, the silent witness of the heavens evokes
wonder for the creation in the psalmist. He is driven by this
contemplation to question the enigma of man's existence posing the
question taken up by Koheleth:

> Also he has put עוֹל (eternity) into man's mind yet so that he cannot
> find out what God has done from beginning to end (Eccl. 3.11).

Here the psalmist's focus on man's existence concentrates on his
exaltation by God, the first horn of Koheleth's dilemma, rather than
his frailty. As Anderson and Eaton suggest, the psalm was probably
written for the autumn festival with v. 2 providing a covert reference
to the election of Zion. Eaton[48] makes the interesting suggestion that
the psalm was for recitation by the king, but it seems more
straightforward to see the piece as the composition of and for
recitation by the temple singers.

Psalm 145 similarly reflects many of the themes of the great annual
festival and may have the post-exilic version of this feast as its
context in the cult. The acrostic structure, the language of the psalm
and allusions to other pieces are all evidence of a late date however.
The psalm singer himself comes to the fore at the beginning and at
the conclusion of this complete hymn of praise. The evidence of the
Qumran text of the psalm suggests that this piece, like Psalm 136,
may originally have been provided with a refrain.[49]

The two remaining hymns which deal with creation are even more
strongly influenced by the wisdom style than Psalms 8 and 145.
Psalm 146 is numbered among the wisdom psalm by Crenshaw and
contains instruction (vv. 3f.), an אשרי (Blessed ...) saying and a
fourfold description of the actions of Yahweh. However, as the psalm
is cast as praise rather than instruction it is grouped here with the
other pieces in which the 'I' is a leader of worship rather than a
teacher. Finally, *Psalm 104*, the lengthy hymn celebrating the
creation and the works of God, also contains evidence of wisdom
influence, particularly in v. 24:

> O Lord, how manifold are thy works,
> In wisdom thou hast made them all.

However, this psalm also is primarily a song of praise and in fact
contains a vow by the psalmist to 'sing to the Lord' as long as he
lives, perhaps indicating an origin among the temple singers.

Two of the three psalms which use the themes of the cultic prophets rather than the wisdom writers are similarly grouped here as hymns and are part of what may once have been a short separate collection of Psalms 103–106. It is probable that these two pieces are also post-exilic in origin. *Psalm 103* begins with an invocation to praise Yahweh and runs over a series of blessings enjoyed, rather than an autobiographical testimony (hence the psalm cannot be seen as a song of individual thanksgiving, contra Anderson, *ad loc.*). The central section of the psalm reveals Yahweh's nature in his dealings with the nation (as opposed to the individual). The permanence and steadfastness of Yahweh is contrasted with the impermanence of man in verses reminiscent of Deutero-Isaiah's prophecy. The conclusion of the psalm returns to a note of praise, summoning all the servants of Yahweh to bless the Lord and concluding with the phrase which began the psalm: 'Bless Yahweh O my Soul'.

Verses 26 and 27 of *Psalm 106* presuppose the exile. The psalm singer appears in the psalm after the introductory invocation, as a member of the chosen people whose fate is tied up with theirs. Anderson's suggestion that the prayer was a kind of Levitical sermon recited annually to draw repentance from the people is attractive yet the post-exilic origin of the psalm indicates that we should see its author as one of the guild of temple singers rather than a cult prophet.

Psalm 135 brings together all these themes of creation and redemption in what is probably, by reason of the critique of idols in vv. 15ff., a post-exilic hymn of praise. After the introductory invocation there is reference to creation (vv. 5ff.) and to the exodus and conquest (vv. 8ff.). Praise of Yahweh's name is followed by scorn of the gods of other nations. In its bringing together of these three themes the psalm may well have been influenced by the prophecy of Deutero-Isaiah. The psalm singer himself appears in v. 8 where, on behalf of the congregation, he proclaims his faith in Yahweh's might.

Finally, for the sake of completeness, mention should be made here of *Psalm 45*, which demonstrates the degree of overlap between prophet, wisdom writer and psalm singer. In the manner of the cultic prophets, the psalmist gives pronouncements of victory and prosperity to the king and his bride; in the manner of the wisdom writers he begins the song by saying:

My tongue is the pen of a ready scribe;

yet the subject matter of the psalm indicates that the song will have
been composed by professional musicians of the temple for the royal
wedding. This psalm, like the others discussed in this section, sounds
a note of caution to any who try to distinguish too finely between the
activities of the cult prophet, wise man and psalm singer. Although
separate styles and functions can be distinguished to some degree, we
must allow for a fair measure of overlap in both of these respects.

Three testimonies of the temple poets (Pss. 84; 42–43; 137)

Although the dating of psalms is always hazardous, the three full
testimonies of the temple poets which have survived fall into a fairly
obvious and straightforward chronological order, and this will be the
order of the discussion here. *Psalm 84* is clearly a pre-exilic psalm
intended for use in some capacity at the festal worship. The prayer
for the king makes this clear (v. 8) as does the delight in the temple.
There is also reference to the kingship of Yahweh (v. 3) and, as
Johnson points out,[50] to the autumn rains which would follow the
festival. The description of Yahweh as שמש (sun), the only such in the
Old Testament, is also indicative of an early date for the psalm. Once
this has been agreed, scholarly opinion is fairly unanimous in seeing
Psalm 84 as a song of pilgrimage, likening the piece to the songs of
Ascents.[51] However, it seems to me that this interpretation is
somewhat awkward, as this would be the only pre-exilic 'pilgrimage
song' preserved in the psalter, and that the psalm is better seen as a
song of joy which does describe the feelings and impressions of the
people who have come to the temple but which also expresses the joy
of the singers themselves. After the opening song of joy the psalmist
then goes on to bless three categories of men associated with temple
worship and it is significant for the interpretation of the psalm that
those who are first mentioned are 'those who dwell in thy house ever
singing thy praise'. The composer of the psalm is surely one of this
group rather than a member of the next, the pilgrims who come up to
Zion. The third blessing, in the form of a prayer, is asked for the king
himself. Again, the psalmist expresses his desire to dwell in Yahweh's
house and the psalm concludes with a reminder that Yahweh's
blessing is given only to those who walk uprightly, in preparation for
the festival which follows. Psalm 84 then comes directly from, and
expresses the piety of, the temple singers of the pre-exilic period.

Several commentators have drawn attention to the similarity in tone between Psalm 84 and the next psalm in this series, *Psalm 42-43*, which also has the heading 'Of the Sons of Korah'. The similarity in style and piety would support the view that the psalmist here is once again the temple singer. Eaton places the lament prayer in his less likely group of royal psalms.[52] Although there is evidence for this in some of the language used, all the other arguments Eaton adduces, such as the psalmist leading worship and the danger faced being a corporate danger, could equally well indicate that the 'I' in the piece is a temple singer. In addition v. 5b is particularly awkward in Eaton's interpretation. He has to resort to the suggestion that the king may be in a field campaign in northern Israel (but it is unlikely that this would produce such desolation and longing for the temple) or to the notion that the psalmist is speaking figuratively of the entrance to the underworld.[53] If this is the case, why does he evoke the beauty of the scene with obvious longing and use proper names? Added to these arguments, the meditative nature of the psalm is unlike that of the rest of the royal psalms, which tend to be direct and urgent prayers, but is very similar to the communing with the soul found in other psalms from the singers.

Weiser, Jacquet and others see the psalmist as a Levite in exile in northern Israel. This is nearer the mark but is somewhat pedantic. The consideration that the distress is something more than personal and the repearted taunts of the adversaries (vv. 3b, 10; 43.2) would tell against this also. The most natural interpretation of the psalm would seem to be to see the prayer as one composed by the temple singers from the situation of exile.[54] The joy of dwelling in the temple expressed in Psalm 84 here becomes a deep longing for the living God in the place of exile. In his meditation the psalmist remembers the great festival in Jerusalem in which he took a leading role and also, in vv. 5-7, the beauty of his native land; yet even in exile the psalmist has his song and prayer (v. 8b). In the second half of the song the mood changes to one of direct intercession and pleading with Yahweh in phrases borrowed from the festal cult. Significant, however, is the fact that when the psalmist is again led back to Jerusalem his first action will be that of a temple singer:

> Then I will go to the altar of my God,
> To God my exceeding joy,
> And I will praise him with the lyre,
> O God my God.

The lyre (כנר) is the instrument of the psalmist which is the symbol of his art (cf. Ps. 137.2). Again the hope of the psalmist, expressed throughout in the refrain, is not to govern or to live or to fight but simply again to praise Yahweh. Psalm 42–43, therefore, is best seen as the composition of a temple singer from the exile in which he gives expression to his private grief which mingles with the grief of the nation, just as a private joy mingles with the joy of the nation in Psalm 84.

Psalm 137, the third and final psalm in the group, clearly reflects the experiences of the temple singers and equally clearly can be dated to the early years after the return from exile.[55] The excellence which led Hezekiah to send Hebrew singers to Sennacherib as part of his tribute in 701 no doubt pertained during the years of the exile. Certainly singers are mentioned in the lists in Ezra as having returned from Babylon (Ezra 2.41).

The same love for the singer's native land is present in this piece as is present in Psalm 42–43. The self-cursing which the psalmist includes would affect the two means by which he played his art—his lyre playing and singing. There is of course great artistry and imagery in the psalm—again placing this piece in the same bracket as Psalms 84 and 42–43: in particular there is the recurring theme of remembering and forgetting. The picture of the harp on the willows can be likened to the nature images of Pss. 84.3 and 42.1. Again as in the other two psalms the emotion of the people is taken up and poignantly summarized in the emotion of the temple poet. In this sense, and in the sense that all three were probably used in public worship, Psalms 84, 42–43 and 137 are not mere private poetry or meditation; they are songs written for public use; yet they reflect, more than most of the psalms of the individual preserved in the psalter, the true emotions and piety of the men who composed them.

IV. CONCLUSION

Although the majority of individual psalms in the psalter were composed for the use of either the king or the ordinary worshipper in the cult, some nineteen of these psalms will not fit easily into either of these categories. In these psalms the voices of the ministers of Israel's cult are heard directly. In the majority of the cases the motive which directs the psalm is not one of prayer or praise but of teaching the assembled congregation. This appears to have been the task of the cultic prophets, by and large teaching from Israel's historical traditions in the pre-exilic period and of the pious wise men in the post-exilic era. Although these two groups between them were responsible for the composition of a large number of psalms, a third group of temple singers can be identified as taking a large share in this work of composition both before and after the exile. Their voice is heard in the introduction and/or conclusion to several hymns of praise and also in three psalms which bear direct witness to the piety and emotion of these poets but which were composed, nonetheless, for use in public worship. In fact, this chapter has argued for a place in public worship for all of the psalms of the individual with the exception of the two late pieces, Psalms 39 and 119.

CONCLUSION

This enquiry began with the question which must be asked by every person who reads the Psalms today: 'Who is the individual who speaks through these pages?' This complex question of the identity of the individual in the Psalms has been answered with a solution which, if complex, at least attempts to come to terms with all the facets of the problem and all the available evidence. Almost all of the individual psalms were written for use in the temple cult: a great many of those which have survived were intended for use by the king as he led the public worship, particularly on the great festal occasions; others were provided for use by the ordinary worshipper; in the third group those who speak are the ministers of the cult, cultic prophets, wisdom teachers and temple singers.

The Psalms as a whole, but particularly the psalms of the individual, have provided a tremendous resource for Jewish and Christian devotion over the whole period of their existence. In the light of this study, and indeed of the past century of critical research on the Psalms, the question must be asked: whose piety, whose spirituality is here? To what group should we look, if not to David or to other individuals, as the fountainhead of so much prayer? The answer, once again, is somehwat complex, and it seems to me that we should see at least three streams of spirituality operating whenever one of the psalms discussed above was recited: that of the person or group who composed the prayer (the temple poets, cultic prophets or wisdom teachers); that of the person who delivered the psalm in the cult (in the case of the royal psalms the special relationship between God and the king would feed into the psalm as it was being composed and surfaces as the royal style identified in Chapter 3); and that of the assembled congregation which would feed into, and be fed by, the faith of those who composed the psalms for public worship.

The cult itself, therefore, should be seen as the medium for the transmission of the spiritual traditions of the people. This tradition, or common ground of belief, formed the basis on which the psalm-composer worked. These groups, who were particularly well-instructed in the traditions of prayer, would reshape the tradition into new prayers to be delivered in the cult by king or commoner or into psalms of instruction to be delivered by the cultic ministers. These prayers would then be recited in the cult by the appropriate individual and so teach the congregation, indirectly, how to pray. Thus the new insights of the psalm composers would be fed back into the traditions of the congregation. This process of transmission could be shown as follows:

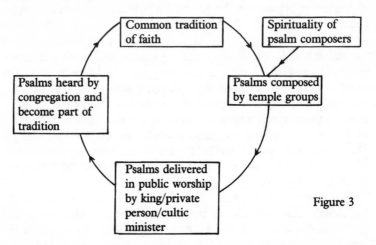

Figure 3

As can be seen from the diagram, the creative contribution in the whole process is the spirituality of the temple-based groups of psalm-composers.

This picture of the spirituality of the psalms adds, it seems to me, another rich dimension to our understanding of the individual in the psalms. To a great extent, the voices which we hear in the psalter are different voices in different psalms: that of the king, the private person, the cultic minister, as has been shown above. However, at a different level the voice we are hearing in the psalms is one voice, the voice of the accumulated tradition of a nation and religious community at prayer: the voice of Israel responding to her God.

Psalm		Description	
2 (P)		RP	Ritual (confirmation of kingship)
3		RP	GH Prayer for aid in battle
4		CM	Wisdom teacher (didactic psalm)
5		RP	Ritual (preparation)
6		PP	General petition
7		RP	Ritual (preparation)
8 (P)		CM	Temple singer (incidental app.)
9–10		RP	Ritual (own category)
11		CM	Wisdom teacher (didactic psalm)
13		PP	General petition
16		RP	Psalm of assurance
17		RP	Ritual (preparation)
18		RP	GH (thanksgiving after battle)
19		CM	Wisdom teacher (hymn)
20	(a)	RP	2nd person (prayer for aid in battle)
	(b)	CM	Cultic prophet (oracle)
21		RP	2nd/3rd person. Ritual (confirmation of kingship)
22		RP	GH (prayer of siege)
23		RP	Psalm of assurance
25		'other'	Post-exilic prayer by non-royal spokesman
26		RP	Ritual (preparation)
27		RP	Ritual (preparation)
28		RP	GH (sickness)
30		PP	Thanksgiving after illness
31		RP	GH (prayer of siege)
32		CM	Wisdom teacher (didactic psalm)
34		CM	Wisdom teacher (didactic psalm)
35		PP	Prayer in persecution
36 (P)		CM	Cult prophet
37		CM	Wisdom teacher (didactic psalm)
38		RP	GH (sickness)
39		CM (?)	Wisdom teacher (protest poem)*
40		RP	Ritual (confirmation of kingship)
41		PP	Prayer in sickness
42–43		CM	Temple singer (testimony)
44 (P)		RP	GH (prayer for aid in battle)
45 (P)	(a)	RP	Royal wedding song (2nd person)
	(b)	CM	Temple singer (incidental reference)

49		CM	Wisdom teacher (didactic)
51		'other'	Exilic prayer by non-royal spokesman
52		CM	Cultic prophet
54		PP	General petition
55		RP	GH (prayer against treachery)
56		RP	GH (prayer for aid in battle)
57		RP	GH (prayer for aid in battle)
59		RP	GH (prayer for siege)
60		RP	GH (prayer for aid in battle)
61		RP	Ritual (confirmation)
62		RP	GH (prayer against treachery)
63		RP	Psalm of assurance
64		PP	Prayer for persecution
66 (P)		RP	GH (prayer of thanksgiving after battle)
69		RP	GH (prayer for aid in battle)
70		PP	Prayer in persecution
71		RP	GH (prayer against treachery)
72		RP	2nd/3rd person. Ritual (confirmation of kingship)
73		CM	Wisdom teacher (didactic psalm)
74 (P)		CM	Cultic prophet
75 (P)		CM	Cultic prophet
77		CM	Cultic prophet
78		CM	Cultic prophet
81		CM	Cultic prophet
83		CM	Cultic prophet
84		CM	Temple singer (testimony)
85 (P)		CM	Cultic prophet
86		PP	Prayer in persecution
88		PP	Prayer in sickness
89		RP	GH (prayer for aid in battle)
92		RP	Ritual (confirmation of kingship)
94		RP	Ritual (preparation)
101		RP	Ritual (preparation)
102		'other'	Exilic prayer for non-royal spokesman
103 (P)		CM	Temple singer (incidental reference)
104 (P)		CM	Temple singer (incidental reference)
106 (P)		CM	Temple singer (incidental reference)
108		RP	GH (prayer for aid in battle)
109		PP	Prayer in persecution
110	(a)	RP	2nd/3rd person. Ritual (confirmation of kingship)
	(b)	CM	Cultic prophet
111		CM	Wisdom teacher (hymn)
116		RP	GH (thanksgiving after illness)
118		RP	Ritual (procession and battle)

119 (P)	CM (?)	Wisdom teacher (meditation)*
120	PP	Psalm of Ascent
121 (P)	PP	Psalm of Ascent
122	PP	Psalm of Ascent
123	PP	Psalm of Ascent
130	PP	Psalm of Ascent
131	PP	Psalm of Ascent
132	RP	2nd/3rd person. Ritual (preparation)
135	CM	Temple singer (incidental reference)
137	CM	Temple singer (testimony)
138	RP	Psalm of assurance
139	RP	Ritual (preparation)
140	RP	GH (prayer for help in battle?)
141	RP	Ritual (preparation)
142	PP	Prayer in persecution
143	RP	GH (prayer for help in battle?)
144	RP	Ritual (confirmation of kingship)
145	CM	Temple singer (incidental reference)
146 (P)	CM	Temple singer (incidental reference)

Ninety-eight psalms are included in the list, of which three do not mention an individual but refer to the king in the 2nd/3rd person.

Totals
Royal psalms	47 (of which 6 refer to the king in 2nd/3rd person; 3 of these psalms are also listed as 'CM' psalms)
Private person:	18
Cultic ministers:	33
'Other' psalms:	3

Abbreviations used here
RP	Royal psalm
PP	Private person psalm
CM	Cultic minister
GH	General historical
*	indicates that the psalm does not appear to have been composed for public worship in the temple.
P	indicates that the 'I' occurs in part of the psalm only.

NOTES

Notes to Introduction

1. So J.H. Hayes, *An Introduction to Old Testament Study* (1979), p. 293; J.H. Eaton, *The Psalms and Israelite Worship* in *Tradition and Interpretation*, ed. G.W. Anderson, p. 255. The other key issue is, of course, that of the relationship between the psalms and the annual festal ritual.

2. It is not my purpose here to reiterate the detailed history of the debate. Such a summary can be found in most of the major commentaries, in the two articles mentioned above, and Eaton's major work, *Kingship and the Psalms* (*KP*) (1976; second, revised edition, 1986).

3. H. Birkeland, *Die Feinde des Individuums in der israelitischen Psalmenliteratur* (1933) and *The Evildoers in the Book of Psalms* (1955).

4. H. Birkeland, *Ani und Anaw in den Psalmen* (1933). Although this work is earlier than *Die Feinde* and presents different conclusions, following the theories of Birkeland's teacher Mowinckel that the 'I' in the psalms is predominantly a private person, the two books taken together do illustrate the importance of these two related questions for the study of the identity of the individual in the Psalms. Cf. C. Schultz, *Ani and Anaw in the Psalms* (1973).

5. Particularly in A.R. Johnson, *Sacral Kingship in Ancient Israel* (*SKAI*) (1952; 2nd edition 1969) and Eaton, *KP*.

6. So H. Schmidt, *Das Gebet der Angeklagten* (1926) and L. Delekat, *Asylie und Schutzorakel* (1967).

7. So, for example, R. Smend, 'Über das Ich der Psalmen', in *ZAW* 8 (1888), pp. 49-147.

8. So Birkeland, *Evildoers* and Eaton, *KP*.

9. A full list of these psalms is given in the summary of results. Psalms 9–10 and 42–43 are each reckoned throughout as one psalm.

Notes to Chapter 1
The Antagonists in the Psalms

1. E.g. G.W. Anderson, 'Enemies and Evildoers in the Book of Psalms', *BJRL* 48, (1965-66), pp. 18-29.

2. Mowinckel's comment on Birkeland's work quoted from G.W. Anderson, *Enemies*, p. 27.

3. Birkeland would here use the word 'enemies'; however, following Rosenbaum, I have subsituted the neutral word antagonist for reasons of

clarity in the arguments which follow; S.N. Rosenbaum, *The Concept 'Antagonist' in Hebrew Psalm Poetry: A Semantic Field Study* (1974) *passim*.

4. Mowinckel, *PIW*, I, p. 227 n. 4; see also *PIW*, I, pp. 197, 207f., 245; Eaton, *KP*, *passim*.

5. Mowinckel, *PIW*, I, p. 197.

6. Mowinckel, *PIW*, II, Additional Note 32, pp. 256f.

7. Particularly that of Sawyer, *Semantics* and also T. Donald, 'The Semantic Field Rich and Poor in Hebrew and Accadian Literature', *Oriens Antiquus 3* (1964), pp. 27-41

8. Rosenbaum, *Antagonists*, pp. 58-64.

9. Indications that the piece is a wisdom psalm include the opening beatitude, the dichotomy between the righteous and the wicked and the fine phrasing and polished style, an example of which is the fact that the first begins with א and the last word with ת—perhaps signifying completeness within the psalm itself. The issue of the wisdom influence on the psalms is discussed in Chapter 5 below.

10. This is one example of their failure to distinguish between the experience of the writer of the psalm and the purpose in the cult for which the piece was written.

11. A.A. Anderson, *Psalm, ad loc.*; Eaton, *TBC, ad loc.*; Johnson, *CPIP*, pp. 296-302.

12. Reading, with RSV, לְעֵת מָצוֹק for MT לְעֵת מְצֹאַרְק (at a time of finding only); so Anderson, *ad loc.*

13. Invocations to learn are of course a distinct wisdom form in themselves and make up much of the collection in Proverbs 1-9; cf. R.N. Whybray, *Wisdom in Proverbs* (1965).

14. The different concepts of judgment operating in the psalms are discussed in detail by R.L. Hubbard, *Legal and Dynamistic Language in the Book of Psalms* (1980). He discusses the distinction between legal and dynamistic language: in the former justice is attained by appeal to Yahweh and by his direct intervention; in the latter there is built into the universe a dynamic whereby the effects of sin will rebound onto the perpetrator. He argues sensibly that these two views are not opposed in the Psalms or on the rest of the Old Testament but are two sides of the same coin. Yahweh occasionally intervenes to set right injustices which the dynamic has not corrected but for the most part his justice works through that dynamic. Hence both legal and dynamistic language are found in most of the Psalms, as here.

15. This conclusion is reached after a thorough investigation of this *crux interpretum* by B. Renaud, 'Le Psaume 73: méditation individuelle ou prière collective?', *Revue d'Histoire et de Philosophie Religieuses* 59 (1979), pp. 541-50.

16. Surprisingly, Birkeland does not discuss Psalm 50 at all in *Die Feinde*

but he deals with the psalm at length in *Evildoers*. He regards the piece as the one genuine prophetic oracle which has slipped into the social religion so prominent, he thinks, in the psalms. The effect of this oracle has been tempered by the insertion of these words by later hand (p. 64).

17. Johnson, *CPIP*, pp. 22f.; Eaton, TBC, *ad loc.*

18. The role of the cultic prophet in teaching the people is taken up below in Chapter 5.

19. So Johnson, *CPIP*, p. 317. Eaton's argument that the speaker in this psalm is the king is not convincing. How could the king be said to steady the earth? (Eaton, *KP*, pp. 55f.).

20. A full discussion of royal style, together with a context in the ritual for Psalm 94, is given in Chapter 3 below.

21. This psalm, like Psalm 94, is given a setting in the royal ritual in Chapter 3.

22. See the discussion of royal style below, pp. 76ff.

23. Eaton, *KP*, p. 5; Mowinckel, *PIW*, I, p. 217.

24. It would be valuable to note here the various hints in the psalms so far discussed which suggest how the people conceived of their relationship to Yahweh and in particular what the relationship of sin was to the nation's plight and deliverance. Psalm 74 presents an attitude of incomprehension in what amounts to a confession of innocence:

> Why dost thou cast us off for ever? (v. 1)
> Then we will never turn back from thee,
> Give us life and we will call on thy name (v. 18)

—a verse which implies continued worship in exchange for military aid. Psalm 44 has a tone similar to that of 74:

> All this has come upon us though we have not forgotten thee or been false
> to thy covenant. Our heart has not looked back, nor have our steps departed
> from thy way (vv. 17f.).

This time the confession of innocence is made explicit and again the question 'Why?' is on the lips of the psalmists. The inference is that *had* the people forgotten Yahweh, been false to the covenant or spread forth their hands to a strange god, then their plight would have been deserved or expected. The sin here is that of the nation. Psalm 66, which reflects the rather different situation of thanksgiving for answered prayer, turns on the same theology:

> If I had cherished iniquity in my heart, the Lord would not have listened,
> But truly God has listened, he has given heed to the voice of my prayer
> (vv. 18f.).

25. The rather complex uses of the terms for poor in this psalm are discussed below.

26. Of necessity many of the arguments presented here anticipate conclusions reached in Chapter 3.

27. So Eaton, *TBC*, *ad loc.*
28. Eaton, *KP*, p. 54.
29. Rosenbaum, *Antagonists*, Chapter 6.
30. Psalms 9–10 are the psalms on which Birkeland and others who have followed his theory have largely based their case, for in this psalm, if the MT reading is correct, the equation גוים=רשעים=איבים appears to hold true. There have been several attempts, notably by Ginsberg and by Rosenbaum, to emend the text to read גֵּאִים 'arrogant ones', for גוֹים, but these attempts are awkward and are based more upon a desire for consistent theories than a respect for the text itself. The suggested emendation has no support at all in the MSS and versions. Furthermore, the text does make sound sense as it stands: the natural conclusion to draw from v. 6 alone is that the רשעים are the nations. However, as has been shown in the preceding inquiry, Birkeland's own theory that the psalm reflects a pattern, a stereotyped and formal way of referring to foreign antagonists, is equally dissatisfying. In fact, as will be argued below, Pss. 9–10 appeal for Yahweh's aid both against the nations and against the wicked in the land. Cf. H.L. Ginsberg, 'Some Emendations in Psalms', *HUCA* 23 (1950-51), pp. 74-101; S.N. Rosenbaum, 'New Evidence for Reading Ge'im for Go'im in Pss. 9–10', *HUCA* 45 (1974). pp. 65-72.

Notes to Chapter 2
The Poor in the Psalms

1. See for example, Pss. 40.17; 69.29; 70.5; 86.1; 88.16; 109.22.
2. Comprehensive accounts of the history of this question are found in Schultz, *Ani and Anaw in the Psalms* (1973), pp. 1-21; in A.R. Johnson's valuable essay on psalm criticism in H.H. Rowley (ed.), *The Old Testament and Modern Study* (OTMS; 1951), pp. 198-204; and in the work of J. van der Ploeg, 'Les Pauvres d'Israël et leur piété', *Oudtestamentische Studiën* 7 (1950), pp. 236-42.
3. A. Rahlfs, עני *und* ענו *in den Psalmen* (1892).
4. Birkeland's original position was based on that of Mowinckel in *Psalmenstudien I* and followed from the view of the enemies as sorcerers (פאלי און)—hence the poor were seen as pious individuals appealing to Yahweh for aid. His later work again follows the view developed of the antagonists in the psalms, this time of the enemies as the nations.
5. Schultz, *Ani and Anaw*, pp. 225f.; see also pp. 133-38.
6. Schultz, *Ani and Anaw*, p. 138.
7. Isa. 32.7; Amos 8.4; Ps. 9.9; Job 24.4 (though the textual tradition varies in the latter case).
8. Schultz, *Ani and Anaw*, pp. 53-54.
9. Schultz, *Ani and Anaw*, p. 97.

10. Isa. 3.15; 10.22; 14.32; 49.13; 51.21f.

11. O. Keele, *The Language and Imagery of the Biblical World: Ancient Near Eastern Iconography and the Book of Psalms* (1978).

12. G.B. Caird, *The Language and Imagery of the Bible* (1981), pp. 151, 157.

13. R.C. Culley, *Oral Formulaic Language and the Biblical Psalms* (1967) and I. Ljung, *Tradition and Interpretation: A study of the use of oral formulaic language in the so-called Ebed Yahweh Psalms* (1978).

14. Caird, *Language and Imagery*, pp. 148f.

15. Caird, *Language and Imagery*, pp. 148f.

16. Caird, *Language and Imagery*, pp. 150f.

17. Compare the use of the term 'bread' in the Christian tradition which can call on a great number and history of different interpretations depending on the context in which it is used.

18. Caird, *Language and Imagery*, pp. 151f.

19. 'To refer to the two constituent elements of the metaphor, Ogden and Richards invented the useful terms vehicle and tenor: vehicle being the thing to which the word normally and naturally applies and tenor the thing to which it is transferred' (Caird, *Language and Imagery*, p. 152).

20. So F.C. Fensham, 'Widow, Orphan and Poor in the Ancient Near Eastern Legal and Wisdom Literature', *JNES* 21 (1962), pp. 129-39; J. van der Ploeg, *Les Pauvres*.

21. Eaton, *TBC, ad loc.*, and also in his 'Some Question of Philology and Exegesis in the Psalms', *JTS* n.s. 19 (1968), pp. 603-609.

22. This suggestion is also upheld by R.E. Murphy, *A Study of Psalm 72* (1948).

23. So A.A. Anderson, Weiser, Eaton, Mowinckel etc.

24. Eaton, *KP*, p. 54; Mowinckel, *PIW*, I, p. 3; *PIW*, II, p. 212.

25. Schultz, *Ani and Anaw*, pp. 74-76.

26. Schultz realizes that the identity of the poor in Pss. 9–10 turns on the identity of the רשעים who hotly pursue the עני (pp. 46-50). Anxious to preserve his conclusion that עני never refers to the nation, he takes refuge in the textual emendation suggested by Ginsberg and supported by Rosenbaum of emending גוֹיִם to גֵּאִים throughout the psalm. The merits of this view are discussed above (ch. 2 n. 30). The term עניים occurs four times in the psalm, although in only one place (10.17) is the reading unchalleged by a Kethib/ Q'ere variant. Here the use of the term is consistent with that found above: עניים refers to the faithful in the congregation at prayer (cf. 22.27; 69.32). In 9.18 (MT 19) it seems that Q'ere of עני is to be preferred, giving the more usual parallel with אביון. In the two remaining instances (9.12 [MT 13] and 10.12) where עניים is the Q'ere reading it seems best to leave the text as it stands: the meaning in context here is more 'afflicted' than 'humble' or 'meek'.

Notes to Chapter 3
The Individual in the Psalms as the King

1. Accounts of this are found in Eaton, *KP*, pp. 1-20 and in *Tradition and Interpretation*, ed. G.W. Anderson, pp. 250-55.

2. Originally Pss. 2; 18; 20; 21; 45; 72; 101; 110; 132. Pss. 89 and 144 were added later.

3. Eaton, *KP*, pp. 5-11.

4. Eaton, *KP*, pp. 24f.

5. T.N.D. Mettinger, *King and Messiah* (1976), p. 306, gives a useful list of connections between king and sanctuary.

6. Less sure, however, is Eaton's argument from homogeneity and continuity. He argues (pp. 22f.) that:

> there is a prevailing similarity which is in accord with an origin within a
> restricted range of royal and national cultus . . . It is difficult to accept . . .
> that among similar psalms some, by hair-splitting arguments, can be said to
> belong to the specialised situation of the ordeal trials and others elsewhere.

As was mentioned above, this argument is a nonsense unless Eaton is prepared to argue that *all* the psalms are royal. The following two chapters attempt to show that clear differences do emerge between royal psalms, psalms of the private person and psalms composed for ministers in the cult and that these distinctions are based upon rather more than 'hair-splitting arguments'.

7. Naturally, great care must be taken to identify the situation envisaged in a psalm but to abandon this task altogether, as is often done with Psalm 22, for example, is to abandon the task of interpretation itself.

8. Eaton, *KP*, pp. 23f. and Chapter 4, *passim*.

9. Psalms 2; 18; 89; 118; 144 (from Gunkel's original group); 91; 28; 63 (which also mention the king—for exegesis see below); 3; 9–10; 22; 27; 44; 56; 59; 66; 69; 108 (set against a background of battle); and 94 (the liturgy for the renewal of the king's vocation).

10. The ark procession is acknowledged and affirmed, by among others, Mowinckel, *PIW*, I, pp. 172-74; Weiser, *Psalms*, pp. 40f.; H.J. Kraus, *Worship in Israel* (1966), pp. 184f.; and H. Ringgren, *Israelite Religion* (1966), p. 60. The cultic use of the ark has been examined in detail and confirmed in a doctoral study by T.E. Fretheim, 'The Cultic Use of the Ark in the Monarchic Period' (1968).

11. This understanding, which best accounts for the 'lament tone' of Ps. 132, allows for the translation of קומה ל as 'Arise on behalf of . . .' rather than 'Arise, go to . . .' which most translations have adopted. This translation will be discussed in detail below.

12. So, among others, J.R. Porter, 'The Interpretation of II Samuel 6 and Psalm 132', *JTS* 5 (1954), pp. 163-73.

13. The enemies who are defeated here are the kings of the earth, Israel's military foes, not the forces of chaos opposed to the god in other ancient Near Eastern festivals. In accordance with the general tendency in Israel the myth of the surrounding culture has been historicized. However, vestiges of the mythical viewpoint remain in the Psalms which has led some scholars to the view that the whole ceremony was one in which Yahweh regained his kingship each year rather than it being reaffirmed. In the course of this process the forces of chaos were defeated annually and the order and prosperity of society were maintained for a further cycle of the seasons. This view has been propounded by the 'Myth and Ritual' group of English scholars, led by S.H. Hooke and by a number of Scandinavian writers including Engnell and, to a lesser extent, Mowinckel, but has not come to command general acceptance. The basic approach of the Old Testament was to historicize the myths of the surrounding nations. Kraus and others have argued persuasively that the autumn festival celebrates the once-and-for-all victory of Yahweh in creation, communicating this afresh to each generation. His arguments are supported in the work of Halpern, who draws attention to a distinction in the Psalms between descriptions of Yahweh's victory over chaos where the scene is mainly static, i.e. no actual battle is described as such (eg. Pss. 29; 93; 97) and descriptions of his victory over the nations, which is actively described in several psalms.

14. A.R. Johnson, *Sacral Kingship in Ancient Israel* (*SKAI*) (2nd edition, 1967), pp. 85ff. The existence of the ritual battle is also supported by Mowinckel (*PIW*, I, pp. 182ff.) and others.

15. Following Johnson's discussion of דמינו in *SKAI*, p. 88.

16. K.W. Whitelam, *The Just King* (1979).

17. The debate on the antiquity of the covenant concept in Israel lies outside the scope the present work. Whatever terminology as used however, it is clear that Israel perceived herself to be in some form of judicial relationship to Yahweh from the earliest period and, therefore, that this was reaffirmed annually in some way in the context of the festival.

18. A.R. Johnson, 'The Role of the King in the Jerusalem Cultus', in *The Labyrinth* (1935), ed. S.H. Hooke, pp. 77-113.

19. J.H. Eaton, *'Festal Drama in Deutero-Isaiah* (1979), p. 9; cf. *KP*, pp. 130f. Of the definite group, Psalms 75 and 92 have vanished without trace, as have Psalms 52, 57, 61, 86, 116, 120, 130 and 139, all the 'possible group' in the earlier book.

20. Mowinckel makes his position clear thus:

> As long as the 'suffering' of the king in a majority of the psalms must be referred to actual historical disaster or real prosaic illness, strong positive arguments are needed in order to prove that the suffering in other psalms, which is referred to in a perfectly analogous way, have to be referred to ritual sham sufferings (*PIW*, II, pp. 253f. n. 31).

Whilst Mettinger, although he finds some support for a ritual of humiliation in the lament metre of Psalm 101, writes:

> The evidence remains inconclusive. A cultic suffering on the part of the king would perhaps not consitute a wholly inconceivable element in Israelite kingship. However, as far as I can see, there is a lack of positive evidence for such a practice in ancient Israel (*King and Messiah*, p. 307).

21. J.B. Pritchard (ed.), *ANET*, p. 334a.
22. Eaton, *KP*, p. 130.
23. Eaton, *KP*, p. 132.
24. See below, n. 26.
25. Even more dubious is Eaton's view that the king was also involved in rites of atonement (*KP*, pp. 181ff. and *Festal Drama*, pp. 35f.) which may or may not have been linked with the royal humiliation described above. The evidence for the priestly acts on the day of atonement being taken over by the High Priest from the king himself which he attempts to bring forward is not wholly convincing in itself. In particular Ezek. 47.17, it seems to me, does not envisage an atoning role for the prince, as Eaton makes out, but merely states that the prince shall furnish the offerings for the temple on behalf of the people. Even if this could be shown to be the case, however, we would have nothing other than Eaton's own interpretation of Psalms 51 and 102 to indicate that the king took upon himself the sin of the community and suffered on their behalf. Such an understanding again seems to derive more from a desire to seek the roots of the cross in the Old Testament kingship rites than from the evidence itself.
26. In his recent study on Israelite kingship, Baruch Halpern has established two points which support this contention. In the first place, he argues convincingly that there is a common ancient Near Eastern myth which can be recovered from the Enuma Elish, the Sumerian Lugal, the Ugaritic myths of Baal-Yam and the Old Testament sources which describes the victory of the (storm) god over the god of the sea. A common structure emerges from each of these myths: danger threatens the cosmos; a hero is designated to meet this danger and to do battle with the forces of chaos; he defeats these forces and returns to be enthroned and acclaimed as king and to pronounce judgment over the earth. In the Old Testament the myth of the Divine Warrior is changed in most sources so that the enemies defeated by Yahweh are not the mythological forces of chaos but Israel's historical foes (however there are vestigial traces of the original myth in several of the psalms, eg. Pss. 89; 74); this defeat of the foes is still associated, however, with Yahweh's being proclaimed king and winning for himself a sanctuary (cf. Song of Deborah, 33.2-5; Ps. 44.1-5; Exod. 15.1-18; Halpern, *Constitution*, pp. 61-85). This observation therefore validates the threefold structure of the festival given above.

Second, Halpern clearly establishes a connection between the myth of the

Divine Warrior and the establishment and renewal of the human monarchy. This was clearly the case in Babylon: the three themes of the establishing of the human monarchy, of the temple at Egigi and of Marduk's kingship over the cosmos are linked together in the Babylonian akitu festival at which the Enuma Elish was recited before the god. Halpern also brings forward other evidence to support this connection. It is thus all the more reasonable to suppose a common ground between the affirmation of Yahweh's kingship and that of the Davidic ruler and this interpretation is borne out in the exegesis of the psalms which follows. It also represents a further demonstration that there was in fact a fair degree of common ground between the Babylonian akitu celebration and that practised in Israel (B. Halpern, *Constitution*, Chapters 3 and 4, pp. 51-125).

27. Although Eaton does not include Psalm 26 in his group of royal psalms in *KP* he does favour the possibility that the suppliant here is the king in his earlier Torch commentary.

28. A.A.Anderson suggests that Deut. 17.8-13 provides a context in life for a psalm such as this, but this seems unlikely to me. In Deuteronomy it is the Levitical priests who must judge the case and to whom appeal must be made, rather than to Yahweh himself.

29. J. Gray, *I and II Kings* (1977), p. 125.

30. Johnson connects the psalm with a king's prayer from a ritual of incubation but, like Eaton, does not connect the psalm with the kingship ritual.

31. Cf. K.W. Whitelam, *The Just King* (1979).

32. So 1 Kgs 13.1-10 (the unnamed prophet to Jereboam at the festival); 14.10-16 (Abijah to Jereboam); 17.1 (Elijah against Ahab) and 1 Kings 22, the story of Micaiah, bearing witness to the fact that prophetic opinion was not uniform but some would be for a given king and some against: v. 20, 'He never prophesies good concerning me'. This list could be greatly extended. There is less direct evidence for the process of accusation against the kings in Judah but there seems no good reason to assume that independent criticism of the king by the prophetic movement was confined to the Northern Kingdom.

33. RSV 'groanings' seems rather strong here as a translation of 'הֹגִי' in view of the context; NEB has 'inmost thoughts' here.

34. Halpern, *Constitution*, pp. 1-13.

35. Judg. 11.1-12.7; Halpern, *Constitution*, p. 115.

36. Judg. 6.11-8.35; Halpern, *Constitution*, pp. 116f.

37. Eg. that of Joash, which contains the elements of designation by anointing, cultic and political purge and then (only) the king 'took his seat on the throne of the kings' (2 Kgs 11.19; Halpern, *Constitution*, pp. 140ff.). According to Halpern also (p. 146) the investiture of Joshua the High Priest in Zechariah 3 may also shed light on the designation part of the kingship rites: the removing of dirty garments and the putting on of clean ones is here

given the symbolic significance of the removal of sin, which would seem to support my own contention that the Israelite rites, like the Babylonian, involved some form of confession by the king.

38. Eaton, *KP*, p. 60. Despite noting this Eaton does not use the psalm in his reconstruction of the royal ritual. Halpern similarly alludes to the psalm as being associated with the festival but does not explore its significance further: *Constitution*, pp. 95-97.

39. So among the judges Gideon degrades himself (Judg. 6.15) at his call (as indeed does Moses in Exod. 3.11); Saul's words on being anointed echo Gideon's (1 Sam. 9.21) whilst the narrator himself imparts a similar sentiment to the story of David's first anointing (1 Sam. 16.6-13); David also, according to the narratives, humbles himself before the Lord on several occasions in this fashion (eg. 2 Sam. 8.18ff.).

40. Mettinger, *King and Messiah*, p. 307.

41. The Hebrew literally translated here would read:

> Let the oil of the head never anoint my head.

The RSV sensibly follows the LXX and other ancient versions in reading רָשָׁע for רֹאשׁ, giving the contrast with צַדִּיק and חֶסֶד in the first half of the verse.

42. The RSV translates, in rather a tame fashion, the Hebrew לֶאֱכֹל אֶת־בְּשָׂרִי as 'uttering slanders against me' and confines the vivid metaphor of 'eating up my flesh' to the margin. The metaphor of wild beasts approaching the suppliant here, as elsewhere in the psalter, would seem to denote a military aggressor (whether historical or ritual) rather than simply slander (cf. Pss. 22; 59).

43. The phrase זִבְחֵי תְרוּעָה provides further supporting evidence that Psalm 27 was used in the ritual. תְרוּעָה seems to have been a technical term for 'victory shout' as used in several different texts. 1 Samuel 4 is particularly interesting as the תְרוּעָה is given in response to the arrival of the Ark:

> When the Ark of the covenant of the Lord came into the camp all Israel gave a mighty תְרוּעָה and the earth shook.

תְרוּעָה is also used of the shout given when the Ark was brought into the temple (1 Sam. 6.15, par. 1 Chron. 15.28) and according to the Chronicler, at the rededication of the temple in the time of Asa (2 Chron. 15.14). In the Psalms the word is used, significantly, in Psalm 47 which would seem to have been sung as Yahweh, his presence symbolized by the Ark, went up to the sanctuary after the ritual battle:

> עלה אלהים בתרועה
> יהוה בקול שופר (Ps. 47.5, MT 6).

תְרוּעָה is also used in Ps. 89.16—in the first half of the psalm which would seem to have been taken from the festival rites (cf. below, pp. 118f.). All these considerations taken together have the effect of strengthening the association of Psalm 27 with the festival and with the rising up of Yahweh to fight on behalf of Israel and the king.

44. Two texts which support the case for linking the phrase בקשו פני with the Ark are 2 Sam. 6.4-5—where David and all Israel are said to be making merry לפני יהוה and the context clearly indicates that this means before the Ark—and Ps. 24.6:

זה דור דרשו מבקשי פני אלהי יעקב

following, with RSV, the LXX tend in omitting the suffix from פני and inserting אלהי. Psalm 24 is the psalm most often associated with the ascent of the Ark into the temple. These two texts, with other less convincing evidence, are quoted by T.E. Fretheim in support of his case that פנים can be a synonym for the Ark (*The Cultic Use of the Ark in the Monarchic Period*, Chapter 1).

45. D.R. Hillers, 'Ritual Procession of the Ark and Psalm 132', *CBQ* 30 (1968), pp. 48-55.

46. So Johnson, *CPIP*, p. 70 n. 7. In particular he argues that we would have expected מן here if the meaning 'from' had been intended.

47. So BDB, p. 515 col. b.

48. Halpern records that being granted a temple is closely connected with a god being recognized as king throughout the ancient Near East. In Enuma Elish Marduk's reward is the construction of a palace (Ee 6.39-66; *ANET*, pp. 68b-69a); Baal receives the grant of a temple from El after defeating Yam in the Ugaritic texts (Halpern, *Constitution*, p. 21) and Yahweh's shrine is itself associated with his kingship and with victory in war (Exod. 15.17; Pss. 46; 48; etc.).

Again Halpern has argued, convincingly, that the temple is the bond between the king and the god. The Babylonian king is always a temple builder and the Israelite kings seem to have regarded the founding of a sanctuary as of the utmost importance in securing the permanence of the dynasty. Excuses have to be made for David's not having built a temple; Solomon is the temple builder par excellence, etc.

49. So Pss. 46, 48 etc.

50. Psalms which may be assigned to the festival at this or any other point (such as Psalms 24 and 68) but which are neither psalms of the individual nor directly concern the king's involvement in the ritual have not been discussed here.

51. The RSV translation is given here except that I have retained (with NEB) 'I am anointed', the literal rendering of the Hebrew בלתי (RSV's translation: 'Thou hast poured on me') since the NEB seems to make better sense in view of the interpretation of the psalm put forward above. The RSV, with several other translations, sensibly supplies the word 'downfall' in v. 11 (MT 12) (so NIV, GNB).

52. It is worth noting generally the frequency of direct oracles from the cultic prophets in these ritual psalms here and in Pss. 2, 132 etc. which supports the general case for reading Psalm 94.16 as a word directly from Yahweh.

53. Anderson and Jacquet, *ad loc.*, both give excellent reviews of the evidence in favour of the unity of the psalms and Jacquet provides a list of link phrases.

54. This song of thanksgiving answers the king's cry for judgment given in Pss. 7, 17, and 27 above.

55. *Ps. 9.4 (MT 5)*. This verse would be more literally rendered by 'Yahweh take your throne, a judge of righteousness'—i.e. a righteous judge and hence to give righteous judgments.

56. *Ps. 9.6 (MT 7)*. A case can be made, as is noted by Anderson (*ad loc.*) for re-ordering the phrases in this verse to that the phrase 'everlasting ruins' is applied to the fate of the cities rather than the enemies. The verse would then read:

> The enemy has vanished,
> The very memory of them has perished
> Their cities thou hast rooted out,
> They are ruins for evermore.

Again, Anderson notes the suggestion that the Hebrew word המה at the end of this verse (which the RSV takes as emphasizing the pronoun 'them') may be equivalent to the Ugaritic *Hm* meaning 'behold' and may therefore belong to the next verse.

57. This judgment is itself portrayed in Pss. 58, 75, 82 and 97.

58. *Ps. 9.9 (MT 10)*. The Hebrew here reads—ויהי יהוה. It seems sensible to follow the RSV emendation to ויהי: 'Yahweh is . . .' (so Anderson, *ad loc.*, GNB, NIV).

59. *Ps. 9.12 (MT 13); 9.18 (MT 19); 10.12*. For a discussion of the Kethib and Qere variants in these verses see Chapter 2, n. 35. In 10.12 RSV retains אל, probably correctly, in spite of the BH suggestion that the word should perhaps be dropped on the evidence of the Targum.

60. So *BH, ad loc.*

61. So BDB, *ad loc.*

62. As regards those royal psalms which are not assigned here to the ritual a useful distinction can be made between 'general historical' and 'particular historical' pieces. The term 'particular historical' is used of those few psalms which appear to have been composed in response to some particular historical event. Examples of this category include the Song of Deborah in Judges 5 and Psalms 74 and 137, psalms referring to the destruction of Jerusalem and to the exile respectively. The majority of non-ritual royal psalms, however, are general in reference, in that they appear to have been composed not in response to a particular historical event but to have been

delivered in a general type of crisis such as defeat in battle or sickness befalling the king. It appears that the psalter would hold in its repertoire songs relating to a limited range of such crises to be used as and when the need arose.

The distinction between psalms used in the annual ritual and psalms used only when the need arose, although a useful one and made by a number of scholars (including Eaton, *KP*, p. 131) clearly cannot be pressed too far. There would certainly be nothing to prevent prayers for Yahweh to arise in the ritual being used in response to historical disasters and vice versa. The principle followed here, however, has been to assign to the royal rites only those psalms which contain positive evidence in favour of such an association and to leave all others in the general historical group.

63. Threat of violent revolt was particularly acute in the Northern Kingdom: in the course of the 200-year life of the northern monarchy the succession was only secured for more than one generation by two families. There were six military coups in this short period (terminating the reigns of Elah, Jehoram, Zechariah, Shallum, Pekahiah and Pekah) and one extended period of civil war between Zimri, Omri and Timri (1 Kgs 16.5-20). The security of the Davidic dynasty in Judah would have been much less apparent to the kings themselves: that security was made possible, in part, because of the strong propaganda effect of the royal ideal in the cult and the linking in of promises of prosperity to David's successors. However, there is a strong tradition of revolt even in Judah, including Absalom's revolt; Adonijah's attempt to seize the throne; Solomon's purge of rivals; Athaliah's coup (2 Kgs 11.1) and the counter-attack led by the priests (11.13ff.); and three recorded conspiracies against Joash (12.20f.), Amaziah (14.19) and Amon (21.23f.).

64. So Eaton, *KP*, pp. 27f. and *TBC*, and *ad loc.*; A.A. Anderson *ad loc.*; Weiser, *ad loc.* Mowinckel sets the psalm in his group of national psalms of lament in the I-form (*PIW*, I, p. 220) in which the speaker is most likely to be the king.

65. I do not find attractive the suggestion that Psalms 3 and 4 are a pair: a morning and an evening psalm, respectively, for reasons which will be explained in Chapter 5 in the exegesis of Psalm 4.

66. A festal, though non-royal, interpretation of Psalm 44 has recently been put forward by M.D. Goulder. Goulder's general thesis is that all of the psalms headed 'For the Sons of Korah' have their origin in the northern sanctuary at Dan. Moreover the psalms as arranged at present comprise two separate collections. Pss. 42–49 are a complete festal liturgy in themselves whilst 84, 85, 87, 88 and 89 are older psalms also originally used in the great festival at Dan. Certain aspects of Goulder's thesis are very attractive, in particular the alleged northern provenance of many of the Korah psalms; his reconstruction of the history of the Korahite priesthood and his contention that we find evidence in the psalms not only of the festival as celebrated in

Jerusalem but also of other, slightly different, festivals celebrated elsewhere, of which the one at Dan, the main shrine of the northern kingdom for many years, would surely be the most important. However, Goulder's contention that all of the Korah psalms should be attached to the festival has two main weaknesses: in the first place his reconstruction of the Dan liturgy depends to a great degree on the assumption that the Korah psalms have been handed down in the order in which they were originally used; in the second he assumes that the only Korah psalms which have survived came from the liturgy of the festival. It seems to me that, whilst there are common elements between some of the Korah psalms, these are not sufficient to tie all the psalms into the same liturgy, given the great differences which also exist. Hence I would maintain that Psalm 44 is, because of its great urgency, a psalm more suited to be used in an actual historical situation of need than in the annual liturgy (M.D. Goulder, *The Psalms of the Sons of Korah* [1982]).

67. The point has been well made by R.J. Clifford, 'A Lament Over the Davidic Ruler's Continued Failure', *HTR* 73 (1980), pp. 35-47.

68. A useful review of solutions is provided by Jacquet, *ad loc.*

69. Mowinckel, *PIW*, I, p. 49.

70. Eaton, *KP*, p. 75.

71. Johnson, *CPIP*, pp. 331f.

72. Birkeland, *Die Feinde*, pp. 92f.; cf. Eaton, *KP*, p. 52; Pritchard, *ANET*, p. 418b.

73. So, for example, in Isa. 8.8; Pss. 18.5; 66.12; 124.4.

74. Cf. Psalm 44, where the same accusation is levelled against God in a military situation:

> For thy sake we are slain all the day long and accounted as sheep for the slaughter.

75. The only possible objection to this view, turning on the translation of גזל (v. 5) by 'steal' is effectively countered by Eaton in his translation of the word by 'taken by plunder'—a translation supported by LXX, which has ἁρπάζω rather than κλέπτω at this point.

76. R.J. Clifford suggests the translation:

> The people acknowledge Yahweh marched,
> In the effulgence of your face they walked

which, he feels, further stresses the processional nature of the festival described. This reading substitutes אָשְׁרוּ (they marched) for אַשְׁרֵי in the MT and gives better parallelism, though whether this gives us sufficient grounds for emendation must be questioned. The emendation also involves moving תרועה (shout) to the end of v. 17. Clifford's article is useful in drawing together the essential unity in the psalm and the correspondence between the past tradition appealed to and the present dilemma but he never addresses the central question of whether the psalm is a ritual or a general historical piece (R.J. Clifford, 'A Lament Over the Davidic Ruler's Continued Failure', *HTR* 73 [1980], pp. 35-47).

77. Goulder may well be correct in arguing that vv. 1f. and 5-18 represent the oldest, originally separate, part of the psalm and that these originated in the northern shrines rather than at Jerusalem. In particular this would account well for the mention of Tabor and Hermon in v. 12. (*op. cit.*, pp. 211-38).

78. J.M. Ward, 'The Literary Form and Liturgical Background of Psalm 89', *VT* 11 (1961), pp. 321-41, 335.

79. A.R. Johnson, 'The Role of the King in the Jerusalem Cultus', in *The Labyrinth*, ed. S.H. Hooke, p. 101.

80. Johnson, *CPIP*, p. 377 n. 5.

81. It is easy to imagine how this reading became confused as the original significance of the psalm was forgotten in its adaptation to general usage. As a first stage the short line אָכְלוּ וְשָׁתוּ would have been transposed and read as the first part of the long line following. The imperative אָכְלוּ would then be changed to an indicative שָׁתוּ receives an additional וַ to bring the first half of the new line into parallel with the second and giving the confusion of the present Hebrew text (which is also reflected in the Greek).

82. Eaton's arguments are: the description 'servant' which is suggestive of a royal relationship; the claim the psalmist makes to a covenant bond (vv. 1, 8, 11, 12), God's promise to conduct the psalmist by his angelic spirit and his desire to do God's will, as well as the affirmation 'Thou art my God' (but on this see above pp. 155f.).

83. Johnson, *CPIP*, pp. 266ff.

84. Eaton, *KP*, p. 80.

85. Pritchard, *ANET*, p. 390.

86. So, for example, A.A. Anderson, *ad loc*.

87. A.H. Johnson, *The Vitality of the Individual in Ancient Israel* (1961); H.W. Wolff, *Anthropology of the Old Testament* (1973).

88. D. Jones, 'The Cessation of Sacrifice after the Destruction of the Temple in 586 BC', *JTS* n.s. 14, (1963), pp. 12-31.

89. Eaton, *KP*, pp. 71f.

90. The arguments in favour of a royal attribution are set out above, p. 44; cf. Mowinckel, *PIW* I, p. 219.

91. Cf. Eaton, *KP*, pp. 49f.

92. So Engnell and, to a lesser extent, Eaton, *KP*, p. 131.

93. Verse 6 (MT 7) is a notorious *crux interpretum*. Later Christian tradition (cf. Heb. 1.8) and the LXX, possibly influenced by that tradition, suggest reading אלהים as a vocative, giving the translation: 'Your throne, O God, is for ever and ever'. This, however, would be a statement of the royal ideal, seeing the king as divine, which goes way beyond the normal understanding of the king's nature found in the Old Testament. It seems

better, therefore, with the RSV, to see אלהים used as an adjective here, referring not to the king but to his throne (and therefore to his office) which was instituted by and under the protection of Yahweh and therefore ordained עולם. Such an understanding of כסאן אלהים also gives a better parallel with שבמ מישר in the second half of the verse.

Goulder has recently revived the theory that Psalm 45 is a festal psalm and that the ritual marriage of the king played some part in the annual royal ritual at Dan. He puts forward the view that Psalm 45 may have been originally written for the marriage of Ahab and Jezebel at the northern shrine. The psalm may indeed have had an original setting in the north and have been written for such an occasion. It is also not unlikely that royal weddings took place at the same time as the main festival. However, it is difficult to find any trace of this aspect of the royal ritual in the Jerusalem rites or to imagine how the worship in Jerusalem would be content with the accompanying ideology, which is closer to the idea of the Canaanite fertility ritual which orthodox Yahwism repudiated from earliest times (M.D. Goulder, *The Psalms of the Sons of Korah*, pp. 121-37).

Notes to Chapter 4
The Individual as a Private Person

1. A number of writers of the topic of prayer and the psalms have shown great carelessness in dealing with the evidence from the psalter, in particular J.L. Haddix, *Lamentation as a Personal Experience in Selected Psalms* (1980), who insists on seeing the psalms as the individual creations of pietists describing their own spiritual experiences and so invalidates his arguments; V.J. Bredenkamp, *The Concept of Communion with God in the Old Testament* (1975), who, again, selects his psalms for discussion on the grounds of their 'personal content', irrespective of whether or not the pieces were actually composed for us by a private person; and H. Vorländer in *Mein Gott—Die Vorstellung vom persönlichen Gott im Alten Orient und im A.T.* (1975), selects a group of 'personal psalms' for evidence in his enquiry almost arbitrarily and with no consideration of the possibility of their being royal—although he does discuss the question of the enemies at length (pp. 248-58), concluding, wrongly, that the enemies are real demons.

More balanced and comprehensive studies of prayer in the Old Testament and the background in the ancient Near East include C.W.F. Smith in the *Interpreters' Dictionary of the Bible*; W.W. Hallo, 'Individual Prayer in Sumerian', *JAOS* 88 (1968), pp. 72-89; E.R. Dalglish, *Psalm 51* (1962), pp. 8-56.

2. Johnson, *CPIP*, pp. 359f.

3. Eaton, *KP*, p. 73.

4. That is, each half of the verse not only means the name but contains

the same parts of speech in the same order.

5. R.C. Culley, *Oral Formulaic Language in the Biblical Psalms* (1967); I. Ljung, *Tradition and Interpretation* (1978).

6. As has already been noted, the opening verses of the psalm indicate that the suppliant is envisaged as a man of some substance, who has the means to be generous to the poor. Hence it is not unlikely that such a man would have enemies who would want to cast him down from this position.

7. H. Schmidt, *Das Gebet der Angeklagten* (1928); L. Delekat, *Asylie und Schutzorakel* (1967).

8. Eaton discusses and dismisses these theories in the course of his setting out the case for a substantially royal interpretation of the psalms (Eaton, *KP*, Chapter 1).

9. E.g. Prov. 16.7; 24.17f.; 27.16.

10. E.g. Prov. 6.16; 14.5; 25; 19.5; 28; 21.28; 24.28.

11. Cf. Ps. 35.4 with Ps. 70.3. Evidence such as this supports the theory mentioned above that the psalmists drew on a common pool of, say, curse phrases or beseeching phrases in their method of composition.

12. Particularly in v. 21; cf. Ps. 70.4.

13. Comparison with Psalm 70 is again instructive. Cf. 35.27 with 7.5.

14. H.L. Creager, 'A Note on Psalm 109', *JNES* 6 (1947), pp. 121-23.

15. The arguments for and against this position are aptly summarized by E.J. Kissane, 'The Interpretation of Psalm 109', *Irish Theological Quarterly* 18 (1951), pp. 1-8, especially pp. 3f.

16. Eaton, *KP*, p. 85.

17. Eaton, *KP*, pp. 79f.

18. This is clearly the case in Psalm 40, since part of the psalm is actually preserved elsewhere as Psalm 70, and it may also be true of Pss. 31.1-8, 9-24; 35.1-10, etc., all of which could stand as complete, if brief, psalms of petition.

19. I.e. Isa. 2.3f. par. Mic. 4.1f.; Zech. 14.16f.; etc.

20. A useful summary is provided by C.C. Keet, *A Study of the Psalms of Ascent* (1969), Chapter 1, pp. 1-17.

21. In Pss. 122.4; 123.2; 124.6; 129.6; 133.2; BDB (p. 979 col. a) describes the particle as 'in usage limited to late Hebrew passages and passages with a N. Palestinian colouring'—the latter remark evidently does not apply to the Psalms of Ascent with their frequent references to Zion.

22. Keet, following Gesenius (who saw in this feature an explanation for the superscription), cites as examples Pss. 121.1-2; 122.2ff.; 123.2ff.; 124.1-5; 125.2f.; 126.2f.; 129.1f. (Keet, *op. cit.*, p. 7).

23. Eaton, *KP*, pp. 82f.

24. Eaton, *KP*, p. 83.

25. The domestic and agricultural images used in the Psalms of Ascent are those of: the glowing coals of the broom tree, as a punishment for a lying

tongue (Ps. 120.4); the eyes of a maidservant (Ps. 123.2), for Israel's relationship to God; the metaphor of rejoicing at harvest, for a change in Israel's fortunes (Ps. 123.2); a quiver of arrows, for sons (Ps. 127.5); vine and olive shoots, for wife and children (128.2); the plough's furrow, for national suffering (129.3); the watchman, as an image of salvation (130.5); the weaned child, for peace and contentment with God (131.2); anointing oil and dew, as symbols of unity (133.2). These images are not found elsewhere in the psalter and to a large degree contribute to the charm as well as the distinctiveness of the Psalms of Ascent.

Notes to Chapter 5
The Individual as a Minister of the Cult

1. The precise nature of the wisdom teacher's involvement with the cult will be explored below in more detail. It seems unlikely that the cult 'employed' such teachers in any professional capacity in the temple as it employed both cultic prophets and musicians, but conversely the presence of wisdom psalms in the psalter indicates that there was a degree of formal involvement by the wise in the religion of Israel.

2. Also discussed in this section, although briefly, are psalms in which the singer appears, as it were, incidentally as an 'I' in the psalm, i.e. Pss. 8; 45; 103; 104; 106; 145; 146. Psalms 20 and 110 are mentioned briefly for the same reason in the section on cult-prophetic psalms.

3. A.R. Johnson, *The Cultic Prophet in Ancient Israel* (*CPAI*) (2nd edition, 1962).

4. The following psalms are included and discussed in detail:

(a) as illustrating 'the responsibility of the cultic prophet for the life of society as recognisable in regular worship':
Pss. 81; 95; 50; Song of Miriam; 78; 132; 89; 110; 24; 15.

(b) illustrating 'the responsibility of the cultic prophet for the life of society as recognisable in times of national crisis':
Pss. 74; 80; the Song of Deborah; the Song of Moses; 60; 20; 91; 90; 85.

(c) illustrating the 'responsibility of the cultic prophet for the life of the individual as recognisable in times of personal crisis':
Pss. 28; 86; 6; 17; 5; 143; 63; 30; 32; 130; 75; Song of Hannah; 56; 27; 61; 54; 116; 22; 60; 49; 51.

Royal psalms are included in all three groups and include most of the individual psalms discussed. There is no indication in Johnson's work as to whether this list is meant to be exhaustive of the psalms which reflect the cultic prophets' influence.

5. These include particularly the use of the emphatic particle הוא; the concern with the שלום of the individual and of society and the oracle form which appears in several psalms.

6. In particular I would disagree with his early dating of many of the psalms, which seems, in the first place, in many cases to be based on a 'There is no reason why not. . .' argument rather than positive demonstration and, second, to cut against many of the accepted conclusions of Old Testament scholarship without any attempt to justify this (cf. A. Philips' criticism of the book in *JTS* 31 [1980], p. 127). I would also disagree with Johnson on the designation of certain psalms as royal, as has been explained above, and also on the proposed context of many of the royal psalms. The work suffers from a tendency to see this question of the cultic prophets in isolation from other questions in psalm studies and also from a desire to link up psalms, wherever possible, to particular events in Israel's history, a process which reaches its climax in the assignation of Psalm 51 to David himself and its context to David's sojourn at Manahaim while he awaited the outcome of Absalom's revolt. As Philips remarks: 'We seem at this point a long way from Gunkel'.

7. A.F. Kirkpatrick, *The Book of Psalms* (1902), pp. 428f.

8. Cf. above pp. 24ff.

9. The image is used frequently by, for example, Micah, Jeremiah and Ezekiel.

10. A similar homogeneity has been noted by M.J. Buss among the psalms headed לבני קרח (Pss. 42–49; 84; 85; 87). Buss thinks that these psalms also were written by the ministers of the cult for recitation by that group in the temple services and he may well be right. He notes that 'the strong personal element in these psalms points to a connection with the cult organisations' and suggests that the whole group of Asaph and Korah psalms should be seen as 'clergy psalms' rather than 'lay psalms', a point which is substantiated in this chapter. A similar point is made of the Korah psalms by Goulder, *The Psalms of the Sons of Korah*, who argues that the 'I' who speaks in many of these pieces is a representative leader of worship in the temple cult. As will be argued below, the Korah psalms seem to represent more the interests and concerns of the musicians of Israel where the Asaph collections have preserved psalms with a more cult-prophetic interest (M.J. Buss, 'The Psalms of Asaph and Korah', *JBL* 82 [1963], pp. 382-92).

11. For example, neither de Vaux nor Ringgren, who have both written standard works on the subject, pays any significant attention to the role of the cult in either education or social control.

12. The only alternative would be proclamation, which was doubtless used on various occasions as in Hezekiah's unsuccessful attempt to invite the northern tribe to Jerusalem to celebrate the passover, recorded in 2 Chron. 30.1-12.

13. According to the Deuteronomic History, for example, many solemn

warnings are delivered to Israel by her leaders at times of national festival (e.g. Joshua 24; 1 Samuel 12; 1 Kings 8); although the composition of these speeches is Deuteronomistic the tradition of historical review seems to be an ancient one. The Deuteronomistic writers take up a concept made explicit in Deuteronomy itself that teaching is central to the faith (Deuteronomy 31.10f.; 33.10.) From a different strand of Israel's tradition the classical prophets delivered their oracles of warning and judgment at the great national festivals (Amos 7.10; Jer. 7.1; 26.2; 36.1ff.). Also in the prophets, the guardians of Israel's religious traditions, both priest and cultic prophet are severely censured because they have ceased to teach the people (Hos. 4.6f.; Jer. 7.8: Mal. 2.6f.). Finally, teaching, and particularly the teaching of Torah, assumes an even greater importance in the period of the exile and afterwards, as several oracles of salvation reveal:

> Come let us go up to the house of the Lord,
> That he may *teach us* his ways
> And that we may walk in his paths,
> For out of Zion shall go forth the תורה (law). (Isa. 2.3, Mic. 4.2, following
> Kaiser's dating of the text to the post-exilic period).

14. Cf. Johnson, *CPIP*, p. 29 *et passim*.

15. Eaton, *KP*, p. 79.

16. Somewhat surprisingly, the psalm is not discussed at all by Johnson in *CPIP*.

17. Notably Pss. 74; 79; 80; cf. Kirkpatrick, *Psalms*, p. 430.

18. Johnson, *CPIP*, p. 321.

19. Again somewhat surprisingly, Johnson does not deal with this psalm in a significant way in *CPIP*.

20. Eaton argues (*KP*, p. 69) that Psalm 36 is a royal psalm although placed in his 'less sure' group. However, there is no evidence for this view which cannot be taken also, in this case, as evidence for the psalm being delivered by a cultic prophet: both king and prophet are witnesses to Yahweh and can identify their own fate with that of the nation. Also, positive indications that the psalm is royal, such as evidence of royal style, are lacking here.

21. A clear discussion and summary of the debate on the wisdom psalms is provided by Leo G. Perdue in his stimulating examination of the whole relationship between the wisdom schools and the religion of Israel: *Wisdom and Cult* (1977).

22. To summarize Perdue's overview, the following scholars identify the following pieces as wisdom psalms:

>   Gunkel: 1; 37; 49; 73 112; 127; 128; 133.
>   Mowinckel: 1; 34; 37; 49; 78; 105; 106; 111; 112; 127.
>   Johnson: 1; 37; 49; 73; 91; 112; 127; 128.
>   von Rad: 1; 34; 37; 49; 73; 111; 112; 119; 127; 128; 139.
>   R.E. Murphy: 1; 32; 34; 37; 49; 112; 138.

J.L. Crenshaw: 1; 19; 33; 39; 49; 104.

K. Kuntz: 1; 32; 34; 37; 49; 112; 127; 133.

Perdue himself included the following psalms as wisdom pieces: 1; 19A; 19B; 32; 34; 37; 49; 73; 112; 119; 127.

23. A useful list of elements in these three areas is provided by P. Rowantree, 'Wisdom in the Psalms: an examination and assessment of the evidence of wisdom material in the psalter', unpublished M.A. thesis, University of Wales (Cardiff), 1969.

24. As in the often quoted parallels between Prov. 22.17–24.22 and the Egyptian 'Instruction of Amen-em-opet'.

25. Sirach 24; cf. Perdue, *Wisdom and Cult*, pp. 189f.

26. So W. McKane, *Prophets and Wise Men* (1965).

27. Mowinckel, *PIW*, II, pp. 111f. The only wisdom psalms which seem to have been non-cultic are the two late poems, Pss. 119 and 39.

28. Perdue, *Wisdom and Cult*, pp. 266ff.

29. Particularly strong evidence for this development is found in the importance given by the Chronicler and Ezra-Nehemiah to teaching in the cult.

30. The idea of personal testimony is, of course, extremely prominent in the teaching style of the wisdom schools, whose whole philosophy was built upon experience.

31. Transposing על מות from the end of Psalm 48 to the beginning of this psalm, following Perdue, p. 340, who follows Gunkel, *Einleitung*, p. 348.

32. This theme is so pervasive through the psalm and the stress throughout so much didactic that I am unable to accept Goulder's suggestion that the psalm should be seen as arising from the royal cult in the northern kingdom (*The Psalms of the Sons of Korah*, pp. 181-95).

33. יגר (v. 13) is listed by BDB (p. 430) as a Late Hebrew word common in Zechariah 9–14 and Esther but not elsewhere.

34. The forms include instruction (vv. 8-10), two sayings and an example testimony (v. 36).

35. Eaton, *KP*, pp. 29f. In particular 'what is said about prayer, earlier experiences of grace, sleep, the "many who say", glory and derision'.

36. Weiser's commentary states that the LXX has all the verbs in v. 2 in the third person perfect. In fact this is not the case: οἰκτίρησόν and εἰσάκουσον preserve the imperative now found in the MT. However, the fact that the LXX translator has preserved the imperative in v. 2b can only be an indication of his faithfulness in the transmission of the text and caution in harmonization. The other indications that v. 2 should be in the past tense throughout are so strong, however, that we can only conclude that the text was partially corrupted when it came into the translator's hands.

37. Cf. Pss. 9–10 above, pp. 108ff.

38. So Weiser, Anderson, Mowinckel (*PIW*, II, p. 267), Perdue (pp. 216, 319), etc.

39. Cf. Psalm 89, discussed above pp. 118f.

40. On wisdom in creation see Prov. 8.22-31; Job 28.23-27; Wisdom 7.22f. On wisdom/torah see Sirach 24.

41. For a list of wisdom features in Psalm 119 see Perdue, *Wisdom and Cult*, p. 312.

42. There are, of course, examples of protest literature in the wisdom writings of other nations; cf. the Akkadian 'Dialogue of Pessimism' and the Sumerian Job story.

43. J.L. Crenshaw, *Old Testament Wisdom* (1982), p.82.

44. Mowinckel, *PIW*, II, pp. 85-95.

45. The arrangement of the Levitical guilds in the post-exilic age, for which we have the information given in Chronicles—Ezra—Nehemiah, has been discussed in some detail by H.G.M. Williamson, *I and II Chronicles* (1982), pp. 119ff. He concludes that the lists in Chronicles do not shed very much light on pre-exilic practices.

46. So A. Sendrey, *Music in the Social and Religious life of Antiquity* (1974) and *Music in Ancient Israel* (1969). Sendrey writes from the perspective of the musicologist and many of his insights are helpful. However, although he has a basic awareness of Old Testament scholarship he makes uncritical use of many of the sources. Further insight into the importance of music in ancient Near Eastern culture is provided by Curt Sachs, Sendrey's mentor in *The Rise of Music in the Ancient World, East and West* (1943) (although Sachs's assumptions about the origins of music are viewed with some scepticism by contemporary musicologists) and F.W. Galpin's study, *The Music of the Sumerians* (1937). Some useful illustrations are given in O. Keele's study of iconography, pp. 335ff.

Three insights emerge from Sendrey's work which are helpful in understanding the Psalms:

(1)   It appears, from various references, that singing was primary in the temple worship; instrumental music was an accompaniment to the singing.

(2)   The music itself may well have been in the 'makamat' style in the manner practised in many Near Eastern countries today, whereby the performer plays variations on a simple melody rather than following a set score. If so, the musical accompaniment to the psalms may well have set the mood (of either lament or rejoicing) and the pace but not dictated the 'melody' (as we know it today), leaving the singers free to develop a theme under inspiration.

(3)   Finally, Sendrey argues, the collective nature of the enterprise means that, of necessity, a school of musicians and singers would need to have been established in the temple, probably from Solomon's time, to pass on the necessary skill and expertise from one generation to another.

Eaton's recent work, *The Psalms Come Alive* (1984), also gives a useful discussion of the music of the psalms (pp. 72-101).

47. Additional evidence for this view is provided by the notes in the psalm headings, the most reasonable explanation for which seems to be that they indicate musical accompaniment in some way.

48. Eaton, *TBC, ad loc.*

49. So Eaton, *TBC, ad loc.*

50. Johnson, *SKAI*, p. 94.

51. So Anderson, Kraus, Weiser, Jacquet, and Goulder, who argues, convincingly, that this psalm comes from the northern Shrine (*op. cit.*, pp. 37, 51).

52. Eaton, *KP*, pp. 69f. Mowinckel (*PIW*, I, p. 219) supports the view that this is a national lament in the 'I' form.

53. The most reasonable explanation of these verses seems to be that provided by Weiser: 'the thunder of the torrents (of the Jordan) becomes to the psalmist a symbol of his own adversity, a symbol in which he cannot help seeing a punishment which the hand of God has inflicted upon him' (*Psalms*, p. 350). Thus the psalmist evokes both the beauty of the land he loves and the symbolism of the waters as signifying deep distress in the space of two verses.

54. This suggestion is supported by a number of older commentators, including T.H. Robinson (in *The Psalmists*, ed. D. Simpson, p. 42) and by the heading in the *Good News Bible*. Whilst Goulder and others are probably right in once again arguing for a northern origin for the psalm (in which case the exile might be that of the northern praise singer exiled to Jerusalem) I cannot myself see that this psalm was taken from the festival. The distress envisaged is acute; the tone is so different from Psalm 84 and more akin to other cries from exile preserved in Psalm 137 and Lamentations (Goulder, *op. cit.*, pp. 23-37).

55. So Anderson, Weiser, *et al.*

BIBLIOGRAPHY

Anderson, A.A. *The Book of Psalms* (New Century Bible), London: Marshall, Morgan and Scott, 1972.

Anderson, G.W. 'Enemies and Evildoers in the Book of Psalms', *BJRL* 48 (1965-56), pp. 18-29.

Bardtke, H. *Biblia Hebraica Stuttgartensia, 11, Psalmi.* Stuttgart: Deutsche Bibelstiftung, 1976-7.

Birkeland, H. *ANI und ANAW in den Psalmen*, Oslo: Jacob Dybwad, 1933.

— *Die Feinde des Individuums in der israelitischen Psalmenliteratur*, Oslo: Grondahl and Sons, 1933.

— *The Evildoers in the Book of Psalms*, Oslo, 1955.

Bredenkamp, V.J. 'The Concept of Communion with God in the Old Testament with Special Reference to the Lament Psalms and the Confessions of Jeremiah' (Ph.D. thesis, Princeton University), Ann Arbor: Xerox University Microfilms, 1970.

Brown, F., Driver, S.R. and Briggs, C.A. *Hebrew and English Lexicon of the Old Testament*, Oxford: Oxford University Press, 1907.

Buss, M.J. 'Psalm of Asaph and Korah', *JBL* 82 (1963), pp. 382-92.

Caird, G.B. *The Language and Imagery of the Bible*, London: Duckworth, 1980.

Clifford, R.J. 'Psalm 89: A Lament Over the Davidic Ruler's Continued Failure', *HTR* 73 (1980), pp. 35-47.

Crenshaw, J.L. *Old Testament Wisdom: An Introduction*, London: SCM, 1982.

Creager, H.L. 'A Note on Psalm 109', *JNES* 6 (1947), pp. 121-23.

Culley, R.C. *Oral Formulaic Language and the Biblical Psalms*, Toronto: University of Toronto Press, 1967.

Dahood, M. *The Psalms*, (Anchor Bible Commentary), New York: Doubleday, 1966-1970.

Dalglish, E.R. *Psalm 51*, Leiden: E.J. Brill, 1962.

Delekat, L. *Asylie and Schutzorakel.* Leiden: E.J. Brill, 1967.

DeVaux, R. *Ancient Israel*, 2nd edition; London: Darton, Longman and Todd, 1965.

Donald, T. 'The Semantic Field "Rich and Poor" in Hebrew and Accadian Literature', *Oriens Antiquus* 3 (1964), pp. 27-41.

Eaton, J.H. *The Psalms* (Torch Bible Commentary), London: SCM, 1967.

— 'Some Questions of Philology and Exegesis in the Psalms', *JTS* n.s. 19 (1968), pp. 603-609.

— *Kingship and the Psalms*, London: SCM Press, 1976 (second [revised] edition, Sheffield: JSOT Press, 1986).

— *The Psalms in Israel's Worship* in *Tradition and Interpretation*, ed. G.W. Anderson (Oxford: Oxford University Press, 1979), pp. 238-74.

— *Festal Drama in Deutero-Isaiah*, London: SPCK, 1979.

— *The Psalms Come Alive*, London: Mowbray, 1984.

Elliger, K. and Rudolph, W. *Biblia Hebraica Stuttgartensia*, Stuttgart: Deutsche Bibelstiftung, 1976-77.

Engnell, I. *Studies in Divine Kingship in the Ancient Near East*, Uppsala: Almquist and Wiksellis, 1943.

Fensham, F.C. 'Widow, Orphan and Poor in Ancient Near Eastern Legal and Wisdom Literature', *JNES* 21 (1962), pp. 129-39.

Fretheim, T.E. 'The Cultic Use of the Ark in the Monarchical Period' (Ph.D. thesis, Princeton University), Ann Arbor: Xerox University Microfilms, 1968.

Galpin, F.W. *The Music of the Sumerians*, Connecticut: Greenwood Press, 1970 (originally published by Cambridge University Press in 1937).

Ginsberg, H.L. 'Some Emendations in Psalms', *HUCA* 23 (1950-51), pp. 74-101.

Goulder, M.D. *The Psalms of the Sons of Korah*, Sheffield: JSOT Press, 1982.

Gray, J. *I and II Kings*. 3rd edition; London: SCM 1977.

Gunkel, H. *Die Psalmen* (Handkommentar zum Alten Testament), Göttingen, 1926.

Gunkel, H. and Begrich, J. *Einleitung in die Psalmen* (Handkommentar zum Alten Testament), Göttingen, 1933.

Haddix, J.L. 'Lamentation as a Personal Experience in Selected Psalms' (Ph.D. thesis, Boston University Graduate School), Ann Arbor: Xerox University Microfilms, 1980.

Hallo, W.W. 'Individual Prayer in Sumerian', *JAOS* 88 (1968), pp. 71-89.

Halpern, B. *The Constitution of the Monarchy in Ancient Israel*, Chicago: Scholars Press, 1981.

Hayes, J.H. *An Introduction to Old Testament Study*, Nashville: Abingdon Press, 1979.

Hillers, D.R. 'The Ritual Procession of the Ark and Psalm 132', *CBQ* 30 (1968), pp. 48-55.

Hooke, S.H. (ed.) *Myth and Ritual*, Oxford: Oxford University Press, 1933.

—*The Labyrinth*, Oxford: Oxford University Press, 1935.

— *Myth, Ritual and Kingship*, Oxford: Oxford University Press, 1958.

Hubbard, R.L. 'Dynamistic and Legal Language in Complaint Psalms' (Ph.D. thesis), Ann Arbor: Xerox University Microfilms, 1981.

Jacquet, L. *Les Psaumes et le coeur de l'homme*, Gembloux, Belgium: Duculot Press, 1975-1979.

Johnson, A.R. 'The Role of the King in the Jerusalem Cultus', in *The Labyrinth*, ed. S.H. Hooke, pp. 73-111.

— 'The Psalms', in *The Old Testament and Modern Study*, ed. H.H. Rowley (Oxford: Oxford University Press, 1951), pp. 162-209.

— Review of H. Birkeland, *Evildoers in the Book of Psalms*, *JSS* 3 (1958), pp. 307ff.

— *The Cultic Prophet in Ancient Israel*, 2nd edition; Cardiff: University of Wales Press, 1962.

— *Sacral Kingship in Ancient Israel*, 2nd edition; Cardiff: University of Wales Press, 1967.

— *The Cultic Prophet in Israel's Psalmody*, Cardiff: University of Wales Press, 1979.

Jones, D. 'The Cessation of Sacrifice after the Destruction of the Temple in 586 BC', *JTS* n.s. 14 (1963), pp. 12-31.

Kaiser, O. *Isaiah 1-12*, London: SCM, 1972.

— *Isaiah 13-39*, London: SCM, 1974.

Keel, O. *The Symbolism of the Biblical World: Ancient Near Eastern Iconography and the Book of Psalms*, London: SPCK, 1978.

Keet, C.C. *A Study in the Psalms of Ascents*, London: Mitre Press, 1969.

Kirkpatrick, A.F. *The Book of Psalms*, Cambridge: Cambridge University Press, 1902.

Kraus, H.J. *Worship in Israel*, Oxford, Basil Blackwell, 1966.

— *Psalmen* (Biblischer Kommentar Altes Testament), Neukirchen: Neukirchener Verlag, 1st edition, 1960; 5th (revised) edition, 1978.

Kuntz, J.K. 'The Retribution Motif in Psalmic Wisdom', *ZAW* 89 (1977), pp. 223-33.

Ljung, I. *Tradition and Interpretation*, Lund: C.W.K. Gleerup, 1978.

McKane, W. *Prophets and Wise Men*, London: SCM, 1965.
— *Proverbs—A New Approach*, London: SCM, 1970.
Mettinger, T.N.D. *King and Messiah*, Lund: C.W.K. Gleerup, 1976.
Mowinckel, S. *Psalmenstudien I–VI*, Kristiania, 1921-24.
— 'Tradition and Personality in Psalms', *HUCA* 23, (1950-51), pp. 205-31.
—*The Psalms in Israel's Worship*, Oxford: Basil Blackwell, 1962.
Murphy, R.E. 'The Faith of the Psalmist', *Interpretation* 34 (1980), pp. 229-39.
— 'A Consideration of the Classification "Wisdom Psalms"' in *Supplement to VT IX*, ed. G.W. Anderson *et al.*, Leiden: E.J. Brill, 1963), pp. 156-67.
—*A Study of Psalm 72*, Washington: Catholic University of America Press, 1948.
Perdue, L.G. *Wisdom and Cult*, Missoula: Scholars Press, 1977.
Ploeg, J. van der 'Les Pauvres d'Israël et leur piété', *Oudtestamentische Studiën* 7 (1950), pp. 236-71.
Porter, J.R. 'The Interpretation of II Samuel 6 and Psalm 132', *JTS* n.s. 5 (1954), pp. 163-73.
Pritchard, J.B. (ed.) *Ancient Near Eastern Texts Relating to the Old Testament*, 2nd edition; Princeton: Princeton University Press, 1955.
Rad, G. von *Wisdom in Israel*, London: SCM, 1972.
Rahlfs, A. (ed.) *Septuaginta*, Stuttgart: Deutsche Bibelgesellschaft, 1935.
Renaud, B. 'Le Psaume 73: Méditation individuelle ou prière collective?', *Revue d'Histoire et de Philosophie Religieuses* 59 (1979), pp. 541-50.
Ringgren, H. *Israelite Religion*, London: SPCK, 1966.
Rosenbaum, S.N. 'The Concept "Antagonist" in Hebrew Psalm Poetry: A Semantic Field Study' (Ph.D. thesis, Brandeis University), Ann Arbor, Xerox University Microfilms, 1974.
Rowantree, P. 'Wisdom in the Psalms: An examination and assessment of the evidence of wisdom material in the psalter' (M.A. thesis, University of Wales [Cardiff]), 1969.
Sachs, C. *The Rise of Music in the Ancient Near East*, New York: Norton, 1953.
Sawyer, J.F.A. *Semantics in Biblical Research*, London: SCM, 1972.
Schmidt, H. 'Das Gebet der Angeklagten im Alten Testament', in *Old Testament Essays*, ed. D.C. Simpson; London: Charles Griffin, 1927.
Schultz, C. 'ANI and ANAW in the Psalms' (Ph.D. thesis, Brandeis University), Ann Arbor: Xerox University Microfilms, 1973.
Sendry, A. *Music in Ancient Israel*, New York: Philosophical Library. 1969.
— *Music in the Social and Religious Life of Antiquity*, New York: Farleigh Dickenson University Press, 1974.
Simpson, D.C. (ed.) *The Psalmists*, Oxford: Oxford University Press, 1926.
Smend, R. 'Über das Ich der Psalmen', *ZAW* 8 (1888), pp. 49-147.
Vorländer, H. *Mein Gott: Die Vorstellung vom persönlichen Gott im Alten Orient und im Alten Testament*, Neukirchen: Neukirchener Verlag, 1975.
Ward, J.M. 'The Literary Form and Liturgical Background of Psalm 89', *VT* 11 (1961), pp. 321-41.
Weiser, A. *The Psalms*, London: SCM, 1972.
Whitelam, K.W. *The Just King*, Sheffield: JSOT Press, 1979.
Whybray, R.N. *Wisdom in Proverbs*, London: SCM, 1965.
Williamson, H.G.M. *I and II Chronicles* (New Century Bible), London: Marshall, Morgan and Scott, 1982.
Wolff, H.W. *Anthropology of the Old Testament*, London: SCM, 1973.

INDEX

INDEX OF BIBLICAL REFERENCES

INDEX OF AUTHORS

JOURNAL FOR THE STUDY OF THE OLD TESTAMENT
Supplement Series

* Out of print